TO THE

CROSS

AND

BACK

TO THE
CROSS
AND
BACK

AN IMMIGRANT'S JOURNEY
FROM FAITH TO REASON

FERNANDO ALCÁNTAR
FOREWORD BY DAN BARKER

PITCHSTONE PUBLISHING
DURHAM, NORTH CAROLINA

Pitchstone Publishing
Durham, North Carolina
www.pitchstonepublishing.com

Library of Congress Cataloging-in-Publication Data

Alcántar, Fernando.
  To the cross and back : an immigrant's journey from faith to reason / Fernando
Alcántar ; foreword by Dan Barker.
      pages cm
  ISBN 978-1-63431-048-2 (pbk. : alk. paper)
  1. Alcántar, Fernando. 2. Atheists—United States—Biography. 3. Christianity and
atheism. I. Title.
  BL2790.A38A3 2015
  211'.8092—dc23
                        2015015162

Front cover design by Mark Rantal

CONTENTS

FOREWORD

This might be my fault.

If I had not started taking students from Azusa Pacific on short-term missionary trips to Mexico in 1968, the year I enrolled there, it is possible that faculty member Carolyn Koons would not have had the idea to start Mexico Outreach, and young Fernando Alcántar would not have met those preaching gringos in Mexicali whose testimony led not only to his conversion but also to his eventual graduation from Azusa Pacific, U.S. citizenship, and this wonderful book.

Carolyn had other influences besides me, of course, and she was a much better organizer than I was, so I can't take the credit (or the blame), but I was there at the very beginning, before it was called Mexico Outreach. Some of the California congregations we worked with—such as Chapel in the Pines—were churches that I had been involved with in Mexico outreach since a few years before. I knew the Mexicali area and some of the pastors. I knew the warden of the Mexicali jail and was able to negotiate to have the Azusa Pacific basketball and soccer teams compete against the surprisingly talented prisoners within those overcrowded walls. I became acquainted with a couple of "coyotes," young men with cars and TVs who described to me how and where they helped immigrants cross the border. I had already visited some of the orphanages. I had spent time ministering at La Granja ("The Farm") just south of Mexicali in Colonia Ahumadita where delinquent Mexican boys were being "educated" behind barbed wire.

And I knew the language. I had been preaching in Mexico since 1964.

I was fifteen years old in 1964 when I accepted what I was convinced was a "call to the ministry" during a sermon at Anaheim Christian Center. I had already been involved with local ministry, having played the piano since 1963 for the Peralta Brothers Quartet in Hispanic churches in southern California, but after "the call," I started carrying my bible to school, ministering to students and eventually convincing my Spanish teacher at Anaheim High School to give his life to Christ. Another student invited me to join Youth Unlimited Gospel Outreach, a short-term missionary group, during their next outreach to Mexico. It was a convenient four-hour drive to the "foreign mission field"—at that time, we took the route past Palm Springs, Indio, and Coachella, skirting the dry and forbidding Salton Sea heading toward Calexico—and I was happy to fulfill my calling to spread the "good news" of Jesus to the desperate needy Mexicans south of the border. Mexicali, the most northerly city in Latin America, was "easy pickings" for us zealous Protestants, like the fruit dangling from the date palms we passed on the way there.

I preached my first public sermon during Thanksgiving weekend that year, when I was still fifteen, before a small crowd on the dusty bank of an irrigation canal in Ejido Morelia, a few miles south of the border. It was not a great sermon. Since I was still learning Spanish, I wrote it out and read from a pencilled piece of paper. I don't remember if we had any converts that day, but I do recall how interested the people were in us Americanos descending on their tiny village. Especially the children.

Most of those children in the *ejidos* south of Mexicali were barefoot and many were shirtless, but they were smiling, singing, laughing, happy to take our handouts and participate in the arts and crafts that illustrated the teachings of the bible. They did not appear to understand how depressed they were supposed to be due to their poverty and false religion. When we asked how many of them wanted to accept Jesus as their personal savior, every hand shot up: "*Yo! Yo!*" We were pleased to return home to report that we had led hundreds of souls to Jesus on the mission field.

The kids up in the city of Mexicali, where Fernando Alcántar was eventually born, were usually better dressed, but just as excited. When Fernando describes meeting the American missionaries in Mexicali more than two decades later, I can picture the scene perfectly, since I had been one of those gringos, playing my accordion and leading the children singing "Soldado Soy de Jesús" ("I Am a Soldier of Christ") hundreds of times, just as he describes in this book. Sometimes a few kids stood back a bit, watching us foreigners with cautious curiosity. I can see the observant (in both senses of the word) Roman Catholic Fernando Alcántar lingering there, taking in the strange and noisy American Protestant rituals.

I spent a total of more than two years as a missionary in Mexico, spread over two decades, much of it as a team leader and pianist with the Frank Gonzales Evangelistic Association, and some of it on my own initiative. (I describe some of those proselytizing adventures in my book *Godless: How an Evangelical Preacher Became One of America's Leading Atheists*.) We took American high-school and college students on school-break and summer-long tours all across the country, from Tijuana to the Yucatán. When Fernando describes his years in Sinaloa, along the eastern side of the Gulf of California, I can conjure images of the days I spent preaching in Los Mochis, Navojoa, and other towns in that area. In 1970, after I was elected Spiritual Life Director at Azusa Pacific, I took a team of about fifteen APC students on a Tres Estrellas de Oro bus all the way to Mexico City where we preached and sang in a number of churches during Christmas break.

For many years after I left Azusa Pacific, I continued to be invited by the very capable Carolyn Koons and the inspirational professor/administrator Ron Cline to help with Mexico Outreach, which was growing into a huge endeavor. I was often the music and worship leader of the now-massive crowd of students sitting on the dry corn fields barely south of the border, an army of "*soldados*" invading and conquering a dark and lost country for Jesus.

Fernando Alcántar's story is the flip side of mine. Just as the contrived-name cities of Calexico and Mexicali straddle the border of two very different countries like mirror images, I can see Fernando's face reflected in mine. We both know English and Spanish, though we didn't start with the same first language. He was raised Catholic and I was Protestant before we became evangelicals. We both spoke in tongues. He plays guitar and I play piano. I entered Azusa Pacific the year Francis Schaeffer's influential *The God Who Is There* was published; Fernando entered Azusa Pacific the year *god Is Not Great* by Christopher Hitchens was published. We were sincere believers who dedicated our lives, resources, and even our health to the cause of bringing souls into the Kingdom. We were both involved in scary automobile accidents in Mexico, and both inside Mexican prisons. We both ministered to Mexicali children and adults, and continued our missionary outreach to other parts of the world.

We took similar paths to freethought. "Religion and Reason have been demons and angels standing on each of my shoulders fighting for my identity," Fernando writes, and I can identify with that struggle. I know exactly what he was thinking when he said to Jesus: "I have been your faithful friend. And you have been in stories, sermons, and hopes, but not in real life. It is way overdue. Jesus, my dear fantasy, we are friends no more." We both now agree that not only is God not great, but he is also not there at all.

Others have told similar stories. The Protestant missionary and linguist Daniel Everett relates a dramatic tale in his book *Don't Sleep, There Are Snakes* about how he failed to convert a single member of the Amazonian Pirahã tribe to Christianity and ended up becoming a convert himself: to atheism. Héctor Ávalos, a pentecostal child preacher born in Nogales, México, has become one of America's leading experts on the bible and is now an admired atheist professor of religion at Iowa State University. Steve Benson, grandson of Church of Jesus Christ of Latter-day Saints president Ezra Taft Benson, was a Mormon missionary to Japan who eventually abandoned his faith when he realized the teachings of his church are false. (Steve, now an outspoken atheist, is the editorial cartoonist at the *Arizona Republic*.) The Clergy Project, founded in 2011, now contains more than 650 former or current ministers, missionaries, priests, and rabbis who have abandoned their belief in the supernatural.

Each one of us who has trudged the dusty trail from faith to reason has a fascinating saga to relate, but none of them is more poignant than Fernando Alcántar's. He started off as a fruit (or victim) of missionary efforts, became a missionary himself, and then carefully, painfully, untied all the knots, unloosened the mask of faith and the cloak of religious submission, and let them drop to the floor so he could see in the mirror: we are simply biological organisms in a natural environment. And that is wonderful. Real love for real humanity is what matters most in the real world.

"We also see those who give love a face," Fernando writes, "regardless of creed and doctrine, and add value to our lives. I chose to hold on to the latter, as we healed from the past, and learned to see through masks. I wanted to be one of them, the rescuers, the real ones, the believers, the people of love."

Where does the urge to missionize come from? The Catholic Spanish priests who brought the faith of the "one true church" to the Americas certainly possessed a strong conquering ("conquistador") impulse. So did the Protestant English colonists who "civilized" my native American ancestors. (Hence our respective birth languages.) Muslims practiced "*dawah*" ("inviting") when they invaded North Africa, Spain, and Persia. Most of us understand the natural human desire to convince others to think like we do. But why reach out? Why start a Crusade? Why start a Mexico Outreach?

Certainly, when Fernando and I felt "the call" to the mission field, we sincerely believed we were in possession of a beautiful truth that the whole world needed to hear. But that is common to all faiths. Our love for Jesus, the desire to glorify God, and the concern for millions of souls who might be lost for eternity were powerful motivators, but they were basically beliefs, essentially no different from Allah, Muhammad, or the Virgin Mary. Belief can be inspiring, but belief is not knowledge.

I think there is a huge egotistical streak across our species. Perhaps it comes from tribalism, which has bequeathed us with instincts that protect the "in crowd" from the "other." As a Protestant boy, I thought Catholicism was strange, foreign, intrusive, superfluously elaborate, complicated, and bloody in its imagery. I simply did not like it. But now I see that this was because I had been conditioned by my religious upbringing. Maybe it is like our food taboos, which we obtain during a window of time during our childhood, and then become fixed. We just seem to maintain, most of us, a "my way is the right way" mentality. That attitude probably served our struggling primate ancestors very well, but today it seems, well, tribal.

Looking back on it, it seems silly that I felt the drive to drive down to Mexico to try to turn Catholics into Christians. It was all so arrogant and condescending. So "American." We Protestant missionaries truly believed we were doing the world a wondrous favor. It made us feel special—as I'm sure those thousands of young people who travel with Mexico Outreach feel special—to be delivering the precious truth to a lost, dark country a whole ten miles south of the border. And Fernando is absolutely right to point out that most of those who go on those APU short-term "missionary" trips are not really concerned about the souls of lost Mexicans. If they were really worried that the world should not perish but have everlasting life, they wouldn't have to travel long distances to do it. They would keep it up after they return home. I bet less than 5 percent of those students actually care as much about real mission work as Fernando and I did. "Saving souls" is merely a pretext in Mexico Outreach. There is certainly some educational value in such cross-cultural experiences, and a few of the participants are indeed charitable and compassionate toward real human needs, but Mexico Outreach is mainly a Spring Break for evangelicals, a Christian Camp where American youth can "get away" for a while and reevaluate their lives and purposes in the pretense of doing good work for needy people.

I am now deeply embarrassed by my paternalistic attitude toward a whole *country.*

That's why I was excited to accept the invitation of the newly formed Atheists of Mexico (Ateos y Librepensadores Mexicanos) to speak at their inaugural meeting in Mexico City in 2010. That was my first return to Mexico, more than a quarter century after I had preached there, and my first visit as an atheist. When I started my lecture before that group of intelligent and caring Mexicans, I asked them for absolution. I explained what a horrible condescending attitude I had held toward those beautiful people. I admitted I was wrong to do what I did. I confessed my sin and begged for their forgiveness. They applauded and some stood up as they yelled "We forgive you!"

Fernando Alcántar is now doing the same thing. He is apologizing and asking for forgiveness, not from an imaginary deity, but from those who really matter—real caring and hurting human beings. I can guarantee you that his story has the ring of truth. It is honest, exciting, informative, moving, and courageous. As you read it, you may visit locales that seem familiar, but I can promise you will also be taken places you never imagined visiting.

I can't resist offering Fernando some avuncular advice: stay away from boulders!

—**Dan Barker**, co-president, Freedom From Religion Foundation

INTRODUCTION

To my friends who remain faithful to Judeo-Christian traditions and a submission to the cross, I have one thing to say, I love you. You have been part of my life since the moment I knelt next to my bed and prayed a word of repentance. I grew in the faith and you taught me what community was and you trained me to become the leader I am today. In my depictions of my journey through faith, I have tried to remain faithful to the true sentiment of the born-again experience. I found myself spending days going through journals and memories so I could place myself emotionally in that stage of my life and retail the stories just as I felt them. I know that the Christian path is, for the faithful, a true experience of love and a relationship with the divine—as real as the one they have with fellow humans. Salvation, doubt, fear, forgiveness, community, and sacraments are very tangible emotional experiences for those who, like you, believe in the deity of Jesus Christ. And I respect that.

For some of you this book may seem like an act of betrayal, and you may post messages and responses on social media that will align me with hedonism, or start a campaign of prayer and intercession to save my soul from the lake of fire. I appreciate your concerns, but please believe me when I say that my decisions are not about a desire to sin or any other such charge, and that I am well.

This book simply tells my story, as I lived it, as I experienced the holy, and as I discovered myself with and without the lens of religion. Reason is not something anyone should ever apologize for and, as a friend, I challenge you to read to the end of this book, and not simply nitpick the parts that will fire up your conviction for apologetic conversation—to read not just through the eyes of personal opinion, but through the eyes of rational thinking.

If the truth shall indeed set us free, should we ever fear its result? If God is the real source of truth, then in theory any exploration of truth should lead us to him. But if truth should lead us to reason, why should we sacrifice understanding for the sake of maintaining a status quo?

To my friends who lie on the side farthest away from the cross, this story is also for you. For some, this material might tempt you to boast that another mind has been freed from the merciless shackles of religious oppression. I would challenge you to move past the sounding of trumpets, and to move closer to a call for tolerance. One of the greatest pieces of evidence against the divine is the tolerance of massacres in the name of gods who stand silent as death and torture are delivered on their behalf. Why should we add fuel to the fire?

For those who have once walked the path of the cross and now reside in Reason, you understand its sweetness and grasp. You feel for me and my pain as I experienced the guilt and shame of accepting my doubts, and the consequences of departing from faith.

For those who have never stepped onto this enigmatic road of mysticism, I hope that it will give you an empathetic look into the lives that your fellow brethren of earth experience every day. They are not willfully ignorant individuals who wake up wondering how they can limit people's free will and abolish their liberties with moral holograms. They live a personal reality that is based on the same desires you have for community, growth, and significance, and they have found a source that attempts to make sense of the chaos they see around them—just like you do.

And to those who are in between, those of you who secretly doubt elements of your identity, be it religious commitment, sexual identity, or cultural allegiance, I hope these stories may help you process your own journey. Many times when I have sought mentoring opportunities I found that the most helpful question was, "How did you do it?" We all live our own lives with our own sets of experiences, but history has taught us that often the best way to move forward is to first learn how others have done it before.

Finally, this is a letter for anybody who has ever experienced pain, loss, and regret. This is not necessarily a book about religion, but a book about a journey where religion has taken center stage and molded my decisions, in one way or another. I share the most intimate and darkest secrets of my heart. I also share the most heartbreaking memories of sorrow and defeat—stories that have left blood, sweat, and tears on this book's pages. Opening up my life like this for people to pick apart is an excruciatingly difficult and terrifying thing to do. I ask for respect and sensitivity as you learn about who I am and how I have learned.

The book is written in a hybrid of chronological and thematic narratives. Each chapter covers a major stage in my life or a series of related events. As a result, the book flows thematically, not in a day-by-day retailing of events. I have not included all of my lessons, all of my successes, or most certainly all of my mistakes, but it covers the main experiences and decisions that have made me the person I am today. As I wrote it, I tried to picture you next to me witnessing what I saw, and feeling what I felt. I am hoping that as you read it you take the time to put the book down at the end of each chapter and process the concepts presented as they pertain to your life, your relationship with the holy, and your relationship with one another.

I once shared one type of "good news," which I thought was the truth. By chronicling my story here, I am sharing another powerful form of news—the value of common sense, research, introspection, and reason. They might, if given the chance, be able to free us from the boundaries of restricted thinking and judgment toward that which we might not yet understand.

I now welcome you on this journey of discovery, love, and adventure, which took me . . . to the cross and back.

Part I: The Way to the Cross

*"It's a dangerous business, Frodo, going out your door.
You step onto the road, and if you don't keep your feet,
there's no knowing where you might be swept off to."*
—J. R. R. Tolkien, *The Lord of the Rings*

1

GENESIS

"Before you judge me, try hard to love me,
Look within your heart then ask, Have you seen my Childhood?"
—Michael Jackson, "Childhood"

The Motherland

Mexico is a land full of contradictions. We honor and revere the ancient traditions of the great Aztec and Mayan civilizations, but we sometimes fail to honor our responsibility to continue to achieve in the present day. We take great pride in our culture, music, food, and rituals, but today we look north of the border for an example of greatness and hopes of a better life. Some people go as far as believing that today there is no such thing as a "Mexican Dream"—that any such dream is only about crossing over the fence to fulfill the "American Dream." I have always wished for a renewal of Mexico's dreams and hopes. And, as a boy, that is why my eyes first looked up to the heavens for inspiration. In a way, they still do.

My birthplace, Mexicali, is herself a land of contrasts, reflected in the city's very name—"Mexi" for Mexico and "Cali" for California. It sits on the border of two of the most culturally polarized neighbors in the world. Built on a low and dry desert, it was originally founded by illegal Chinese immigrants who were driven underground when it was demanded the land be owned only by Mexicans. Its temperatures have reached 128°F, and its earthquakes have been as high as 7.2 magnitude, both of which surprise but do not shock her inhabitants. On May 28, 1977 (a month earlier than expected), with a loud cry followed by sweet giggles, I became the newest member of this kind community of contrasts.

From peninsula to peninsula—Baja California to Yucatan—all Mexicans are connected by a web of invisible bonds. We wave our flag and flood the streets after a tie or victory of *El Tri*, the national soccer team. We are enlivened by the trumpet-led sounds of our country. We may not own a Mariachi CD, or even think of attending a Mariachi concert, but we'll have a Mariachi band present at weddings and graduations and sing every song by heart. We grow up with the familiar sights of large cathedrals that host an image of a barely clothed man nailed to a cross and a woman in a teal robe, clothed with the sun, the moon beneath her feet.

My identity, like the identity of nearly every Mexican child, was interwoven with each of these bonds—often without question. Except for funerals and the occasional mass, my family would almost never attend church, but one thing I knew for sure: if I was Mexican, then I was Catholic just as much. My mom said so. TV said so. School said so. I learned that, in 1531, a decade after the Spanish conquest of the Aztec Empire, La Virgen de Guadalupe stood on the Hill of Tepeyac and appeared to Juan Diego, an uneducated and humble native, asking for a church to be built on that spot in her name. As miraculous proof of this vision, he presented Spanish flowers from the usually barren hill and her image painted on his cape.

The Catholic Church canonized Juan Diego in 2002—his sainthood demanded by the faithful masses. Since that momentous day on the hill, the blood flowing through Mexico's veins have had an innate Vatican rule.

A Little Boy's Prayer

Being the sinful ten-year-old that I was, I understood early on that there was something wrong with me. Why would my life be so miserable then, if not because of the wrong of my doing? I understood clearly that if I prayed, God would come to my rescue. If he didn't, it was obviously, *obviously,* because there was too much filth in my life and He wouldn't care for any soul unless it was all clean and shiny.

My father abandoned both my mother and me at the news that I was in her womb. Unable to ask him to stay, or to communicate the consequences of growing up fatherless in a world of men, I was born at the end of a warm spring day without a paternal guide.

I have this vivid recollection of playing at a playground near my house back in good-ole fourth grade. My friend, she had a dad. He pushed her on the swing and she would rise up in the air along with the sound of her laughter traveling through the park. Dang, she looked so happy. I stood there as a silent witness and felt a void grow inside of me—or maybe just a realization that the void had been there all along. My eyes got really big when she told me her last name came from her dad. It wasn't just given to us like our first name. There's actually a reason behind it. I thought, where did my last name come from then? I mean, I didn't have a dad.

So I understood early on what the word *bastard* meant. And that's how I felt.

But if God loved me, then He must have seen something wrong with me that would explain why I grew up without a father. My mother had to work all the time because she wanted to provide for me and my sister. But why did I often fear her when she was around? I didn't yet understand mental illness or parental dysfunction. All I knew is that I was a kid and that nightmares were real, even when I was awake. Without a clear pattern, for seemingly insignificant things, she unleashed anger at me with her hands, shoes, belt, and, worst of all, that ceaseless shouting. It was not until years later, during one of those late nights around the kitchen table with a cup of hot chocolate, that I learned she would cry herself to sleep asking, "How could I have done that to my little boy?"

And I prayed.

I didn't know what the worth of a little boy's prayer was to God. It was unknown to me. I was baptized as a baby, and though I have no recollection of them, I know I have a godfather and a godmother somewhere. I had been brought to the altar of God and presented as a tribute to Him, with requests for His protection and validation. So the deal was sealed—or so I was told. But yet, there was no God in my life. And the prayers of a little boy, scared, bruised, fatherless, and insignificant, were not enough to compel the God of Heaven to take a break from shining in Glory to let him know that he was something valuable, or at least that he would grow up to be valuable.

I went through Confirmation as well, though I don't remember it. How do I know? Because there was another man I called "nino" (short for *padrino*—godfather). My nino would give me gifts here and there. He worked with my mom at the same Holiday Inn where she met my father.

Despite my upbringing and surroundings, I still understood there was good in the world, even if I didn't see it. I could definitely feel evil and pain. No one had to tell me my situation was bad—I felt it. I felt it with the intensity no child ever should, with nightmares that never left even when the lights came on. I grew up as a skinny, ungroomed child, always teased for his messy hair, his above average height, his low weight, his lack of masculinity—the little boy with those gentle golden-brown yet sad puppy eyes.

And I prayed, "Why?"

Over the Wall

My mother started dating an American man, Don, when I was in fifth grade. He was white, blond, and blue-eyed, the embodiment of the great American stereotype we had grown to admire—one of wealth, looks, and power. They met at the hotel where she worked. My sister, Carolina ("Caro") (who has a different father than I do), and I were thrilled at first. He brought us candy, took us out to eat, and gave us presents.

Fifth grade was different in many ways. Primarily because it would be the last time we saw home as it was—as we knew it.

With the promise that we were going to Disneyland, Don and my mother packed our things. "But why are we packing the bed if we're going to Disneyland?" Selling it? Yeah, right. I overheard a phone conversation between my mom and my Aunt Aide, where she told her that she was telling us a story so we wouldn't complain. Lying was mom's way of getting us to do something. She wholeheartedly believed that lying to children was fair game and that we would soon forget any false promise, as she thought children did.

I knew Disneyland was nothing but a lie. Maybe out of spite, or out of dim hope, I kept asking Don about it on the way up. "But this map says Disneyland is coming up." "The map says this is the exit." And he kept saying I was wrong, that I was "being stupid." Awkward, since, as far back as kindergarten, I had always obtained the highest GPA, not just for my grade, but for the entire school—my picture always on the top of the honor's board. A kid genius, many thought, even the school's principal. So I could most certainly read a map.

Finally, we arrived at our new apartment in Port Hueneme, California. Though we didn't get to say goodbye to our friends and family, we pretended to be happy. Mexicali was definitely not the Promised Land; *Gringoland* was always supposed to be it. Otherwise, why did so many people want to swim the dangerous river, walk the blazing desert, or hop the high fence, to get to the other side? If that's the place where dreams—American Dreams—come true, why wouldn't we be happy there?

We ran toward Don, hugged him, and cheered. Maybe if we acted like it we would soon believe it. The people we had built memories with, the people we had learned to laugh with, to play hide and seek with, to write our ABCs with—all gone. Our childhood was not too important in contrast with their adult plans—not important enough for an explanation anyway.

Indeed, life seemed better in California. There were palm trees and the beach was in walking distance from our place. Everyone spoke English and was white. The streets were clean, and grown-ups wore slacks and dress shirts when they left their homes. The air smelled fresh, and our apartment had a carpet. Maybe we did move to the Promised Land.

But the nicer cars, nicer walls, nicer brands, and nicer looks didn't tell us right away that what had been promised was not as originally advertised. It didn't take long for nightmares to come back in a whole new form.

How many times did my little sister, six years younger than me, beg me at nights to tell her a bedtime story? Again and again she asked for stories that I had often told the night before. "That one about Cinderella." "The one about the dwarfs." I had never been told stories as a child, but now I was the adult trying to feed someone else's childhood so it wouldn't perish before it got a chance to bloom—so it would take longer for her to feel the effects of the shadows that lived beyond our bedroom walls.

Soon after we began living with Don, we learned that he was an avid drinker. He filled our space with smoke, lighting a second cigarette before he'd put down the first. He bragged at the kitchen table about how loud his farts were, even when we refused to eat anymore out of disgust. We tried to ignore the yelling—the shouting that seemed to go on for hours, the slamming of doors, the screams . . . again, that ceaseless shouting. I could feel it vibrating through the walls and doors. Or was it just in my heart and ears? It had to echo beyond our apartment. The walls we shared could not have been so thick as to shield us from witnesses. I hoped that if I remained silent, somehow by doing that, my little sister would be immune from the noise.

I walked into the kitchen one day. Mom was sitting in the living room with, in retrospect, a static idle sadness. I ventured into the refrigerator with hopes there'd be a misplaced slice of cheese, a forgotten half orange, a cracker hidden behind a jar. I put my right hand on the door. I placed my left hand on the plastic edge trying to reduce the noise to zero as I, very, very slowly, pulled the door open softly and quietly. You'd think I was pulling wires from a bomb and any wrong move or sound would detonate it. It kinda did. There wasn't another sound in the apartment. I breathed in trying to somehow absorb the fridge's sucking in of air. But my mom's voice immediately responded from the living room. I know she hadn't moved an inch in the quiet room. It wasn't so much the words, but the hopelessness, coupled with a tat of anger, in her voice. "Why are you opening it?" She said. "You know there is nothing in there."

I was hungry. But the feeling I felt was an odd one. I felt not sorry, but guilty. Not because I thought somehow I had broken some rule, but because

I had brought out again in my mom the acknowledgment that she couldn't provide for us. Her relationship with this guy was supposed to be the light at the end of the tunnel, and America the Promised Land. She had no friends here. She didn't understand the language. She couldn't work. She brought us here and we had found nothing but unanswered questions.

Even stability was something she couldn't assure us. This fear became real one day when Caro and I played at the wall that separated our apartment complex and the dirt field next door. We'd use a large block of wood on our end to hop over it. The dirt level was a few feet higher on the other side, so we didn't fear falling. As we played, the police showed up on the side of the dirt field. Mom heard the sound and came running outside. The police officer never got out of the vehicle, but asked only where we lived. We pointed to our apartment, the one closest to the wall. He advised us to be careful and to not be hopping over any more walls. He then drove away. Mom came toward us and brought us together. She said something I hadn't thought of before, "You have to be careful. Don't you see that we are here illegally and they can kick us out back to Mexico?"

"Illegally?" I kept thinking.

She looked honestly concerned and worried. I walked over to our room with that hovering over my head. What did she mean by "illegally"? And how careful did we need to be?

It didn't take long to learn that there was a subculture of kids, just like us, who were brought here by other parents with hopes that they'd have a better life than the one they had in Latin America. But even then, as a sixth grader, I remember feeling uncomfortable. The palm trees are nice, and so is the beach. It's cool that you can drink the water from the faucet without getting sick and play on sidewalks that aren't cracked—but should we really be doing something "illegal"? What kind of people does that make us? Are we criminals? Are we bad people?

I didn't have an answer. I was still trying to figure out what kind of family we were on either side of the wall.

Christmas Eve

In the lead-up to our first Christmas in the United States, we did not have any nice decorations to put on walls or windows, but our kindly neighbors let us borrow some of theirs. We kept staring at how shiny they were. "Like real snow!" Caro and I said through giggles. Don's mom went through her storage and gathered an artificial Christmas tree and plenty of ornaments—all golden.

We plugged in the lights and they glowed like the entrance to a park of angels. At first we thought the bottom of the tree would remain empty, until Don's family visited and placed wrapped boxes under it. I looked at my little sister and saw a spark in her eyes—a spark I too felt inside. It might have been the reflection of the tree lights, or maybe signs that Christmas had arrived.

We looked at the wrapped boxes. The bows are bright—some with sparkles. We looked at the names on the cards and giggled. We shook them and tried to guess what was inside. Though we weren't the closest of siblings, she was my best friend. She was the one to share my smiles with, and I was the one with whom she shared hers. With those wide smiles, we pretended we could smell the tree's fresh scent. We looked at the lights wrapped around the tree and imagined they were stars in the sky on a beautiful, scandalous night.

On Christmas Eve, though, mom sat on the couch with a bleak look on her face, the room dimly lit by the tree. I knew that there was no party we had to go to, and we definitely had no loved ones stopping by. We tried to interact with her, cheer her up, but she waved us off.

Where was Don? I didn't know.

What could I do? I had to think of something. Though I, as a boy in a strange country, had my own needs, I felt it was my responsibility to care for my lil' sister and make her smile. I asked her to join me by the tree. We sat on the carpet next to the gifts that, according to American tradition, we had to open on Christmas morning and not on Christmas Eve like we did in Mexico. Even in the most humble situations during the holidays, back home we could hear someone singing, at least some kind of joy coming from the television or someone stopping by for a quick visit and a hug. *"Feliz Navidad."* "Merry Christmas." Unfortunately, we had none of that here.

I grabbed one of the Christmas cards we had received. When I opened it, a song began to play. Our eyes opened wide. We had found treasure. Being the only sound in the house, it was the loudest. I looked behind me and saw mom sunk in the couch, her face resting on her fist, far too deep in thought, a shadow resting on her eyes. I turned my head back and continued giggling. My sister didn't speak much English, but some tunes were easy; plus, we had learned some of them from American movies and commercials. And so we sang, *"Jingle bells. Jingle bells. Jingle all the way. Oh what fun it is to ride on a one-horse open sleigh. Hey!"*

We also sang in Spanish, *"Na-vi-dad. Na-vi-dad. Pronto llegará. Es un día de alegría y gran felicidad. Hey!"* which translates as, *"Christmas. Christmas. It will soon be here. It's a day of joy and great happiness. Hey!"*

Our innocence made us believe that was the way it worked. To the tune of "Jingle Bells" we sang over and over, smiling, swaying our heads from side to side. Christmas was almost here, and it is a day of joy and great happiness. *Hey!* We laughed. We giggled. As I bumped my shoulder against Caro, I looked at her, and she beamed—as little sisters do. She was with me and I was with her. The boxes with bows winked at us. We had a sky of lights before us. We had music in our hands. Most importantly, we had each other. Joy and great happiness had arrived. *Hey!*

Finally, the front door opened. Don had been drinking, and he was not alone. A couple and their two kids had come with him. He was a former drinking buddy, and she was his tolerant wife. The boy, whom I had tried to befriend on previous visits, was hyperactive and defiant. The girl knew exactly the way things had to be done and when they had to be done. My mom didn't understand a lick of what they said. Don would drink with his bud, while my sister and I would put up with the kids' heavy attitudes. We dreaded being with them, even though they were kids like us. They exhibited dysfunctional behavior that even we felt uncomfortable with, but that Christmas Eve, it was my family's turn to put on a show.

My mom and Don began to shout at one another. I kept trying to distract my little sister from their arguing, "Look at this light. Look at this ball. It's so pretty." I started singing, and she followed, *"Na-vi-dad. Na-vi-dad. Pronto llegará."* The family just stood there—uncomfortable, I imagine. *"It's a day of joy and great happiness."* Mom ran to her room and slammed the door behind her. *"Hey!"*

I don't remember the rest of the night, but it remains forever scarred in my mind, in my heart. Most stories I can remember from that period had a similar feeling—us children holding on to innocence and fighting for joy with our bare hearts, only to be blindsided by the shadows of adult decisions.

Soon after that, I said goodbye to the few buds I had made in school—mostly immigrants like me—and we packed our things again and headed south, the Promised Land in our rear view mirror. I sat quietly staring out the window, thinking of the large block of wood, the nightly fairytale stories, the empty fridge, the golden Christmas tree, and the prayers my little sister and I would pray at night. Any of those moments would have been a perfect time for God to show up and do His thing.

I think.

2

THE PEOPLE OF LOVE

"Toto, I've a feeling we're not in Kansas anymore."
—Dorothy, in *The Wizard of Oz*

Charay

Neither my mom nor Don, who continued to stay together, told us where we were going—not for feedback, not even as an FYI. As in many other cases, I only learned of our destination by overhearing them in conversation. I couldn't believe it.

Charay (*Cha-rah-ee*) is a humble, tiny, rural town in the state of Sinaloa, Mexico, in the Gulf of California. It currently has about 3,000 people. Back then it had to be half of that. I spent every summer as a kid, and all of third grade, in Charay. Summers were fun, but third grade wasn't really. You could walk from one end of town to the other on its one paved road in less than thirty minutes (and that's with child-sized legs).

Many houses were built entirely of clay. Ours was half clay, half brick. The more humble single-room homes were made out of cardboard or sheets of synthetic material. The larger yards were filled with fruit trees, including mango, tamarind, guava, and lime. The road that connected us to the rest of the world had no traffic lights nor stop signs (though it had some speed bumps). When nighttime came, someone would grab a long stick and press the switch high up on a light pole, turning the street lights on. There were a few mom and pop stores where we'd get our supplies, but we'd need to take the one-hour bus ride into Los Mochis, the nearest city, if we needed something extravagant like shoes.

The residents were hard-working folks who mostly lived off the land. We had a hen house and a couple of cows that supplied our eggs and milk. Once a month we'd chase a chicken around the yard and turn it into chicken soup.

Local entertainment included horse races and the monthly dance that was held at the *plazuela*, the gazebo plaza.

Back then, most people in the town had an education no higher than sixth grade—if that. They married and conceived young and had to worry about providing for their offspring. Thus, work was not reserved only for grown-ups; as soon as a child was capable of breaking fruit off the plant, he or she would likely be enrolled in the workforce, as my cousins and I were. They'd wake us up with shouts at the butt-crack of dawn and we'd jump in the back of a truck that would take us to the *bajio (ba-hee-oh),* the fields. We'd all line up with a bucket at the entrance to a *surco*, an aisle in the plantation, and work our way to the end. We'd sit on the bucket, search the plants on both sides for fruit (green beans, pumpkin, and corn), drop the plucked fruit in the bucket, stand, take a few steps forward, and do it all over again.

At the end of our hard work we were "paid" a thousand pesos, which in those days allowed us to buy a cold Coke and a bag of Principe, a round cookie with a hint of cinnamon at each end and chocolate caramel filling at the core. Though we worked a lot, we ate humble meals, sometimes eating beans for breakfast, lunch, and dinner, so those cookies sure tasted like heaven. When you work your young ass off you learn to appreciate the little things and never take them for granted.

Now that mom was pregnant with her third, Don's family was concerned that we were moving to a place that had one single telephone for the entire town. It was at the local store, and people came and paid by the minute. I remember when it arrived. We all stood there as the company guy drove up, pulled those cables out of the truck, climbed that latter, did his thing, and brought the cables back down. It had a booth and everything. For some kids in town it was like watching fire for the first time.

Although at the time I wasn't pleased about our move to Charay, looking back now, I see it was a special place, especially for a kid. It was a place with few rules, where a child's imagination could run wild on the limitless scenarios nature offered. Long before technology would hold our attention captive in the palm of our hand, we looked outward for fantasy and adventure. I had some of the most memorable moments in that little town. Friends to this day envy my stories the same way they might envy the tales of Huckleberry Finn. Stories about learning how to swim in a canal while trying to evade a stray alligator, riding cows out in the open field, or building castles and swinging from branches on giant trees in the middle of the untrailed forest. There was no limit to what we could do when we set our imagination free—and free we were.

"The Jews"

Dozens of men, teens, and little boys who often have a *manda* to fulfill, participate in a "sacrificial pilgrimage" during the Easter season in Charay. A *manda* is a promise you make, most commonly to the Virgin of Guadalupe (Virgin Mary), or to one of the saints (surprisingly seldom made to Jesus or the Father), in return for a fulfillment of a favor—a miracle. They hide their identity under a mask made of animal skin or wood painted with exotic colors, symbolizing spirits, demons, or sins they were repenting from. Sometimes they created just the wackiest, most random array of colors and arrangements they could think of. They wore lines of wooden bells around their ankles, sometimes going up to their knees. Sometimes barefoot and shirtless, most often wearing plastic sandals and wrapped in blankets, they held a drum in their hands and beat and rattled their way in a parade of incomprehensible sounds all the way around town.

The first time I saw them, deeply baffled, I pulled on my Aunt Miralda's shirt and asked, "Who are they?" To this she calmly replied, "They are the Jews." In quick response, I inquired, "What are the Jews?" Her answer made both my mouth and my eyes open wide, "They are the ones who killed Jesus."

Los Judios (Hoo-dee-ohs), "the Jews," come into town each and every year. As children, we awaited their visit with great anticipation. We'd hear first the beat of the drum. Then the shake of the rattle. "*¡Ahí vienen!*" "Here they come! Here they come!" The rain of footsteps, followed by a chant that went something like, "*Tewa, tewa, tewa, te-tewa. Tewa, tewa, tewa. Tewa, tewa, tewa.*"

Kilometer after kilometer, and day after day, they'd journey through most areas of town. If families wanted to be visited by the Jews, they'd place a wooden cross in front of their house. The Jews would march around the cross three times, make their noises, knock the cross down, and head down to the next. People would rush to their doorways, windows, and front yards to witness, with a certain awe, the surreal experience of watching the Jews.

On the last day, on Resurrection Sunday, the Jews would take the straw-filled dummy of Judas Iscariot (the apostle who betrayed Jesus) and carry him on a chariot three times around the Catholic Church while beating him with sticks, shouting, and spitting at him. Afterward, they'd set him on fire behind the church and celebrate his death. They then would come to the front of the church and stage a fight with the shepherds (the ones who witnessed the announcement of Jesus' birth). They'd throw rocks and sticks at each other, leaving a cloud of dust over us. The Jews would then line up on both sides to form an aisle that would lead from the bottom of the stairs up and onto the church entrance. A man dressed in a black robe, who represented the Devil, would then escort the Jews through the aisle, up the stairs to the church entrance, and back several times until finally allowing them to enter. They'd come to the altar, watch the veil be torn in half (symbolizing the ripping of the temple veil at Jesus' death), and come outside for a final cheer. At this point the Jews would take their masks off and show us who they were. We would then walk over to the fair and celebrate with rides, games, and food.

This celebration is fully sponsored by the Catholic Church and the local priest, who have an ironclad cultural hold on the region. For the rest of the world, this tradition may seem to be irreverent and distasteful at best. Indeed, this cartoonized version of "the Jews," which was based on religiously sponsored ignorance, looked very different from the Jews I later saw in movies like *Schindler's List* and *The Boy in the Striped Pajamas*—and, more significantly, from those I came to admire, respect, support, and call close friends. But in a culture with high poverty, low education, corrupt governance, and endless pride in the past, you get traditions like this that, to those who celebrate it, are seen as completely natural, colorful and harmless.

Mom's Journey

When I was in junior college, mom and I chatted at the kitchen table one night. Holding a cup of hot chocolate, she spoke freely from her heart, her eyes focused ahead of her at no particular point. I sat next to her, amazed that history was making a rare appearance, and simply listened. The sands of time rippled through that late night and took us back to the black and white days when she took a risk and moved to the city.

Just like my younger cousins' experiences in Charay today are much different from my past experiences, so too were my mom's experiences as a child significantly different from mine. I've had many conversations with my aunts and uncles, my *tias* and *tios*, about their upbringings in Charay, and their stories always seemed to come from an alternate reality of the place I knew as a child.

Tata (*ta-ta*) Nano, grandpa Fernando, was an interesting character himself. As tall as they come, he eventually hunched over from old age and hard labor. He had a thirst for alcohol and women that the greatest of mayhems could not quench. All of his kids grew up fast and in different directions. Stories of alcoholism, divorce, children out of wedlock, extreme poverty, and many other traits seemed to follow them all. Even so, Tata Nano had little patience when it came to his kids' rebellion. He was comfortable applying physical punishment, be it with a belt, a shoe, or worse. He would even tie them to a tree to teach them a lesson. He once chased me with a bamboo stick when I refused to go back to *el bajio*. He left me beaten and weeping in the middle of the front yard, trembling in the fetal position.

He forced his kids to skip elementary school so they could work the land, with the girls getting the worst treatment. "Why would they need to go to school? They're women!" Tata Nano would unapologetically argue. They would ride carriages pulled by mules on the way to *el bajio* over a dirt road that ran between the canal and the elementary school. The girls would hide, pulling a tarp over their heads, but the kids in school knew that carriage and ran toward the window shouting, "*¡Ahí van las García!*" "There go the Garcías!" The embarrassment was great—not as bad as the labor—but nowhere near as painful as the broken desire to be inside that classroom.

Despite this, they managed to attend school on their days off work. But their dad wouldn't even give them money for the most basic school supplies. My mom recalled getting up early, drinking coffee for breakfast, grabbing eggs from the hen house, and running to people's houses to sell them for just enough pesos to buy a little notebook and pencil before rushing to school. Her professors were understanding and tried to support her as much as possible. "It is a miracle I finished elementary school," mom told me.

I couldn't help but think what a shame it was—how such a young soul could crave education, love, and fair treatment, and get the opposite in return.

As a teenager, she moved to Mexicali, dreaming of a better life. She first worked as a maid and later at the hotel where she eventually met my father.

When I was born, she lived in a small condo surrounded by college students who attended Universidad Autónoma de Baja California (UABC), the main university in the state of Baja California. Very poor themselves, they packed in tiny rooms to save some money while pursuing an education. Mom was alone. She didn't have many friends. My bastard father had abandoned her to face luck on her own. He walked away and never looked back.

Bastard.

Late one night her baby boy would not find sleep. His young belly hadn't had enough sustenance and was incapable of understanding his young mother's predicament. She had been working extra hours and hadn't had much sleep in days. What little money she made went to rent and utilities, and she struggled to put food on the table and inside the baby bottle. Thick veins showed on her forehead, and she felt her hair was losing color. Her hands trembled while hopelessness crawled through her like a spirit overpowering her being. She didn't notice when her tears started hitting the forehead of her frail newborn. She tried calming him with singing, but that singing soon turned into a deep lament that echoed beyond the slim walls and windows of that tiny one-room apartment. She could've been in college just like her neighbors learning about Socrates and Descartes and the laws of Physics, or how to fill out t tables and make a five-axis diagnosis. Instead, she gave way to despair and knew this would be the longest night of her life.

But human hope believes in light at the end of the tunnel. That night, human hope existed inside poor college students who heard our cries and refused to let them go painfully into the night. They knocked on our door and opened their hands to show what they had put together. Some peso bills and coins that she refused immediately. But love is more persistent than that—it always should be. They rushed to the store and brought back baby formula, bread, and ham. And as if that wasn't enough, knowing she could not afford a sitter, they all took turns holding the baby so she could sleep. They later took the baby boy to class, to homework sessions, and even on dates.

She hypothesizes that this was probably the reason why, later in life, the boy would struggle to communicate with kids his own age. At the very mature age of ten, he'd come home mad for losing another friend, but apparently not too disappointed. "They are too immature, mom," he'd explain.

As she sipped on that cup of hot chocolate, sharing these memories and experiences with me, she smiled and added, "If I could find any of them. I would thank them so much. They did so much for me, for us."

I sat there and felt the weight of the past on my shoulders. I knew I'd had it rough. But for the first time I saw a glimpse of *her* past, and once again saw evidence of the true power of the human spirit.

My mom and Don soon decided that Charay might not be the best option and started looking for opportunities in Mexicali. Don got a job at the place he was consulting for when he first met mom. They bought a house four houses away from my aunt. Since the school in Mexicali wouldn't accept my records from the United States, I stayed in Charay to finish sixth grade and returned to Mexicali at the end of summer.

Living in Charay was nowhere near glamorous, but it did teach me a lot of valuable lessons. I learned how to be a kid and to be impressed by the fruit of imagination. But most importantly, I would later see my mother's story— and my journey with her—from a different angle. She had fought her own demons with a sword and shield and had worked to define her life on her own terms. I stand where I am today because of the sacrifices she made, sacrifices I misunderstood for so long. Tears and struggles may have marked the life of my fearless, loving mother, but if you saw her now, you may not guess it. She broke free from the firm grasp of destiny's hell to offer us a chance to write a future of our own. She may never have known where life would take her or her children, but she believes now those tears have been redeemed.

I learned early that fanfare and rattles get attention, that our past has consequences, and that love knows no bounds when pressed to save the lost. In life we see those who wear a mask of godliness but who, following the test of history, are revealed to be nothing more than a spectacle. We also see those who give love a face, regardless of creed and doctrine, and add value to our lives. I chose to hold on to the latter, as we healed from the past, and learned to see through masks. I wanted to be one of them, the rescuers, the real ones, the believers, the people of love.

3

THE BODY OF CHRIST

*"As a child I felt myself to be alone, and I am still, because I know things
and must hint at things which others apparently know nothing of,
and for the most part do not want to know."*
—Carl Gustav Jung, *Memories, Dreams, Reflections*

Terror

Growing up and living with Don, my sister and I lived in what we now call
"a constant state of terror." We never knew when the next outburst of anger
would be, or whether there would even be one. If we left the toilet seat up,
if we showed up two minutes after curfew, if we left a toy in the wrong
place, if we didn't slide the bathroom towel all the way to the right, if we said
the wrong thing, if we glanced the wrong way—we could be grounded for
an hour, a week, or a month. It always depended on our stepfather's mood
and the amount of alcohol in his system. But to be honest, the tone of his
voice, not its volume, and the demeaning, hateful look he'd have in his eyes
was enough to make us tread cautiously. The type of punishment was never
certain, and we never knew how the next shouting match would end, either
between him and us, or between him and mom. During the latter, we would
hide in our doorless room and pretend not to exist, trying to quiet our own
breathing. We would huddle on the bed and place a blanket over our faces, as
if that would somehow protect us from the uncertainty.

One day, when I was in seventh grade, I sat watching TV at my cousin's
house when loud bangs shook the front door. Tia Aide wasn't home, so
my cousin David (*Da-beed*) headed toward the door. He opened it to find
Don's staring eyes with a look quite familiar to my sister and me. He firmly
demanded my presence. David frailly turned to me. Part of him wanted me to
escape, and the other part feared my stepfather's retribution. I stumbled up to

the door to be greeted by Don's hand on my neck, pulling me outside. "What? What happened?" I asked repeatedly. He responded with angry mumbles that I couldn't decipher and then threw me to the ground on the patio in front of the house. Though my eyes asked for help, I couldn't speak. Hopelessly I resigned myself to the familiar situation.

Once we made it to our house, I saw Caro crying her eyes out. My sister had accused me of having done something to her, causing her despair. I later determined that she had done something wrong and started crying as a distraction to avoid his wrath. I kept trying to explain myself—that I hadn't even been around—and eventually convinced him of my innocence. He finally shot me a look of apathy and indifference, as if I were a nuisance. "What do you want, an apology?" he said before walking away. I stood there cold, once again, in the foreign, unwelcoming place that was supposed to be my home.

But I wasn't ready to give up just yet. Others had told me there was someone who could help—if I prayed, and if I believed.

A Higher Help

To my mother's surprise, I signed up for Catechism. It is a normal step in a Mexican kid's life to follow the established steps of Catholicism, but it's usually done as a little kid and I was now thirteen.

I was the oldest in a class designed for children. But my teacher, in all her sweetness, always acknowledged that it was a rare and beautiful thing to pursue a closeness to God, regardless of age.

If He was out there, I wanted to find Him.

I learned the sacraments, the saints, the doctrine, the traditions, and every single prayer, along with everything about the Virgin, the Trinity, the Pope, and the Roman Catholic Church. Week after week I excelled and received praise from my teacher and envy from my classmates. I always showed up early and left late. I was hungry for it.

I observed the images on the church's glass windows when they would take us there—they seemed so holy and anciently mystic. I had hoped that there was something more powerful than the world we lived in, and more powerful than the crap that took place in it. More powerful than the evil that was left as evidence for the greed and sin of humanity.

I was happy that I was not the only older kid in the class. I always sat with Marcos, who was a year younger than me. I'd let him copy some of my answers from time to time. We'd practice the prayers together until we memorized them. He always showed up with more raggedy clothes than me. He often smelled like he hadn't showered in days. He had a haircut that made me wonder if he had cut it himself—he sure didn't comb it. And he seemed to have skipped more meals than he would've liked. He also had a reputation as a troublemaker. The other kids would tell me stories of bad things he did on his block and at his school. But certainly God would be happy that he was there learning about Him.

Although I was always surprised to see him there, truth is I always knew why he came. I could easily imagine that he lived in an environment worse than the one I had—one almost certainly defined by alcoholism, lack of proper food, absent parents, and probably drug use. But behind that tough boy bravado, I could see innocence flicker in his eyes. He was trying to do a final *something* before he fully let go and gave himself to the streets.

To put it bluntly, he looked the way I felt. I knew he was there looking for the same thing I was—hope.

Absolution

I remember one crucial day in our training as if it was yesterday. We were incredibly nervous. We had prepared for days. We knew it was a big deal. They told us so. We hopped on the vehicles and headed toward church. This confession would be our first experience with a ritual that would continue for the rest of our Catholic lives.

For days and nights I had debated with myself about the things I would say, but I knew there was one thing hidden deep in the back of my mind—in my heart—that had to come forward if I was to truly seek purity. Was it guilt? Was it shame? Was it pain? Was it all of the above?

It was.

We all dressed in our Sunday best, with one exception. Marcos smelled dirty and his clothes were wrinkled. People looked at him funny, but I was the only one who did not make a comment or stare in disgust. He was the only one close to my age, and there was always an unspoken understanding between the two of us. I was just glad that he had made it at all. He sat next to me, smiled, and looked down in comfort.

Our hands were shaky when we got to church. Our eyes couldn't stop wandering off. Our giggling was out of control. We kept practicing our prayers over and over. "*Padre Nuestro que estás en los cielos*, hallowed be Thy name . . ." "*Dios te salve, Maria. Llena eres de gracia.* The Lord is with thee. Blessed art thou among women . . ." "*Yo creo en una iglesia, Santa, Católica y*

Apostólica. We acknowledge one baptism for the forgiveness of sins . . ." We learned and practiced the major prayers and even the minor ones. We didn't know which ones we were gonna get.

When my turn came, I walked inside the priest's office. I wondered why we weren't inside the traditional box I had seen in movies. He sat there, ageless in his black outfit and white Roman collar, watching as I made slow steps toward him. He didn't seem puzzled or affected by the sins of the kids who'd confessed before me. I saw a chair in front of me and took a seat. The place looked pretty ordinary. There weren't any cool rays of sunlight coming in, no incense burning, and no aura around his body. He looked so, well, human.

"*Ave Maria purísima,*" he said. "*Sin pecado concebida,*" I replied. *Conceived without sin.* I had been taught these steps, and I didn't screw them up.

"Tell me your sins," he continued.

Oh boy, this is happening. This is it. This is why I didn't sleep last night. This is why I couldn't eat this morning. Would lightning strike me? No. But he is probably going to slap me right across the face. I probably would do the same, I thought to myself.

He seemed unamazed by the various lies and mischief making I confessed to.

No thunder yet.

"Is there anything else?" he asked.

I could so easily answer, "No," I thought. He would never know. He would forgive me of all my sins, right? I would not have to go through the humiliation, and I really wouldn't mind being spared his wrath. But I wasn't sure I would have been able to live with myself. Being thirteen meant I was a big boy now. I knew best. I felt the clock was ticking faster and, if I didn't speak in the next half second, I would have lost my opportunity. But if I told him he would certainly get mad. His eyes would get all big. He might even stand up in disbelief. So I chose to speak, "Well, there is one more thing."

I quickly thought of all the other things I could say instead. There was plenty else to confess, small stuff, but I knew I was supposed to bring up the main ones. This would certainly count—not just as a main one but *the* main one. I could even lie. It wasn't too late. Come on, Fernando. Lie. It's easy. You've done it a million times.

I didn't. I couldn't.

My eyes blurred as the memories surged from the locked vault in my heart, up my throat, and onto my lips. My mouth struggled to speak as my eyes came to focus on the vision of what I knew was my greatest sin.

I was ten and she was fourteen. She took me inside my room's closet, closed the door, and said we would play a game. My pants came off, then my underwear, leaving me vulnerable. I didn't know why she wanted to sit on me, but I knew it felt weird, wrong. She was curious and I was confused. What had just happened?

I wish it had ended there. Her brother, a year or two older than her, later thought that it'd be a good idea to play games of his own. "But I don't want to touch it," I said to no effect. "Please, I don't want to do this."

Later, another boy his age who lived near us had games of his own.

Why can't you all just leave me alone?!

I was asking for help as much as I was confessing.

"Dirty games" is how I described it when words finally came out. My lips trembled. I couldn't look up. When I finally did, he didn't seem confused. But why didn't he look shocked, enraged, disappointed?

He didn't ask about the nights I spent in fear, feeling dirty, thinking it was all my fault.

"Okay, anything else?" he asked. "No," I said. He made the sign of the cross over me and absolved me from *all* of my sins.

But I wasn't ready to feel weightless just yet. I was still surprised, but I was expecting something more. At any second now God would do something that was going to surprise me, scare me, and fill me with awe. Of course I wasn't expecting thunder and smoke to fill the room. But something.

Then he told me to say five Our Fathers and five Hail Marys. He then thanked me and waved me off, remaining seated and unchanged.

"What just happened?" I kept thinking as I walked outside. Sin had left me, but why did I still feel the same?

All my classmates were waiting outside. "Did you tell him everything?" "Oh my gosh, I was so embarrassed." "Were you embarrassed?" "How did it go?"

We then gathered in the sanctuary for our prayer penance. "What did you get?" "What did he ask you to pray?"

I stood still. Wait a second, *all* of us got the exact same penance, the same homework? All of us got five Our Fathers and five Hail Marys? Wait, wait, wait. My young mind started to spin in place. How is it possible that we all had the same penance? Were all my sins equally as bad as his, and his, and hers, and the sins of that guy over there, and that girl too? Granted, I felt I got off a little easy, but I still thought it was odd.

Back in the van, I had to ask my teacher about it. "Why did we all get the same prayers?" "Well, there are only so many prayers so he had to repeat some." "No, I mean, we *all* got five Our Fathers and five Hail Marys as a penance," I said. "I mean, there is no way that we were all equally as bad or good, right?" To which she replied, "Well, maybe he felt that because this was the first time for all of you, and you are all kids, that it was fair to give you all the same penance."

I knew that was as good an answer as I would be able to get at that point, but my mind was not satisfied. In a way, I felt cheated. I wasn't sure, though, and I couldn't have told you at that moment what it was that I was expecting. But then again, the process wasn't over yet.

First Communion

I couldn't be more nervous. I thought I was going to throw up! I was up most of the night again waiting for Communion. My brand-new white clothes, which symbolized how clean my soul was, rested on the chair. I had tried really hard to not sin between my confession and now. We were told not to. I was terrified that I would commit a sin, even a small one, and ruin the whole thing.

"Why don't we confess right before Communion so we don't have the chance to sin with so many hours in between?" I asked. There was no answer that made sense. "God would understand," or "Try not to sin." But this is a big deal! We are going to eat the physical body and blood of Jesus Christ on a little wafer! That's what we were taught. Those little kids may not understand fully, but I did. God was physically going to enter me. He was going to go down my throat, travel through my intestines, and from there He would go into every vein and muscle in my body. He would become part of me! How could anyone take this lightly?!

Morning finally came. Our families packed the church. Well, sadly, not every family was there. Marcos' family wasn't. But he did dress up. He told me that he had borrowed his clothes and that he got them last minute. They weren't really all that white, and they didn't fit him well, but he was there. I realized he had made a much bigger sacrifice than any of us had to be there. He also didn't smell bad this time, and he tried to comb his untrained hair. We both smiled and then laughed really hard—he had even showered!

We stood in line next to each other. I was the tallest, and he was the second tallest, so he waited a step ahead of me. We both knew this was going to be a solemn moment. The saints on the glass-stained windows looked brighter than ever before. The choir's echo seemed to invite the angels to witness our ceremony. Every candle was lit. The priest and the nuns had worn their godly outfits. Every member of the community was in their Sunday best. This was going to be special.

"This is happening. This is happening." I kept saying under my breath. All of a sudden, there we were, on the way to the front, down the middle aisle, permanently recorded by flash photography. Are they going to fall down? Are they going to cry? The youngest and shortest students went first. Getting closer . . . Mom and Don watched me from the side. Even closer now . . . Marcos received the offering. Oh my, what if I forget what I'm supposed to say?! Is it "*Sin pecado concebida*"? Wait, is the "amen" said loudly, or whispered? Do I say "amen" and something else?

The white wafer rests on my tongue. I can feel it dissolving. Could it really happen this fast? God is entering my body like, right now, as we speak. Will something happen even before I get back to my seat? The choir. The guitars. The echo. The candles. The statue of the *Virgen*. The statue of *Jesús*. The saints on the windows. The crowd. The packed aisles. The bumping of shoulders. The line of kids. The looks. I think I'm gonna . . .

I'm back at the *cuadra*—back at my block. Still dressed in white. We walk from house to house sharing the news. "*¿Te bautisaste?*" Did you get baptized? "Yup." "Aha."

It's a memory now. But this much is true: nothing really changed past the fanfare of painful confessions, memorized prayers, white clothes, and thin wafers.

Unable to find what he was looking for, Marcos' life went back to the usual—with his shaggy hair and worn-out clothes. God didn't show up once he took the wafer and went back home. So he ended up seeking peace out on the streets, and at the bottom of a bottle.

We looked for God. We did what we were supposed to. We learned what we were supposed to. We prayed what we were supposed to. We believed what we were supposed to. We painfully confessed what we were supposed to. And lo and behold, God didn't respond how He was supposed to.

As for my shadows, they came back in full force.

Marcos always followed me around in Catechism. He gave it a try, copied from me, and found no fruit. Maybe it was time for me to try it his way. At least I might learn, like him, how to forget.

4

THE EVE OF THE DEATH OF INNOCENCE

"All children, except one, grow up."
—J. M. Barrie, *Peter Pan*

A Second Chance

Eighth grade. Every once in a while Don would sit with me at the kitchen table while I was doing homework. The alcohol would make him nostalgic and lead him to talk about the old days. I can still picture him sitting there, talking in front of me, but not talking to me. He would glance at me from time to time. His blue eyes, shaggy hair, huge mustache—just like Chuck Norris, which is what his friends nicknamed him. He held a beer in one hand and a cigarette in the other that moved along with the story.

It would often get late, but at least there was peace.

I let him talk, partly in fear that he would get mad if I said I had to finish my homework because it was already past midnight. He didn't seem to get what the books, pencils, and notebooks on the table were for. My using the calculator or writing down answers during the small gaps in his stories weren't loud enough clues.

But I also let him talk because I could sense his humanity—a rare sight. Never something too personal. Never a tear. He'd share anecdotes about times with his buddies back in the United States, about the places where he had lived, and about his childhood. Though I didn't get to say much, I knew I was the only one in the family he could speak English with since I was the only one fluent enough. Hence, I became his unexpected, late-night confidant. Through it all, there was something I understood well—he was homesick. He was now the immigrant in a foreign land.

But even though we had our moments, peace never lasted for very long.

Tenth grade. Very late at night. I look over to the other side of the room

41

and my sister is just as awake as I am. We knew mom kept walking around the house, looking out the window, to the couch and back. We had the bed sheets up to our necks, staring at the dark ceiling, pretending to be asleep. We hear a car park in the front of the house. A few seconds later we hear the door.

It started with mom's demand for an explanation. From the sound of his voice and how late it was, we knew he had been drinking a lot. It seemed, by the sound the furniture made, that he was struggling to stand. There were many words shouted.

"Don't you care about the kids?" She asked. She wanted to know why he kept squandering all the money. And then came the kicker: "If you want, you can go find another woman!" She tells him. He could leave the house if he wanted. *"¡¿Otro mujer?!"* He asked in his broken Spanish, his voice cracking at the end. She was sick and tired of it and was way past the ultimatum stage.

Caro and I turned to face each other. We could see each other's eyes wide open thanks to the dim moonlight coming through the window. We were the kids. It was our job to keep our mouths shut and never question the lives of the grown-ups, even if, or especially if, they were screwing up ours. We just laid there in shock, but I'd lie if there wasn't a hint of hope of relief.

The following morning, probably because he knew we must have heard what happened, he seemed contrite. He said he was going to change because he cared for our mother and because he cared for us. *"Yo siento mucho amor por su mamá. Y por su hermana y tú también,"* he said. He felt a lot of love for my mom, my sister, and me.

I wanted to believe it. I really did.

Growing up without a father had been exceptionally hard. He had been the closest thing I'd ever had to one and he was asking for a second chance. I agreed to it, but deep down inside I knew that I agreed not just for him. It was a chance for me—to have what I never had before.

But, though we had our moments, peace never lasted for very long.

A Typical Sunday

Eleventh grade. June 12, 1994. It was a typical Sunday morning. We moved slowly around the house on the weekends. The growing heat anticipated a typical Mexicali summer, but our downstairs window AC unit blew in refrigerated air, helping keep the house cool. I did some chores; played with my little brother, Ernest, who was now four years old; and helped clean a nasty diaper for my newborn baby sister, Sharon (both of these little ones were blond, taking after Don).

We started watching a movie as it came time for lunch. Mom brought the food to us in the living room.

We had been working on building a new bedroom in the back of the house for some time now. I had been helping Don put the wooden ceiling together. It had become a little project the both of us could work on. Those times were actually cool. He seemed to enjoy the help and I enjoyed learning. He would cut the pieces. We would then varnish them and glue them to each other, side by side, until they covered the length of the room. We applied insulation and texture, and he handled the electrical wiring himself. He had experience in that. It started to look pretty good. Definitely something to feel proud of.

Don decided he would work on some of the wiring after lunch. He took his drill and headed outside to the electrical box, adjacent to the neighbor's aluminum fence. Mom and my siblings stayed downstairs, and I headed upstairs to my room to listen to music.

Though the new room wasn't completely finished, mom and Don had already moved into it. This meant I was finally able to have my own room. A teenager could certainly use his own space. I plastered my walls with posters, some of popular *Rock Mexicano* bands like Caifanes, Fobia, and Cafe Tacuba, but primarily with posters of Mexico's pop rock diva, Gloria Trevi. With her tangled hair, ripped pantyhose, weathered shoes, and ever-intense look—she was defiant, blunt, controversial, sexy, and broken. The idol many of us sought after as a means of identification, lost in a world of cultural taboos and expectations.

My window, which faced the front porch, sat open so fresh air would flow freely. I turned the dial on my boombox until I found a tune I liked and sang along. As soon as a song ended, I would start a search for a new one. I was on song two or three that day when a loud noise interrupted my singing. It was a sound that didn't seem natural in the laziness of the day—a loud metal bang accompanied by a very loud scream.

I lowered the volume and quickly formed a hypothesis. The neighbor's fence was an ugly sheet of metal, perhaps seven-feet tall. I knew the bang had to be it. I had heard the sound before when something hit it. The shout didn't come from a parent yelling at a child. It sounded like a something-happened-that-I-didn't-want-to-happen shout. Could it've been a cry of pain? Surprise? I was perplexed. Both the bang and the shout were loud.

As I neared the window to check if I could see anything, I heard Don's drill. He was obviously still working. But still, something just didn't feel right.

I walked out of my room and headed downstairs. "Mom, I think I heard something."

Mom, Caro, and I headed to the front door, walked outside, and looked around. Nothing. We walked toward the right and turned around the corner, and there . . . there he was . . .

. . . lying on the ground. Shirtless with jean shorts. The drill lying next to him, still running. I can still feel its vibration.

Mom gasped and brought her hands to her mouth. Caro stood frozen.

"Don?" I called his name. He didn't respond.

"Don?" I repeated with a more concerned tone in my voice as we got closer. I could now see the huge dent on the metal fence to the left, the wooden table he had been standing on, and the open breaker box on the wall before us.

"Don?" I kept saying, shaking his body and touching his face. He didn't seem to be breathing. I got on my knees, picked up his upper body, and shook him in my arms against my chest as the tone in my voice grew frightened and desperate, "Don?! Please! Don!"

What could I do? What should I do? I've seen this in movies.

We all ran to the front of the house, into the middle of the street, and started shouting, "Help! Help! Help!"

Kids on the street stopped playing. Mothers called out their husbands. Neighbors started coming out and gathered around us. I quickly lost track of where mom and Caro were as the men and I walked in through the fence and stood in front his body. I told them what happened. "What do you want to do?" They asked me. "Help me bring him to the front of the house," was the first thing I could think of. We all took an arm or a leg and carefully brought his body to the front. "Call an ambulance!" I shouted to people, and someone ran to the phone. Those of us who remained around his body tried whatever we could think of. Someone slapped him on his face. "¡Despiértate!" "Wake up! Wake up!"

He was not responding.

I was the only one from my family there. I had no idea where mom went, or where my siblings were for that matter. Dozens of neighbors, children and grown-ups, had blocked the front gate and were sticking their heads above the brick walls on the sides. The men around me were as clueless as I was.

"Where the hell are they?" A lot of time went by. We couldn't believe how slow the response time was for the paramedics. If it had been the United States, it would've been at least a third of the time. How painful it is to sit there, helpless, and know there is nothing else you can do but wait. The hands on my watch let out a ghostly laugh that reminded me I had no power over how long it would take for help to arrive. I held his hand and looked around, trembling, silently begging for a miracle to take place.

There is no way this is real. It was a typical Sunday.

In the distance, we heard an ambulance and wondered if it was the one coming here. I wondered how long it would take to arrive. I had run out of ideas and I was running out of hope.

When the paramedics finally arrived, people moved out of the way to let them in, but otherwise they all remained fixed in place, observant. The paramedics opened their bags and brought out some equipment, including a syringe and a small medicine bottle. They sucked liquid into the syringe and injected it into his left arm. But . . . wait . . . "Why is that happening?" The liquid was not going anywhere. A little bubble inflated right on his vein and chilled still. "Why is it not circulating into the rest of his body?" The paramedic tried to push it along the vein with his fingers—to little effect. The liquid was stuck in the same place where he had injected it.

The harsh reality started to sink in.

I looked above and saw a nearly perfect blue sky extend in all directions, interrupted only by a few small, white clouds floating along. I brought my eyes down and found the paramedic's eyes directed at me. He paused and waited to make sure he had my attention before slowly uttering the words I dreaded would follow, "He's gone."

"No. It can't be," I thought. I quickly pressed my ear to Don's chest in disbelief.

What is that?

"I can still hear it," I said. "What?" They asked. A paramedic checked his heart again and seemed surprised. He pulled something else out of his bag and tried some new trick. I looked around the fence and saw dozens of faces still glued to the scene. I wondered how this whole thing must look to them. I couldn't believe this was happening. How could this not be just a bad dream? I looked back at the paramedic just in time to hear the words, "I'm sorry."

I felt the earth move beneath me.

That is the one thing you cannot say to me. You see, we were having a typical Sunday.

One of the neighbors who had helped me move him asked the paramedics if they had a defibrillator. He shook his head and said, "No, I'm sorry." "How is that possible?" the neighbor asked. The guy apologetically raised his shoulders, his palms curling up. I brought my ear back to Don's chest, seeking some last hope, maybe my own confirmation and . . . and I know . . . I know I heard it. The softest, lightest, glimpse of a heartbeat that kept getting slower . . . and slower . . . and slower . . .

. . . until it disappeared completely.

Defeated, I brought my head back up. Balance was not my ally. I couldn't stand. People in front of me became a blur. Their voices a buzz. Nothing seemed clear. My eyes weren't able to focus on anything.

I brought my eyes back down and saw him. His head facing his left side. His bare chest now turning slightly purple—clear evidence that he had passed regardless of my strong objection. Just like that on a typical Sunday afternoon, just after lunch, his life was no more. Then I set out to look for my mom to have the worst conversation of our lives.

People moved aside, but they kept their eyes on me. I found her leaning on the neighbor's car next door. I sat right next to her. "What happened?!" she demanded. I had no words. I could barely breathe. I held her left hand. What do you say in a time like this? I hadn't read the manual. How do you tell a mother and wife that . . .

I looked forward and in a soft tone said the only thing I felt I could say, "It's gonna be okay." "But what happened?!" she shouted, with tears coming down her face and veins rising on her neck and forehead. I held her left hand with both of mine, and without being able to look her in the eye, I repeated, "It's gonna be okay."

She lost it.

I felt her body shake abruptly. She shouted and slammed the car with her right hand and then brought it to her mouth letting out a cry of deep sorrow. I remained there without letting go of her other hand. Curious eyes still focused on our private moment.

A void inside of me kept getting larger and larger. Like a balloon inflating inside my chest. The space was wide, but hollow. I said everything would be okay, but I had no idea how I was going to pull it off. How was I going to take care of her and my siblings, let alone myself?

What happened after that is all a blur, really.

I received the autopsy report, which gave electrocution as the official cause of death. I had to call his family with the news. I had to talk to his friends. I had to make funeral arrangements. I had to forget I had feelings because, if I did, I might have to take care of them and God knows I wasn't ready for that. I wouldn't know where to begin. At that point I wasn't living,

I was only surviving. I was walking through life waiting for an answer that would never come.

Seventeen

Before the summer of '94 had ended, my mom and siblings found a new home in El Centro, California, just a few miles north of the border. My mom and I decided it would be best for me to stay behind and live with my aunt so I could finish my last year of high school in Mexico. I'd move to the United States once I graduated. My mom said they would visit me every weekend, and she would help my aunt with food and expenses.

They would come on Fridays after Caro finished school and return Sunday evenings. During those two days, packed with many blankets and a small set of kitchen supplies, we would stay at the empty house we had lived in with Don. We never used the bedrooms, though. We were still haunted by ghosts from the past and decided it was better to spend our time together, right next to each other, and give the fog of dark memories some time to dissipate.

We would spread the blankets across the living room floor and lie down for the night, side by side. I slept right below the stairs between the living room and dining room. I would see the street light sneak through the window on my right, hear the restful breathing of my family to my left, and sense the gloomy darkness of the place all around. I would always be troubled with my thoughts until finally the deep night would overcome my consciousness and allow my eyes to close. But on one particular night, I simply couldn't fight the ghosts. We all seemed to have started the process of moving on. The neighbors weren't talking about Don's death as much, at least not in our presence. A new routine had begun to take place. But even if the furniture was all gone and our mail was delivered to a whole new address in a whole new country, every time we walked through those doors, regardless of how many good things had happened there, one fact remained—he had died in that house.

They might be resting peacefully next to me or they might be fighting their own personal war with the past, but my questions kept me awake: How would life have been if he were still around? What would a regular Friday night look like for our family if death hadn't paid a visit?

Part of me thought I could sense him. His alcohol and tobacco breath. His loud obnoxious farts and burps during dinner and his ridiculing laughter that followed. His yells bouncing off the walls. His yellowish teeth snickering after he hurled an insult. His hard judgment for small mistakes. His stumbling walk in the middle of the night. His hands on my neck before slamming me against the ground. His bloodshot eyes. The thick pores on his face. His belittling language and fondness of humiliating me.

Now living on social security, my family had a rather small, but nonetheless secure, income. And my sister and I did not have to fear coming home or keep pretending that we loved the man who made us live in terror.

A large image of the scales of justice formed in front of me. I knew it was an illusion, but it felt so real. The tears from my right eye flowed onto the right side of the scale with bitter memories of the past. The tears from my left eye filled the left side with guilt, thinking of how good life might be from now on. I raised my hands slightly. I could count on one hand the number of times I'd said a prayer without prompting from a priest. I sat there, having something to say, but not sure how to say it.

I turned to my left and saw my family resting there, innocently. Caro and I both knew what it felt like to grow up fatherless. We thought our younger siblings would not have to experience that. Mom had given him the chance to go away, and he didn't take it. He'd be there to teach them to play soccer, or to play catch. He'd be there to talk to him about cars, and to walk her during her quinceañera. He'd be there, as simple as that. And I love them both. Their blond innocent heads, which were now under my care, under my protection. Though with him I lived in fear of the consequences of the next mistake, I wanted them to have the father I never did.

My hands trembled as feelings were forming in my weak heart. My mind shouted, asking my heart to rethink what it was feeling. "It's wrong! You can't! How could you?"

My tears filled both sides of the scales of justice with memories and ethical arguments. I heard a shattering sound inside of me when I noticed the heavier side. I love them more than I love myself. And I even cry at this minute, on this keyboard typing these words, remembering how low I felt. Remembering the clutching feeling. Remembering the dementing thought. I knew the words were coming out of my mouth. I'd only whisper them, but they'd burn like acid on the way out. I was terrified that I might mean them. "No. Please. Don't say it. You feel bad for them," I thought. "But who feels bad about how you felt, what you experienced? Is it possible, maybe?" I had to say it or I might blow up right there and then, "God, I'm sorry that he's gone, but we might be better off now."

I trembled and sobbed in silence, guilty, ashamed, broken. Tears rolled down my face, soaking my pillow, as I clenched the sheet against my mouth.

It didn't matter how old I was—I was still that little boy who needed a father, who was afraid of being hurt.

When the sun came out I still felt guilty, but I couldn't get something else out of my mind. I had seen breath stolen by fate. God had seemed powerless once more against human action. And I was tired of crying. I had no parents watching over me. I had no regrets to learn from. And I had no respect for, nor evidence of, a master of the afterlife. If Life thought it could still control me by pulling the strings of insecurity and ambiguity, it had to find another boy, because this one was tired of being treated like one.

I was going to live, and live free—even if I died in the process.

5

THE GOOD NEWS

"So tell me, since it makes no factual difference to you and you can't prove the question either way, which story do you prefer? Which is the better story, the story with animals or the story without animals?"
—Pi Patel, in *Life of Pi*

Holy Week
Every Spring Break, which corresponded with Easter, my cousin David would invite me to join him at Vacation Bible School—a program for kids held at a local church in Mexicali, Tabernáculo de la Fe (which they nicknamed *El Taber*). Juanita, the hair stylist on our street, would recruit several kids from our block and shuttle them over to El Taber, which was a few miles away. "A bunch of gringos came down to play games," my cousin would say, "and they don't have enough interpreters." But since I lived with a gringo, and my step-family was gringo, I had no interest in going to see a bunch of white people visiting some church. My lack of interest in religion had been growing and, if I understood things correctly, this wasn't even a Catholic church—it was a Christian church.

I had met Protestant Christians—as opposed to Catholics—before. I had visited their churches in the United States, but they didn't seem right. I mean, they didn't have *La Virgen* or saints on their altars and windows. They didn't feel like churches without all the religious symbols. Plus, they didn't have priests or nuns dressed in black, and their leaders were allowed to get married, have sex, and have kids. That didn't seem very holy to us Catholics.

On Wednesday night of Spring Break in 1993, tenth grade, I witnessed something peculiar. I was visiting my friend Javier, who lived across the street from me, and I overheard the conversation a little boy was having with his older sister next door. The boy kept saying something in between sobs, "He is not coming back. He is not coming back." "Who is not coming back?" The sister asked. "Eben is not coming back. He is not sure if he can. This could be the last time I see him." The little boy then broke into tears with a passion that made him tremble in her arms. You'd think he had just lost a brother or a beloved friend. I stood there astonished and wondered, "How is it possible that a bunch of white guys from the United States could have this effect on a group of Mexican kids whom they just met less than a week ago?"

Intrigued by what I'd heard, I finally decided to check the program out. A group of us took the bus to the church, where we arrived late on Thursday—the last day of the Americans' visit.

What I saw at this place was nothing less than surprising. Several vans, all white, sat parked on both sides of the street. A couple dozen American teenagers played with a few dozen Mexican kids. People traded gifts, wrote one another notes, prayed in pairs. The American teens tossed smiling kids in the air. While many ran around the street laughing, some sat crying.

The teenagers dressed in a strange attire. Most of the girls' hair was done in braids. They wore long parachute skirts that went down to their ankles. I'm thinking, "What, did they fly to Mexico and jump off when they saw the church?" Most of the guys had buzzed hair. They wore badly wrinkled jeans that looked like they'd been pulled from a second-hand store. I'm thinking, "Don't they own an iron in the U.S.?"

As soon as Javier saw us walking down the street, he ran toward us and pulled me by the arm. In Spanish he shouted to others, "Dude, this son of a bitch knows English. He can help us now." The gringos looked puzzled but eventually picked up the word, "*Inglés*." "Een-gleech," Javier added. They responded with a sigh of relief, "English? He speaks English? Thank God!"

I immediately began to get pulled from side to side to aid in translation. "Tell him I said I think he is very cool." "Tell her I said that I think she is awesome." "Tell him I will never forget him." "Ask her if she is coming back." "Tell them I said, I love you." "Tell her, thank you so much." Everyone was entrenched in such a frenzy of love, hugs, laughter, and tears that it actually had me thinking, "Holy shit. What the hell is going on? I think these people have all been drugged."

Soon we were called into a gathering on the church patio. Javier and I stood in the back with two other Mexican teenagers and didn't engage much in the program.

Over the ensuing years, I learned their formula. We would be led through a ritual of songs with silly hand movements that had the word "Hallelujah" a lot, along with the shout of, "Hey!" The Americans would play the songs at regular speed, then very slow, then very fast. *"Aunque no marche en la infantería, caballería, artillería."* A soldier of Christ? They'd pretend to have wings, to shoot a gun, to salute in the army, and to march in place. Childish for sure, but everyone ate it up.

Then they would present a Bible story by bringing out several visual aids consisting of pictures from a coloring book and wear sheets as robes. Then we would do a craft with crayons, cotton balls, and glue. I noticed they used a lot of cotton balls. Cotton balls for clouds, for sheep, for angels' wings, for beards, for anything you can think of. Then we'd go play a lot of games at the park, or in the middle of the street. I, and most of the kids, just wanted to play games.

Then we would be called in for the second part of the program. One of the American teenagers would give a "testimony"—stories about their lives that included something bad they had done, or something bad that had happened to them. Then we would do a prayer and they'd ask, "Who wants to ask Jesus into your heart?" A kid or two would raise their hand and they would be called up to the front. Everyone closed their eyes as they asked the kid or kids to repeat a prayer. When the prayer was over, the gringos clapped as if someone had just won a prize and looked at each other very proudly.

Over time I noticed that some of the same kids kept raising their hands to accept Jesus into their hearts every year. When I asked them why they did this, they told me, "It is because I know it makes them happy."

That first year, when it was time for the Americans to leave, I tried to stand toward the back when they started pulling out the cameras, but something weird happened—they kept calling me toward them.

"Here. Here." They put their arms around me and smiled. They gave hugs and high fives. How can they be so welcoming to a dude they just met? Why would they want me in their permanent pictures when I've only been here a few hours, while all the other kids have been here all week? But more importantly, why would these white guys come all the way to this Mexican hellhole and pour so much love on people they didn't even know?

I was both moved and baffled.

"Where do they sleep?" I wondered out loud. "They sleep at a campsite somewhere in the valley with other gringos," I was told by someone from the church. "Wait, so there are other gringos who do this at other churches?" I asked. "Yeah, they are all over the city," I was told. This shocked me. "How many Christian gringos are out there?" I continued.

Apparently there were thousands of them.

When I walked outside my house that's all I would hear kids talk about. "Are you gonna go next year?" they kept asking each other. And I saw more tears, and kids holding on to Polaroid pictures of these guys and girls as if they were looking at professional athletes or movie stars. There was a strange feeling in the air. People cried . . . because they were happy. This was one of the oddest Thursdays I'd ever had.

I went to bed that night with questions and images stuck in my head. But one rare thing did happen, before my eyes closed for the night—I also had a smile.

I went back the following year and, as I will relate, for many Easters after that. Holy week became a refuge where I'd leave my darkness aside for a few days while I basked in the light the American Christians brought with them. We were excited when we saw familiar faces return, and we were heartbroken when loved ones wouldn't.

And such was the case when my closest bud, Matt, said goodbye his last year. They were calling them to go back in the white vans, and we had both been postponing our farewell. We knew it would be hard. He took me to the back of a van and pulled something out of a basket. It was a Chicago Bulls shirt—too tight for me, but he said it would fit and told me to keep it. It was his and now it would be mine. Though I didn't have the muscle to sport it as he would, I treasured that shirt for years as if Michael Jordan himself had given it to me.

I saw the white vans depart, the Americans waving from the inside, us waving from the outside, and all of our hearts torn in half.

When my stepfather passed away a couple of months later, I found myself in a bit of a darker place. Thinking of the comfort I had experienced with the gringos at that Christian church, I sent letters to some of the guys I had gotten close to, including Matt.

I told them there was a chance we'd move back to the United States, and that it meant a lot to know I had great friends to tell my stories to. I was not sharing them with anyone in Mexico. Only one of them responded—Matt's good friend, Scott. He told me he had been busy, that he felt sorry for my pain, and that Jesus loved me. He said a lot had happened since he got back, even that his faith got tested. He included a quote from his daily devotional, *My Utmost for His Highest* by Oswald Chambers, which he had just read that day and wanted to share with me:

Since mine eyes have looked on Jesus,
I've lost sight of all beside,
So enchained my spirit's vision,
Gazing on the Crucified.

I didn't understand the quote; it was too spiritually heavy for my nonreligious mind, but I was touched.

The next year, when the end of Easter 1995 came, Scott and I made a commitment to stay in touch. He also promised that he would somehow bring me to visit their church in Cupertino, California, and that I could stay with him. He said that he would collect an offering at his high school group to pay for my travel and that it was pretty much a done deal. He'd get on it as soon as he got back.

I am just a little kid from a poor Mexican barrio who is getting a chance to return to the Promised Land with the coolest people who ever walked this earth, I thought. I would see where they lived, where they went to school, where they went to church, where they played, where they laughed.

But though I kept sending letters and waiting anxiously for a response, my mailbox never again received a message from Scott or any of my other American Christian friends from those years.

The Fall

After graduating from high school in June 1995, it came time for me to join my family in California and start college.

But this move didn't sit well with me. I went through a deep sadness during those first few weeks. I couldn't sleep. I couldn't eat. I couldn't smile. I had always talked with my friends about going to UABC in Mexicali—where my childhood heroes had gone. We talked about the things we would study together, about the adventures we would have together. The rest of them had the chance to remain together, but I was now in a place that felt more like no man's land than the Promised Land. Even though I now had a green card, and thus lived in the United States legally, being there again wasn't as glamorous as promised. I wasn't a fan of the language. I wasn't a fan of the seemingly money-oriented culture. I wasn't a fan of the lack of community. I hated that I couldn't stay back in Mexico with my freedom, my friends, and live the way I had planned my life to be.

Once the semester started at Imperial Valley College, my days consisted of school, boredom, and waiting for the weekend to arrive so I could head south of the border and feel alive again. My weekend routine consisted of parties, drinking, dancing, and forgetting. Then repeat.

During one of those weekends, four of us, two guys and two girls, decided we'd go check out this new dance club in San Luis in the neighboring state of Sonora. We were dressed to impress and ready to party. Against my mom's wishes, I wore a gold loop earring on my left ear that I had just gotten that afternoon.

We headed east, crossed the state border, and found the place, but we were not very impressed. It looked more like a bar than a dance club, the light show was subpar, and the place wasn't even half full. We had to make up for the lack of energy somehow—so obviously, we drank a lot.

Intoxicated by booze and youth, we decided to leave early and try our usual spot in Mexicali. As we approached the Baja California border, a powerful spot light suddenly glared at us in our truck. My friend, noting a bus pull over on the right side of the road, said, "The light must be for the bus." I nodded, adding, "What's the worst thing that could happen? Just ignore it and keep going. Go! Go! Go!"

Passing the border, we sped away quickly. Exhilarated, we felt like we owned the night. After a few minutes, just as our excitement began to calm, a brighter-than-usual light struck our back window. It couldn't be a UFO, could it? For sure a confused traveler about to pass us?

It grew in intensity as it grew nearer.

Turning, I saw a military truck with a huge light trained directly on us. Shading my eyes, I could make out two men dressed in green camouflage in the front seat. The soldier on the passenger side waved us to pull over. Obeying, my friend directed our truck to the dirt shoulder, with the military truck pulling to a stop just behind us. The two soldiers immediately jumped out of their seats and headed toward us. The driver got to my friend's door first. I saw his door swing open, then a hand come in and pull him out by the collar. The next thing I knew, my door swung open. I saw a pair of angry eyes and then a hand, which grabbed my collar and vigorously pulled me outside. He slammed my chest against the back of our truck and demanded answers. I heard a gasping sound wrapped in pain coming from the other side of the truck. Then a fist hit the right side of my rib cage and a similar sound escaped from my lungs. Next I heard the crunch of metal. Then my head was slammed against the car, making the same noise. The soldiers then threw us back in the truck and told us to follow them. Without resistance, my friend made a U-turn, as we submitted to their demand.

When we got back to the border, their wheels screeched to a halt right next to the bathroom. We parked next to them, filled with anguish. Our eyes became wide as they approached our vehicle. Doors swung open again. Hands pulled us out and pushed as toward the bathroom. Once inside, my friend was pushed against the wall on the right side. My body then was pushed against the wall straight ahead. I briefly saw a tiny window on the left wall and a toilet directly to my right. The guy who seemed to be in charge stood next to my friend. The subordinate stood by my side. They ordered us to keep our foreheads against the wall at all times, and our hands behind our heads. I couldn't see my friend, and he couldn't see me.

From then on it turned into a game of echoes. When I heard my friend gasp after a loud thump, I knew my right ribcage would receive another punch. When I heard his head get slammed against the concrete wall, it meant mine would be slammed against the wall as well.

They questioned us, humiliated us, and hit us consecutively.

At one point the guy in charge questioned the earring I had on. "Are you a fag or something?" He asked. "No, sir," I replied trembling. "Then why do you have that? That's for fags!" he insisted. "I just got it today," I explained. Fist to the ribcage. With my hands still on the back of my head, my legs began to lose balance. "Take if off, then!" he shouted. The fresh puncture in my ear immediately began to bleed as I removed it. But they weren't done. The punching and insulting fest continued. If I turned to see how my friend was, I would get hit. If I moved an inch in any direction, I would have my head slammed against the wall. I wasn't sure how much more we could take. It was painful. It was frightening.

But nothing like what happened next.

I hear the door open and close. One of them might have left the room. I'm trembling.

Agonizing silence.

What is happening?

Then I heard a loud gunshot that knocked the soul out of my body and replaced silence with a ringing I thought meant I would be deafened for life. The echo of the report would not stop bouncing off the enclosed walls. My knees weakened and I doubted whether I could hold my body up much longer.

I was afraid to turn because it would mean one of two things. I'd either receive more physical punishment for my intransigence, or, worse, see his bloody remains lying on the ground. More likely, I knew, both would happen.

I could picture him in my head. His well-dressed body soaked in terrifying red. I couldn't hear anything now, and I couldn't see. One way or another, I knew the end was near.

Seconds went by that felt like hours.

Eventually some life came back to my ears, but not to my heart. I still couldn't see what had happened.

The door opened and a hand turned my body around by the shoulder.

I was terrified.

But what is that? He is alive! He actually looks just the way I did: scared shitless, shaken, and stricken. I look down and I see the remnant of the cherry bomb they threw in the room, which I thought to be a gunshot.

As a final treat, they said they could do us a favor, if we wanted one. The guy in charge said, if they wanted to, they could report us for any number of other things and leave it up to other people to decide what to do with us—that it'd be out of their hands after that. The subordinate just stood there, learning the tricks of the game.

"You want a favor?" the soldier in charge asked. We both nodded. "Then ask for one!" he shouts.

What was the alternative? What else could we say or do? I was too scared out of my mind to be able to speak. My bud opened his mouth, still looking down, "*Sí*." "*¿Sí, qué?*" the leader asked back. "Yes, we want a favor." "Do you want us to let you go?" "Yes, sir, we promise we won't do this again." "Yes, you could get into real trouble for doing this kind of shit. But we think maybe you've learned your lesson. We are good guys and will be magnanimous this one time. So we are not going to press any charges, but you two better not try to pull off something like this again."

They finally released us. As we pulled ourselves back into the truck, the girls were silent. My friend turned on the engine and we drove away. On the way the girls told us they had only been searched by female military guards. Although the situation could have ended up worse, being beaten up by the Mexican Army wasn't necessarily the idea of a good time we had in mind.

When I walked through my front door late that night, I took a few steps and stopped cold. I held the bloody earring in my hand and thought about the army guy's words: "Are you a fag or something?"

I was still shaken from the beating, but also disturbed by the thought. "Why did he have to say that?" People had been calling me names and doubting my masculinity since I was a kid. I realized then that I was shaken by more than just the beating. Had it crossed my mind? Perhaps. But being part of a culture where men of questionable masculinity are harshly caricatured, marginalized, humiliated, and ridiculed, I knew that was something that should never be explored—that should be buried deep within to never see the light of day. Maybe it was because of what happened to me as a child. Maybe because I was fatherless, raised by women. It didn't matter, I was a man. I have a choice to be a man. But still . . . "Why did he have to say that?"

It hurt—deep down, it hurt my pride as a man, because it made me feel less than one.

I walked back toward the window to get some fresh air. I looked out to the night sky and now had a vision of what my life had been like in the last few years, especially after Don's death. Image after image paraded the close calls I'd had with destiny.

During my last year in high school I had spent at least four nights a week, preferably six, intoxicated out of my senses. Once the school's biggest nerd, I had exchanged good grades for rampant displays of buffoonery in search of popularity. I had joined a gang and had barely escaped a battle where I saw knives, rocks, and bottles fly over my head. We had to walk in groups of three because the enemy gang wanted to gut us like fish. I had raced the cops, been chased by the blue and red lights through the dark city. I had just gotten my ribs broken by the Mexican Army—my masculinity challenged because of a stupid earring. And I was just about to lose myself, like many other nights, hugging a boombox with the thoughts of how this seemingly eternal living damnation could come to an end.

I took out the military knife that I'd occasionally rub against my wrist to trace various techniques. Would it be straight down my thickest vein, or would it be across? That night, the slightly pressed knife would leave a red mark that lasted for a day or two, but I feared that the unthinkable, pressing harder, would not be a matter of *if*, but *when*.

I had evaded Darkness' cloak after a few close calls, but I wasn't sure for how much longer. Maybe I had been lucky and outsmarted its cry, but seeing how my days dimmed on hope I feared, oh so gelidly, that its victory would come another way. Maybe, just maybe, by my own hand.

I was barely eighteen. But I had fallen, fallen deep and hard, and I counted the days for the time and the will to not ever climb back up again.

Salvation

I was surprised when the calendar showed Easter 1996 had arrived, because I no longer had Juanita to remind me over and over that it was coming. I went to Mexicali to stay with my cousin David for the weekend. Juanita saw me walk back from the store and asked if I was going. Damn, I had to think about it now. I pondered about it for the night and didn't make up my mind until the following morning. For better or worse, I thought, those Americans were some of the only few honest friends I thought I'd ever had.

So there I was in the morning, dressed and ready to go see them once again, and I told myself, "For the last time."

The Americans arrived a bit late. We were all sitting in the church pews when they finally showed up. We stopped paying attention to the pastor and looked back with expectation as if looking at a menu of celebrities. Who returned? Who's new? I was in a different state of mind than before, though. I still looked with interest, but not excitedly. I knew Eben and Matt weren't coming back, but I did want to see Scott. I wanted to ask him why he never wrote back, even though I kept writing. Why did he ignore me?

One by one, with confused look, they walked in—but Scott wasn't among them. Most were new this year. They had the same look I'd seen before in some of their predecessors. Wide-eyed looks, as if they were observing a new creature at the zoo. Perplexed about where to sit and how to behave. Nervous and shy with their parachute skirts, their buzzed or braided hair, their wrinkled pants, and their plastic wristbands, a different color every year. "Wow," I thought. "This is a waste of time. I knew I shouldn't have come."

When the service ended, we went outside for a quick chat before everyone left. A couple of the girls came and said hi and told me they remembered me from the previous year. I asked them about Scott and they said that he didn't come this year—that he had decided to go somewhere else, Yucatan. This information shocked and hurt me. Not only had he ignored my letters, and didn't come back when he still had the chance to, but he also didn't even send a hello. That was no sign of friendship.

I looked to the right, behind the girls, and I saw this guy. He looked familiar. I had seen him the previous year, but in the shadows of Eben, Matt, and Scott, his light hadn't shined as bright. A scrawny kid with sleepy eyes, freckles, a bandana, baggy clothes, and a humble posture—his name was Joel. We introduced ourselves and talked about all the new faces. I told him that I was in college now and that I probably would not be able to stay for the rest of the week. Joel looked distraught and begged me to please come back. Everybody was new and he could use a familiar face. "I don't know. I'd have to look at my schedule," I said. "Please. Please. Please, come back tomorrow," he begged looking at me in the eye, holding my hand and smiling.

More people spoke Spanish on their team that year, so I wasn't pulled around as much. This gave Joel and me more time to talk. How did I not speak with this guy before? He had not been the rock star personality that others were, but he was down to earth, real, honest, and welcoming. His star may have shone brighter that year, but he still felt human. He felt like just the person I needed by my side with what I was going through. Joel became a light and a hope in the darkness of my thoughts.

At the end of the day I crossed the border and went back home. I looked at my schedule for the week and pondered how I'd do it. I could go before class some days, and go after on others, but this would really be the last time. Make a few memories before pulling the plug.

The gringos acted particularly silly that Monday, which fell on April 1. The rest of us assumed they had some inside joke and just went along, but we didn't understand a thing. Later in life I would learn that there was a verse in the Bible that Christians sometimes refer to when talking about April Fool's Day. "The fool has said in his heart, 'There is no God,'" reads Psalms 14:1. And it couldn't pertain to me more. It had been a season from hell. I had seen life vanish before my eyes, as well as inside them. I felt as though I was hanging off the edge of a cliff and acting out my last hurrahs before going up in a cloud of smoke. I had raised my fist and declared my freedom from the heavens. I had lived foolishly with a heart fed with unfulfilling flares of reckless youth.

Then Tuesday came.

It was a day like any other. The crowd of local kids wasn't as large as past years. Maybe because we were growing up, maybe because less familiar faces had returned, maybe because it wasn't a new thing anymore. I don't know. I got there after class and caught the gringos and kids as they left the church. They had decided to take a break from the program to distribute handouts inviting other kids to Vacation Bible School.

Joel and I walked together and talked most of the way.

The night before had been particularly difficult. I couldn't sleep again. I had so many questions. What was the purpose for my life? What did all of this mean? Should I try something else? It really came to the point that if a change would take place, it would be now or never.

We went around a couple of blocks. My questions flowed: "What is Christianity?" "Do Christians have fun?" "Do you believe in the Virgin of Guadalupe?" "What things can Christians do and not do?" "How can you know for sure that all of that is real?" "Heaven was supposed to be right above the clouds, but where is it now?"

I asked and asked and asked.

Joel seemed caught off guard with the questioning, distracted as we walked and handed out flyers, but he answered as best as he could. He respected Mary as the woman who carried Jesus in his human form. He felt that they could have as much fun as any other person. He said Christianity wasn't a religion, but a relationship with Jesus Christ. He said living life as a Christian was not much different from living it as a non-Christian, but that faith gave Christians a different perspective on life itself. He said that sometimes we had to rely on faith, even when we couldn't physically see the answer with our eyes.

Time went by and, without noticing, we had returned to the front of the church. But I wasn't done. I had a million more questions to ask, and he could tell. Others called us back to continue with the program. Joel was scheduled to lead the next activity, but my hands were up in the air, my eyes were anxious, and my stand was uneasy. He put his hands in front of me as a sign of comfort, glanced behind me at the waiting crowd, and looked back at me with that tender look of his. He then uttered these words—words that to this day remain tattooed in my memory, "*Look man, I don't know a whole lot, but I do know this: If one of these days I go up there* [pointing his right finger to the sky] *and I don't see one of you guys, I'm gonna feel so bad.*" He blinked once, patted me on the shoulder, and headed to the church.

I remained there standing in the middle of the street—frozen in thought. He left me with more questions than answers. What did that mean? Up to this point I had never really thought about the possibilities. Is there really a heaven? And if there is really a heaven, then wait, is there a chance I might not make it up there? And if I don't make it to heaven, then will it be hell? How much longer will it be before that happens? What if right now I was burning in a lake of fire? What if I am wasting my life away with things that don't matter? What if he is right? What if . . . ?

I don't remember what happened after that. I don't know if I went back inside, or how long I stood there in the middle of the street. But next thing I remember is being alone in my bedroom. The blinds are half open and I can see the stars outside from my bed. The clock keeps ticking—now past 2:30 in the morning. My mind can't rest, and I am filled with even more questions that won't wait for daylight.

I started thinking of the last few years visiting the gringos. I started thinking of their testimonies. Eben pulling us under the basketball hoop to confess his sins. Scott telling us he regretted losing his virginity. Matt's tears. I remembered the songs, the skits, the prayers, the smiles, the hugs, the cotton balls. Thousands of memories flooded my mind and nothing could stop their flow. My wide-open eyes moved rapidly, begging for an answer. Suddenly, they stopped. There must be a reason why they would travel all the way from Cupertino, spend thousands of dollars on the trip, eat sandwiches out of a cooler, and sleep in a tent somewhere in the boonies, just to spend time with us. What they talked about must be that important, that real. I leaned forward, looked outside my window one more time, and breathed deeply.

Almost unconsciously, but determinately, I removed the sheets, swung my legs to the side, and went straight down on my knees. I had never really done this. Sure, I'd prayed in Catholic Church, and as a kid with my sister in Port Hueneme, but not alone, not like this. It was different and new. What if I did it wrong? There was no one there to show me how.

I couldn't think of lofty words, so I just said what came natural: "Jesus, if you're there, I'd like you to know me. And Jesus, if you love me, I'd like you to show me."

I couldn't have meant those words any more than I did. I stayed there trembling from its implications. I felt a sudden warmth run through my heart. My eyes began to fill with tears. My head became heavy. I brought it down to my hands, clasped together on the bed. Something was happening inside of me. I didn't know what it was. But it felt like a drug. Like something good started to heal what was broken inside—what was hurting and rotten.

I woke up the next morning and the sun had never shined like it did this time. The energy I had within had a hope foreign for quite some time. I still didn't have many answers, but at least I felt somehow on the right track. I didn't know the lingo yet, but I had heard the Good News, I took it in, and by God's grace my soul was saved.

6

TONGUES OF FIRE

"With great power there must also come—great responsibility."
—Uncle Ben, in *The Amazing Spider-Man*

Changed

The day after the gringos left always felt dramatically different from the day before. Time stood still while we grieved their departure.

This time their departure had slightly greater significance for me. I had to keep discovering what this Christian world was like—this Jesus thing. I just had to.

I asked one of the girls who attended Vacation Bible School what the attendees normally did after the gringos left. I mean, the church didn't close for the rest of the year, did it? She said that the church usually had services on Sunday and that she would go once in a while. She added that many of the kids stop attending until the Americans come back the next year. I realized then that I was friends with those who never attended church outside of Easter, and that I had never been approached by an actual member of the church to attend during the year. She told me to talk to the people next door, the Guzmans, because she normally went with them.

I walked over and knocked on their door. Berta, the mother, opened the door. She expressed surprise when she saw me. "Oh, the gringos are gone," she quickly explained. "They won't be coming back 'til next year." "Yeah, I know," I said. "I was just wondering if someone could still go to church once the gringos are gone." I thought her eyes would come out of their sockets. "Really?! Um, yeah, I think," she says. Once we finished making plans, she closed the door and, as she later told me, leaned back against it still in shock. In however many years they'd been doing this, no one had ever knocked on their door asking to go back to church after the gringos had left.

Some time later they told me they weren't sure if I was playing some kind of prank—or worse. They discussed the possibility that, given my record, maybe I wanted to burn the church down.

The gringoless services were pretty monotonous and boring. The music was far simpler, there were no games afterward, and no one seemed interesting enough to talk to. Without the Americans and the other visiting local kids, the place was almost empty. Only about fifteen people attended on a busy Sunday. How could this be when just last week the place was filled with life? I finally began to notice that the church was in a decrepit state—with old cobwebs, stains, and cracks on the walls. Still, if the gringos had come here, it means they approved of the Christian ways of this church. Right?

As a recovering nerd, I still had more questions than answers about this whole Christian thing. So whenever I had a chance, I would go over to the Guzmans with a new set of questions. They always welcomed me, but I learned later that, after a while, whenever they saw me through the window, they would say, "Oh boy, here he comes again."

Toño, the father, worked at a gas station. He was pretty reserved, some would think moody, but quietly supportive. Berta, the mother, was a kind woman who didn't know many theological answers but spoke of how things felt in her heart. Laura, a year younger than me, had most of the answers and was heavily involved in all things church. And Brenda, three years younger than Laura, was innocent but had a temper like her father. The entire family acted as a devout religious entity of support and faith.

I would show up with my little old orange book of illustrated Bible stories, which had sat unopened for many years. I gave it more use in those few days than in the entire time I had owned it.

My questions seemed unending. "It says here that Joshua made the sun stop in the sky for a whole day, is that true?" "But how is it possible that the sun stopped if the sun doesn't move? It is the earth that moves around it. Doesn't it show they were wrong?" "It says here that Noah got two of each animal in the ark. Was it really every animal, and how could it be every single species in one boat?" "It says here that Samson brought down the temple with strength he got from his long hair. Long hair? Really?" "It says here that fire came from the sky and killed everyone. Why would God kill everyone, even children?" "It says here that Job lost everything, including his sons, but then got new sons and new riches. But why would he have to lose his sons in the first place? Isn't that brutality?" I asked question after question, thirsty for answers.

This was not only an emotional process for me; it was also an intellectual one. But their answers did not always satisfy me. Most of them had to do with trusting God's all-knowing power and plan for people's lives. They seemed so certain about it. They claimed to have a personal relationship with God in the form of Jesus Christ, who had convinced them through a feeling in their hearts that everything in the Bible was true. Witnessing their faith caused these stories, which to me seemed birthed out of fantasy, to become more appealing. But they didn't yet feel real.

The process of my full conversion wasn't a speedy one. At first I continued to go to Mexicali on the weekends after school, party Friday and Saturday, and then join the Guzmans for church on Sunday—many times hungover (which they didn't find out about until years later).

After some time, my high school friends began to notice a change in me that really troubled them. "What do you mean that you can't drink any more?" was among their most popular questions. I kept saying that I would still be the same guy, but that I was trying something out and I had to see what happened. They kept warning me that they had seen this happen to some of their relatives. They had been invited to attend a non-Catholic church and slowly but surely they couldn't do anything fun anymore. They wouldn't even attend certain parties anymore, including weddings and quinceañeras, if they were hosted at a Catholic Church (because they saw the devil worshipped in the shape of saints and the Virgin of Guadalupe) or if alcohol was served at the reception. I promised that would not happen to me at all.

There was no way.

The Big Church

The people from El Taber had another church where they congregated Friday and Sunday evenings. "The big church," they called it—Siete Olivos (Seven Olives). More people went there, about a hundred, including many kids my age, so I had an obvious interest in attending. I expressed my desire to the Guzmans. They looked at each other and decided I was ready.

The church offered an intense music experience, with musicians playing drums, electric guitars, bass, and keyboard and people in the crowd following along with tambourines. I watched as congregants raised their hands up in the air, closed their eyes, and sank into a deep euphoria. Some ladies shook, and some fell on their knees in the middle of the music—an act they called *worship*. "Well, this is new," I kept telling myself. Laura kept telling me that it was all normal, that I shouldn't be weirded out, and that she herself felt as I did when she first attended.

The experience overwhelmed me, but somehow I stuck around.

When May arrived, the church held a special service on a Saturday, followed by a fair, to celebrate Mother's Day. Church members invited family and friends for the occasion. Still relatively unengaged, I sat somewhere in a middle row, next to the wall, so I could lean my head against it. The assistant pastor, Alejandro, preached. I'd heard him speak before, but he seemed zestier this time. A tall guy with a big pear-shaped body that walked with a certain wobble, he couldn't move very quickly around the stage, but he made up for it with brisk arm movements. He'd reach out with both hands, fist pump the air, and abruptly pull them behind him. His waist swayed back and forth as if he were a buoy floating on water. Through his glasses his green snake-shaped eyes darted about his very round face.

He shouted as if the church had no microphone and he had to fill a stadium with the bare power of his lungs. A rain of spit would reach the first row. He'd forcefully wipe his mouth, throw it on the ground, and continue preaching as if his life depended on it. "In the name of Jesus. Halleluuuuujah!" "There is poooooooower in the blood!" He'd march in place, stomping his feet with a wavering movement of his body as he proclaimed, "We will step on the enemy and there will be viiiiiiictory in the Lord! There will be victory for me." Punching himself on the chest, he'd then throw his finger at us. "There will be victory for you. And the rule of the enemy will not prevail! His blood will cover us! It will bless us! It will cleanse us!" Both his arms would swing from side to side as his volume grew higher and higher. His saliva showered like a fountain in every direction. Veins popped all over his face and neck as he got redder and redder. His eyes squinted, and his tongue kept sticking out and flittering outside his lips—just like a snake's.

"And the spirit will fill you up! And it will take control over you! And it will bring glory to the name of Jesus. Hallelluuuuuuujah!" He'd finish his thought with a sentiment I can only describe as animalistic, "Aaaaaagghh!"

His manner scared me.

I started trembling and slowly, but determinedly, walked outside to take a breather. I wasn't sure whether I'd ever be able to go back inside. It was too much. It seemed cultish.

Juanita, who was outside preparing food for the fair, saw me as I rushed out seeking an escape. "Are you okay?" I told her what happened and she told me she understood. Just like Laura, she had also gone through a similar experience, explaining that Brother Alejandro sometimes scares people when he really gets into it. I didn't think there could possibly be a decent explanation for people to act like that. It was supposed to be a Christian church, but in all honesty, I wondered whether he was possessed by the Devil.

Surprisingly enough, as time went by, I got used to the yelling, the spitting, and the convulsing in the name of Jesus. If this was how Christianity worked, I had to get deep into it in order to understand it. And I did. The youth group became one of the closest groups of friends I ever had. The closer we all got, the more fervent our relationship with Jesus became. Every moment we spent together would relate to Jesus in some way or another. If we were eating, we would pray for the meal. If we were traveling, we prayed that His blessings would be on our path. If we were helping at an event, we prayed that God's wonders and miracles would take place. We lived our lives as if at any moment the heavens would split in half and fire would consume us. As if lightning might announce the Second Coming. As if a mighty force would emanate from our bodies and physically affect those we'd touch.

I became a regular at the steps of the altar. My long, skinny body folded into a small, meek, and contrite waterfall of tears. This gave me a safe place to partake in the glories of holy venting. People didn't judge, in part because they didn't know what I cried for. They seemed proud that such a great sinner would be rejoicing at the feet of the cross. But in my heart, I knew.

I did break for the sins I had committed, for the chance to start fresh, but I also cried for the pain I had buried since I was a child. I was raised fatherless. I had always been marginalized, made fun of, for being different. And even as that little child, when choice was taken from me, my small and tender body was used by the despicable to satisfy their carnal desires.

The band played. The lyrics to "Lord, I Lift Your Name on High" in particular struck deep within me, narrating what my lips were too weak to sing. I was glad He was now in my life—glad He had come to save me.

The thankfulness I had was radiating. My life had taken a 180-degree turn and now I was a new creature. When evil people had used me as they would a woman, I thought, when gangs had made me into a vandal, God would make me into a man—a true man. My high school friends started hearing rumors that "Fernando became a Christian." Whenever I would ran into any of them, they had to ask me, "Is it true?" I was so joyful. I could do nothing else but say, "Yes," and try to communicate this feeling to them. "Okay," they would say, nodding—surprised. They had nothing to say. Fernando, the crazy guy, had done the unthinkable.

I would get updates on how their lives had turned out after we split ways: divorce, hospitalization, drugs, jail, and, for some, even death. I even got word that the guy who used to be my best friend in high school had gone haywire and had begun to live as a gay man, even dressing up as a woman. I had been spared of all of that, I knew, thanks to the sacrifice that Jesus made on the cross and to His blood restoring my soul.

The last part of that one song hit me hard every single time. It declared not only God's redemption in my life, but also the purpose I now had.

Lord, I lift your name on high.

Water and Fire

Siete Olivos and El Taber went on a week-long retreat that summer of '96 to Lake Hanson, up in the Mexicali mountains known as La Rumorosa. There'd be some swimming and hiking, but most importantly, those willing would take the "step of obedience" and be submerged in the waters. I knew this is something I had to do.

During the pre-baptism training, church leaders informed me of a particular detail in the Bible. If I wanted to get baptized, I had to remove the earring I had gotten a few months back. I was shown scripture that said that metal through the body of a man was a demonic symbol. I called it rubbish, archaic, old school, and an outdated doctrine. Plus, I had history with that earring. But, they insisted and said that's what would please God.

I took a solo walk around the forest to prepare myself. I decided, as a personal sign of sacrifice and devotion to Jesus—and not because of them— that I would take the earring off. For a while I carried it on a necklace hidden under my shirt, but they even had issues with that.

When the time came for us to go in the freezing-cold water, we could all feel the weight of the moment on our shoulders. The senior pastor, Héctor, called out names one by one and recited a small speech. We each affirmed our allegiance and our love to Jesus. Pastor Héctor and Brother Alejandro then pulled each of us under the water so the lake buried our entire bodies. Pulled back up, we emerged as new creatures. The guitarist played a riff every time someone came out of the water and the crowd cheered.

Laura was the first one to greet me as I approached shore—tears shone in her eyes. She hugged me with pride. It was a day of celebration. We couldn't stop singing, praising, raising our hands, and laughing. God was more evident than ever now that I was walking in His path.

We returned from the camp the next day. In response to our demands for continued celebration, Pastor Héctor called for a vigil. We couldn't get enough of this joy. The music didn't stop. The prayers could be heard a block away. No one had speeches, only weeping and praising. Song after song was offered with our eyes rarely opening. We would get up and fall back on our knees. We would kneel with our heads to the chair, or join a group of friends whose shoulders we'd wet in seconds. God had showed up and we were witnessing His glory. Minutes turned into hours, sometimes in silence, sometimes in a thunderous roar. Sometimes we whispered the most heartfelt song of worship, and sometimes we stomped to the loud frenzy of praise. At times we all fell to the ground unable to escape the fear of clearing our eyes in case we'd see the glory of God and become blinded or death-stricken on the spot.

Sister Esther, the most devout and compassionately dominant elder in the church, stood by the altar with her elbows bent upward like a gray-haired monument of unending and unshakable faith. She spoke in lamenting chants while she interceded for her loved ones, her wholeheartedness undeniable. She believed it. I believed it. We felt, as she did, that she was engaging with a supreme loving power that now flowed through her being. She shook at times as if shocked by a power surge to her shoulders. She'd lose balance and almost fall to the ground. Pastor Héctor remained sitting on the bench behind the pulpit, waving his hand in praise and softly repeating, "*Gloria, gloria, gloria, gloria . . . Aleluya.*" We knew there was a special power in the room that we couldn't see with our eyes, but that we could feel in our souls.

Shaken by the euphoric feeling of intercession, I felt the Spirit of God flow through my veins. It affected me physically. I started uttering sounds that made no sense. Sounds that I had heard come from brethren like Sister Esther. Sounds that I had feared to repeat out loud in case someone identified them as fake or man-made. I had been told these sounds, or language, was a special dialect that God gives His people when they are filled by the Holy Ghost, as it reads in the second chapter of the Book of Acts:

> *And suddenly there came a sound from heaven*
> *as of a rushing mighty wind,*
> *and it filled all the house where they were sitting.*
> *And there appeared unto them cloven tongues like as of fire,*
> *and it sat upon each of them.*
> *And they were all filled with the Holy Ghost,*
> *and began to speak with other tongues,*
> *as the Spirit gave them utterance.*

I was so deeply wrapped into the moment, and so lost in the exhilaration, that I opened my mouth and let my tongue catch up with the thoughts and feelings taking place in my mind. There was no way to come up with prayers that would do justice to the overwhelming presence I felt within. I separated my lips and uttered words that sounded like: *"Hararamasanta Bararaharasanta Mararará. Otikosororonto Roróntomari Kararasamarahasanta Barará. Ararabasanta Hararabasanta Manti Kasanta Barahasario Masanta Harabará."*

My mind thought of the most poetic and melodious sonnets in light speed, and my mouth then used this language to catch up with the tongues of heaven. A lot of our mouths did, as our bodies lay on the ground, unable to regain posture. We shook and twisted to the feeling of a pull in our guts. Every time someone laid hands on another, it was as if a power surge would flow from person to person, making each body convulse and lose composure.

Four months before, on April 2, at the age of eighteen, I had been born again, receiving Jesus into my heart. On August 10, at the age of nineteen, I went under the waters and was baptized as a testimony to the world of my obedience to the Father. A day later I—a devout soul committed to serving his Lord—was given the ultimate gift; I was baptized in the Spirit of God— baptism by fire—baptism by the Holy Ghost.

Liberation
I arrived at church a bit late that Friday. I dropped off my duffle bag and backpack in one of the Sunday School rooms as usual, then turned off the light and headed to the sanctuary.

The service stood somewhere between announcements and songs when I felt my spiritual diabetes kick in.

After a few months of being in this church, a sense of monotony had set in. The gringos left long ago, Brother Alejandro no longer scared me, and Pastor Héctor delivered his bully-pulpit, angry speeches as expected. I sat in my usual seat at the front, struggling to concentrate. I knew the ritualistic parade of church service elements by heart: two songs, welcome, announcements, four songs, testimonies, special songs, offering, sermon, altar call, song, farewell.

I needed to get out of there. Pronto.

I went back to the Sunday School room where I had left my stuff. Entering, I locked the door behind me, but left the lights off. And that's when it started.

I began interceding for the people inside the church temple. I prayed to God, asking Him about my purpose, about His vision, about the meaning behind the gift He had given me. Inside I felt a sense of urgency to reach out to the lost, but I felt I was alone in my yearning. What did He want me to do?

I began to sweat as my voice grew louder. I made a fist with my right hand, swinging it from side to side. I then raised my hands to the ceiling and lowered my knees to the floor. Getting back up, I stomped the ground. I prayed and prayed for an intense forty-five minutes. I felt God listening to me, though He hadn't yet spoken back. I asked for a sign, hoping He'd surprise me.

When I left the Sunday School room, I felt as though I had had a good talk with "J-dawg," but I didn't feel fulfilled—I felt as though something was still lacking.

I entered the sanctuary and found everyone still on their feet. The music pumped through the speakers, but I noticed that only a few of the congregants were actually clapping. Seeing some people at the altar, I figured Pastor Héctor was praying for some of their needs. Rather than make my way back to my seat, I decided to wait at the back of the room till it ended.

Looking more closely at the congregation, I saw fear in their eyes, noticed little children holding on to their parents' legs, all with their eyes locked on the altar.

"What is going on?" I thought.

I took a closer look at the front of the church to see who was praying. I saw the church's leaders and elders, including Sister Esther, Brother Alejandro, and Pastor Héctor, surrounding a man I didn't recognize. Though the band continued to play and sing, their terrified eyes stayed focused on them.

I saw the man's body shake as Pastor Héctor grabbed his hands, raising them up in the air. Poncho, a young recovering drug addict who joined the church around the same time I did, held the guy at the waist with all his might. The leaders prayed fervently, in tongues. I knew then what was going on.

"This is a liberation!"

I don't know what got over me. My mind spent about a second's worth of time with flashbacks of movies and stories featuring such moments, but no more than that, when my feet suddenly swept me to the altar. I walked with conviction past the people on the aisle, moved to the front row, moved past the group leaders, and got right next to Pastor Héctor. I instinctively removed his right hand from the guy's left hand and placed mine on it instead. I didn't wait for a reaction. I got shoulder to shoulder with our senior pastor and looked the man straight in the eye. He immediately gave me a stare filled with darkness, followed by words soaked in rage, "You have no power over me!"

I had no choice. I had to talk back.

"I may have no power over you, but the Spirit of God and the blood of Jesus Christ that is within me give me the power to stand before you and tell you to flee this man's body!"

I reached over and touched him on the forehead. As soon as my skin touched his, he reacted as if I had pressed hot iron against it, with a painful shout originating in his gut.

I didn't feel surprised.

His head came back up, and his eyes quickly looked for mine. As soon as we made eye contact, he let go of our hands and tried to lash after me with brute force. Poncho's older brother, Pancho (also a former addict who understood the feeling of being imprisoned by the past), immediately swung his arms and wrapped them around the possessed man's body to aid in holding him back. The two of them could barely control him as his face came an inch away from mine. I saw up close his desire to rip me into pieces with his bare hands—to bite me. I knew I had entered a real entrenched battle, not just for the man's soul, but for the supremacy of God's glory—I was staring the Devil in the eye.

I could practically see red flames inside those dark brown eyes. His roaring voice emanated from a darker source than his throat. "I know who you are," he howled at me, "You are meek. You are weak. I know your story. I know your mistakes. I know your secrets. And all of us inside of this body are not going anywhere. You have been defeated. Your god has been defeated. And the victory over his soul is ours!"

I had a few fiery words of my own.

"I know I am weak. And I know that I was filthy. I know I have made mistakes. But no, you do not have power over me. You may tell the world what I have done, but I have already confessed my sins to my Creator, who has become my Savior. And though I once was lost, I am now found. And though I was weak, I am now strong. And though I was filthy, I am now clean because I have been washed in the blood of Jesus Christ. And it is in His Mighty and Holy Name that I command you to leave!"

I reached for his chest this time, and the fire seemed to be even more scorching than before. "Aaaaagh!" he shouted, falling to the ground. I knelt down right by his side and placed my hand on his head. I continued to pray,

"Dear Lord, I know you are with us. Free this man as proof of Your mighty power and grace and allow him to join Your family."

Everyone in the church remained on their feet. Pastor Héctor, who was now behind me, moved his right index finger in a circle asking the band to keep playing. The elders and leaders stayed faithfully by the man's side. As the battle continued, I had no idea how it would end.

The normally two-hour service had by this point reached hour four. At times we thought we had won. At times we thought this was going nowhere. For the moment, he had stopped bolting up from the floor, aiming for my throat.

I continued talking to him, "The Enemy has gotten a hold of your heart. I know you must have made many mistakes, things you are ashamed of, but I am here to tell you that doesn't matter any more. Jesus Christ has made me clean, He has made all of us clean, and He can do the same for you. But you have to ask Him yourself. I can't do that for you."

He threw a few more insults at me and condemned me to eternal damnation.

I immediately replied, "You have no power over me." But I quickly shifted my attention to the other person I knew was in there somewhere. "Brother, I know you are in there. You have to fight! Listen to my voice. Accept Jesus Christ into your heart and He will set you free!"

His posture changed, as well as the look in his eyes. He finally reached out, "Help me. What do I need to do?" I quickly answered, "You have to proclaim the name of Jesus Christ. His blood has power to cleanse you, to make you new again. The power of Darkness has no authority over Him. He has defeated him already on the cross. The victory is His. And it can be yours through Him as well. But you have to ask for His blood to cover you. Do it. Do you want Jesus to come into your heart?"

We both dripped in sweat, our veins jumping on our foreheads, extremely exhausted, as the pivotal part of our mystical conversation reached its climax.

He stared at me again. His lips fought against the overpowering demonic instinct still taking hold of his soul. I begged him, "Fight, brother. Fight!" He shouted and growled, "Aaaagh!" I jumped forward to his aid, "You can do it. I am talking to you, Satan. I declare victory over you by God Almighty. I declare power in His Holy Spirit. And I now declare freedom in the blood of his Son, Jesus Christ!"

Suddenly, his shoulders dropped. His lips trembled. His face went down.

"Repeat after me, brother," I said. As he repeated my words, his body seemed to go through a metamorphosis, as if some spirit left him and gave him back the space that belonged to his own thoughts and emotions. "Jesus Christ, Son of God, I declare that you are Lord over my life. I am a sinner. And I repent of my transgressions against you. Please come into my heart. Cleanse me. Make me whole again. I am yours."

To our amazement, he dropped to the ground. He began to convulse violently on that temple floor. I didn't know what was going to happen next, but I knew I wasn't ready for round twelve.

Then, his convulsing stopped.

He got on his knees, still facing down. His body trembled gently, as if something was crawling its way out of him. I wondered whether a flaming creature would emanate from his mouth.

He hunched over and began to vomit a nasty green blob onto the altar floor. We helped him get back on his feet. He raised his hands and began to worship the name of Jesus.

The church audience erupted in cheer and celebration. The band picked up with festive and thunderous praise. The elders and leaders closed their eyes and stomped the ground in a demonstration of victory. I took a few steps back, stood there trying to process what had just happened. Then I raised my hand to the sky and gave glory to Christ. I began dancing and cheering with the rest of the crowd. A soul that was lost had just joined the herd.

When the service ended, Pastor Héctor stood next to the man at the church gates as people walked out. One by one they congratulated him, rubbed his shoulder, gave him hugs, and looked at each other with pride and joy. When I approached him, I said the first thing that I could think of, and I meant it, "Welcome to the family."

I expected a different reaction.

He seemed cold, disconnected, without joy. He showed no fear or nervousness. He stood there like a statue, a shadow of darkness in his semblance. Could there still be a little bit of demonic presence left in him that he will have to battle in the next few weeks? I wondered. After all, I didn't change overnight. But his case did seem much different from mine.

When I finally had a few minutes to myself, I thought about that moment between the vomiting and the dancing—that moment when I stepped back and stood still, questioning what was going on inside me, in front of me.

I had locked myself in a dark room begging God to wake us up from our dormant ways, and to please give me a sign if He wanted me to keep pursuing the risky ways of the Holy Spirit to its full biblical extent. I wanted an irrevocable sign that said, "Be loud, be brave, and be courageous without regrets."

I think I just got it.

Although I had just received such a reply from the Lord, and my ministry picked up in a bold, vibrant, and prolific way, there was something from that day that never left me with a full peace of mind. The Devil and I had waged an epic battle with tongues of fire for the soul of a man . . . whom I never saw again.

Part II: At the Cross

"The Supreme Court has ruled that they cannot have a nativity scene in Washington, DC. This wasn't for any religious reasons. They couldn't find three wise men and a virgin."

—Jay Leno

7

ANOINTED

"Then Samuel took the horn of oil, and anointed him
in the midst of his brothers; and the Spirit of the Lord
came mightily upon David from that day forward."
—1 Samuel 16:13

"It Was Tuesday"

Most people in our youth group had been born and raised in the church, giving me a particularly different outlook on Christianity. Not to mention a clear sense of urgency. For me Christianity was not a culturally mandated process as Catholicism had been, this was a choice, and a tough one at that. Things didn't always make sense, but I had decided to jump in head first and squeeze everything out of it.

But this transformation was harder than I had originally thought. My new faith found itself at odds with my life before the cross.

When I first started my walk in Christianity they taught me that God created music for the angels to worship Him, and for nothing else. Every other kind of music not sung to God was "of the world," and hence "bad for you." In a demonstration of devotion, I shattered dozens of CDs that represented the sin of humanity. Madonna, Ace of Base, Michael Jackson, Mariah Carey, Bon Jovi, Green Day, Alanis Morissette, La Bouche, 2 Unlimited, and many more. One by one I broke them into pieces with my bare hands. Part of my heart broke with each cracking sound. My tears fell down heavily onto the trash bag in which I buried all of these shattered melodies. But I had to continue. Christians told me that if I loved God I should fill myself only with music that glorified God, since everything else was carnal and sinful.

I learned that going to a movie theater was as sinful as going to a bar—that people went there to "fulfill their fleshly desires." If I wanted to be involved in leadership I had to wear a shirt and tie, and girls had to wear a dress because women in leadership wearing pants were labeled "unvirtuous." I used to be considered the best dancer in my high school, but now my movements no longer represented art but rather my flesh's desire to have its way. I had to sacrifice my urge to dance—control it and extinguish it. Dancing had originally given me self-confidence and self-esteem, but I knew now that it opened the door for demons to possess me with vanity and lust.

I lost my friends and distanced myself from my family. I also let go of my dreams and passions. But I remained faithful that God would honor my sacrifice and give me new ones that would blow me away.

So excited with my transformation, I felt a need to call one of the people responsible for my new vision of life—Joel—to share what had happened. Surely if someone would understand my joy and what I was going through, it would be him. From my wallet, I pulled out the picture he had given me with his phone number written on the back. I knew he carried a picture of me in his wallet with my number.

"Hello. Can I talk to Joel, please?" He seemed distracted when he got to the phone. "Hello. Who is this?" He asked. "Hi Joel. This is Fernando," I replied. "Fernando?" He asked. "Yeah, from the church in Mexicali. You gave me your picture with your phone number. Remember?" He seemed even more puzzled now, "Fernando? From Mexico?" "Ah. Well. I'm in California now, but yeah, we have phones here too, dude," I said chuckling at the other end.

I shared with him how, after our last reunion, I had gone back home and decided to give Jesus a try. I told him how I had joined the church in Mexicali and how active I had become in it. I told him how excited and thankful I was for their visits and their ministry all these years.

I expected a quick congratulations. I hoped he'd share amazing stories about his ministry. Instead, he said, "Well, man. Things have been a bit different over here. When we got back from Mexico we were all on fire for a few weeks, but things have changed." "What do you mean?" I asked. "Well, when we're there we're all excited about what's happening and what we're doing. But then we get back and we have to go back to life, and school, and work, and girls, and it's really hard to stay on fire." He said that most people did not remain as involved. That once the "fire of Mexico" had faded away, everyone pretty much went back to normal.

I was beyond shocked. I had greatly admired these guys, the missionaries. I thought they always stayed on fire, changing the world. How could this be?

I let him have it. "I have changed my life for Jesus. I have sacrificed my relationship with friends and family. I have left sin aside and I'm serving Him and growing in ministry. I can't believe this. That day you and I talked was the day that changed my life, and for you, it was Tuesday!"

I hung up the phone, mad, sad, but mostly determined. I had given up a lot. But it didn't matter what happened with Joel; for me, it would never just be Tuesday.

Filled with Power

Two or three weeks after my baptism in the Holy Spirit, I received an invitation to a summer camp Siete Olivos attended in some remote area of the state. The Foursquare denomination, which organized and sponsored the camp, had invited other Pentecostal churches in Baja California to fellowship and to help boost its numbers. Still floating on a strong spiritual high, I immediately accepted, especially since I had never attended summer camp before.

Hundreds of people of all ages from Tijuana, Ensenada, Tecate, Mexicali, and the Mexicali Valley gathered in the Trinity Valley for a week to receive a partaking in the Lord's blessings with no distractions from the world. I, for one, didn't know that many Mexican Christians existed.

The theme for the camp struck me as very odd at first. The camp leadership believed that we could be "*Llenos de Poder . . . Hasta el Fin del Mundo.*" *Filled with Power . . . Till the Ends of the Earth.*

At registration we received a name tag with a round colored sticker on it: red, blue, orange, or green. I got green. Once we finished setting up, the leaders called us into the main sanctuary for our opening plenary. There, they had us split up by sticker color and wait for instruction. It was organized chaos. Everybody seemed to know somebody. All expressed happiness to be there. While we huddled, I decided to take a chance and get out of my shell. If I was going to spend a whole week with these people, I wanted to squeeze as much as I could out of this experience. I started from one end of the line and worked my way to the other, saying hello and introducing myself to everyone on the green team. Although I felt very nervous, my fear of rejection started to quickly dissolve.

Two people on my team stood out to me. They were my age, and they had lighter hair, eyes, and skin tone than the rest, just like me. I introduced myself in English, thinking they were American since they had English names on their tags: Fred and Dan.

Next, the leaders instructed us to select a team captain. Most of the hands on my team started pointing at me. "What? Are you serious?" I asked, shocked. My teammates nodded, saying it had to be me. They said I had proven I was a uniter and had shown a willingness to reach out to everyone. But nobody knew me, a brand-new believer, and they still hadn't seen in me any of the "leadership" qualities that people in my church talked about. Regardless, I accepted, walked to the front, and shook hands with the other three captains, all older and better known than I was. From this point forward I was tasked with organizing my team and leading them in sports competition, worship service programming, cleaning-day strategies, and meal-service planning.

I later found out Fred and Dan were actually Mexican. They just stood out in the crowd for their distinct features. Fred lived in Tijuana and Dan in the Mexicali Valley. They became my greatest allies and partners in leading the crowd. Young, willing, excited, and, above all, friendly, loving, and caring. Dan, a couple of years younger and way flirtier, would disappear to talk to girls at times, until we'd find him to get stuff done. A drummer and a good athlete, he served as our expert on all things worship and sports. Fred, who knew whose shoulder to tap on and for what, handled logistics and connections. I was the charismatic presence, comfortable motivating people and providing the big picture. Whenever the three of us would walk or sit together, the camera flashes would follow. People who didn't know us thought we were brothers, and we played along. We were the darlings of camp, and we milked it for all it was worth.

I'll never forget a couple other characters at the camp, Francisco and Eduardo. Though older than the rest of us, Francisco was the magnetic young leader of the Baja California Foursquare youth. He had huge dreams of achieving things with the denomination that hadn't been done before. He believed in real programing, with big names and big audiences. He got in front of the mic and compelled us to believe that we could indeed achieve anything in the name of Jesus. Eduardo was also a captivating character behind the mic, as well as behind the piano. He led worship in a way I hadn't experienced before. He got us to jump, weep, shiver, and melt at the altar. He became an icon of anointing, and we knew that if he sang, we would experience the presence of the Holy Spirit. We looked up to them, we secretly idolized them, and we trusted them.

The speaker for the camp, a prophet of the Lord, had prophesied that the Spirit of the God would "show up like thunder" and that we would be "blown away." We didn't know how right he'd be. But that first night, we found out.

The wind and rain blew hard outside as the last people from the prayer room (where campers had been interceding in shifts around the clock) arrived, packing the temple. We all felt an electricity in the place. Francisco opened up with a riveting welcome. Eduardo hit a soft Cm chord on his keyboard, signaling we were about to start. Our feet were charged with power we felt come out of the earth. Our eyes were expectant. The drum joined the beat, forcing our hands to clap along. Our butts jumped off our seats and they would not go back down again that night. A group of barefoot dancers joined the stage with white ribbons, dressed in white robes. It looked so holy. Their faces showed dedication. They hopped on one foot, and then switched onto the other waving their hands in worship. We joined in. It was contagious. Old people, young people, the night cared for no age. We raised our hands, moved our feet, closed our eyes, and opened our mouths to sing out loud:

Hay muchas formas de alabar tu nombre . . .

There are many ways to praise your name, and to exalt you, Oh Jehovah.
There are many ways to magnify you, but right now I'll do it like this.

When Eduardo uttered the next words, the place erupted with shouts, praise, laughs, and sweat:

Remolineando. Remolineando . . .

Swirling. Swirling. I will celebrate Jehovah.
Swirling. Swirling.
I will become more vile because of Jehovah.

And we swirled and swirled, hopping in circles. We held hands and danced around, switching hands. Our feet couldn't stand still. A magic moved us beyond control:

Lara. Laralaralara. Laralaralara. Laralalá.

The prophet then came to the microphone and called us all into a greater depth in the waters. I was stunned. How much deeper could we get? We had already lost control without any concern of ridicule.

Eduardo changed the tune and the guitars became melodic:

Al borde de Tu gran trono, me postraré, hoy a Ti . . .

At the edge of Your great throne, I will bow down, today before You.
You reign among principalities, seated at the right hand of God.

An overwhelming feeling like a rushing wind flew through our souls. Our hands shot up in the air. Our heads bowed down. Our tears started rolling down. There was no emotion on earth that made more sense than what we were feeling at this very moment.

Be exalted, oh Great Lamb. You live today, and always will.
Be crowned, with my praise. Your name is, "The Conquerer."

We trembled from the inside out. The flood of worship began to pull our knees down. People started speaking in tongues all around. The music got louder as we became weaker.

The prophet and several elders in the crowd started laying hands on people, who began to praise loudly in reverent blabber, right before being struck by holy lightning and pushed to the ground. One by one it seemed to be the fate of every participant. I saw them fall, those whom I knew, and those I didn't. I stood there with a pull in my gut. I clinched my fists and decided that whatever was gonna happen, would happen. I was not going to walk halfway to the throne. I was going to discover fully what this Holy Spirit was. I had sacrificed way too much, and left too much behind. I had nothing to go back to and this was going to be it. I believed there was a manifestation of God that I couldn't see with my eyes, but that I could feel in my bones. The hands of elders acted as lightning rods for God's power, and it shocked us all.

And then it hit me. Thunder from heaven came upon me as soon as the elder pushed me on my forehead. I didn't think he needed to push me down that hard, the spirit was surely enough. But either way I was now being charged by a refreshing peace as I lay flat on the ground.

The floor ran out of room with so many bodies lying silently. Those who stood kept worshiping the name of Jesus. By the end of the night we had all danced, wept, lain on the ground, and had experienced something special.

Francisco came to the mic and reminded us that the title of the camp was chosen for this very reason. That we could indeed be filled with the power of the Holy Spirit, and then, with that power, reach the ends of the earth to proclaim His name.

What I had experienced was too intense, too real. What I had felt was too good and too out of this world. I had heard the word *missionary* when the gringos came into town, but I never thought that I could become one of them—not in a million years. At the end, what did they have that I didn't? I had *worshipped* them for years, and now the Lord had given me His sign, I was feeling His calling, and I had to find out what to do next.

Days of Pentecost
Visitors were allowed to enter on the last day of camp. A group from Siete Olivos came to check things out. During worship they kept their hands to their sides and behaved like "spectators, not participants"—I had learned that phrase during camp. They seemed like dry foreigners unaccustomed to the camp's vibrant worshipful culture. I wanted to stay there forever.

During the last part of the program, Francisco asked everyone to get into their own church groups so they could pray for one another and take the blessings back down the mountain. I was the newest member in the group, for sure, but I was radiating with willing hope. I was as shocked as anybody when Francisco came down from the altar, opened up a tiny bottle of oil, rubbed some on my forehead, then some on my hands, and said that I'd be praying for my church group. Everyone was wide-eyed with surprise, especially me. My hands trembled as I began praying for my fellow church members one by one, including the ones born and raised in the church and the members of the praise team, even Laura and Brenda. I felt honored, unworthy, and exhilarated. But the kicker came during Francisco's closing remarks.

Francisco brought out a sheet of paper to announce the winning team. I connected looks with Dan and Fred, and we left our church groups to stand next to each other to hear the results together. The green team was definitely the darling due to our special characters. It felt beautifully perfect to stand there holding hands with these situational team members and chosen brothers.

He read the results. Fourth place, the red team. Third place, the blue team. It got down to first and second. We listened attentively. Come on, Francisco, just put the cherry on top of the cake.

"First place . . . the orange team!"

Everyone cheered and clapped. Dan, Fred, and I squeezed each other's hands, looked down, breathed out, let go of our hands, and then raised them to clap for the orange team as well. I'm not gonna lie, it hurt a little. We had done so much, worked so hard, but due to a second-place in volleyball, our score placed us out of our fantasy goal. Still, I was standing with the people I played this game with, and I knew we had tried our best. Our memories would never die.

Francisco emphasized the importance of being filled with power. We had all felt it. We had all experienced it. He also said this camp would be "a launching pad for missionaries all over the world," that this would be "a place where new leadership would be birthed." He said that those around us would one day be the leaders of our churches and of great new ministries. And then he said something that completely caught me off guard, "And one of these days, in the near future, you will see this great leader on stage, leading great ministries, and you'll ask yourself, 'Isn't he the captain of the green team?'"

My eyelids shot straight up, along with those of my church group, who quickly looked my way. Dan and Fred laid their hands on my shoulders in support. I thought he must be referring to another year's captain, or maybe he got the team wrong. He mentioned he had been observing me the whole time. He had seen my determination, my leadership skills, and had seen my openness to let God work His will in me. He said that when that happens, only greatness could be an outcome.

Francisco approached me at the end of his message, looked me straight in the eye, placed his hand on my chest, and reaffirmed what he had said. I felt so immature and inexperienced. I didn't know what that could mean.

I definitely had been on a roller coaster of emotions since becoming a Christian.

And it didn't stop there.

Soon after the camp ended, I became Siete Olivos' youth leader. I made sure that we participated in every single event the Foursquare put together—camps, conferences, retreats, etc. Francisco kept including me in leadership roles. During a winter camp in the city of Tecate, as soon as I arrived, he made me aware of some news. A family emergency had come up and he was going to have to leave immediately. Though he had a most trustworthy crew that had worked with him on planning for months right there, he appointed me as director of the camp, having full faith that I would lead the crowd with efficiency and Spirit-led determination.

Using my creative side, I also developed a strong drama team with my youth group, and we began to perform at events to great response. Eventually we received invitations to perform all over the state. I had become a notable figure in all Foursquare events. People considered me one of the elders, one of the leaders and decision makers along with Francisco and Eduardo.

Francisco always had something new under his sleeve. He dreamt of starting a missionary movement in which members of the Foursquare Church in America served together with their Mexican counterparts. To that end, he made me one of the first Mexican leaders to lead this binational effort.

The word "missionary" became an iconic and idolized word during every single Foursquare event. Leaders lined up flags of countries from around the world across the stage. They would ask us to pray and visualize what country God wanted to send us to, and then to line up in front of the corresponding flag. They would then anoint us and commission us to "*go ye therefore and make disciples of all nations*" (Mathew 28:19). I'd often find myself behind a Middle Eastern flag, since I had become enamored by the idea of meeting Jews and visiting the Holy Land, where it all began.

They also spoke at great length about the need to find purity in our hearts before reaching out to save the world from hell. They called us into abstinence from any sexual experiences until marriage—even masturbation—spoke of the devastating effect alcohol would have on our lips, which some called "liquid sin," and warned against many other "mundane things this world had to offer." They weren't afraid to take a strong stance against cultural trends. For example, they told us how AIDS was God's punishment on humanity for the despicable and disgusting sin of homosexuality, which God called an "abomination."

I found comfort in their words, their vision, and their opportunity for restoration in the eyes of the Lord.

When it came time for Francisco to move on to pastoring and hand off the reins of the state Foursquare youth, he got ahold of me. Although my church was Pentecostal, it was not registered as a Foursquare Church. He inquired if our pastor would be willing to change registration so I could officially take over Francisco's role, but there was no way Pastor Héctor would make such a move. Francisco tried to find a loophole. He said it wasn't that I was the right person to become the leader, but that I basically already was the leader. Though I never ended up taking an official title, he placed me in leadership and asked me to help mobilize things until they selected a successor, which didn't occur until years later, after I had left the area.

His eventual successor, Dan, had already become a very good friend of mine, making me incredibly joyful and proud. When Dan was anointed as the next state leader, I made a vow to Francisco to support him as best as I could—though with Dan being a brother, that would already be a given.

Dan and I remained pretty close for the next few years. We'd share in our struggles and our challenges. I lost track of Fred for the longest time, until LinkedIn found him for me through his old email. Francisco now leads two churches in Tijuana and San Diego. I spoke at his Tijuana church once. Eduardo and I became even closer after we both left the Foursquare. We became confidants, very close friends, and partners in future ministries.

Every time we got together for a meal or a chat, we talked about those days of Pentecost, and how being anointed by God transformed our lives.

Out of all those hundreds of fervent young souls who danced, cried, fell to the ground shaking, and promised to *go ye therefore*, only a handful of us actually did. Baffling, for sure, that anyone could escape the Spirit of the Lord coming mightily upon us and calling us into action like that.

How each of us answered that call, lived out that vision, and cared for our hearts would determine the fullness of our personal satisfaction in the Lord. But of one thing I was sure, once I was anointed by God, that power filled me, and with such momentum and determination I had only one possible path underneath my feet . . . the ends of the earth.

8

EXODUS: THE PROMISED LAND

"But I don't want to go among mad people," Alice remarked.
"Oh, you can't help that," said the Cat: "we're all mad here.
I'm mad. You're mad."
"How do you know I'm mad?" said Alice.
"You must be," said the Cat, "or you wouldn't have come here."
—Lewis Carroll, *Alice in Wonderland*

Shooting Star

Lying on my bed, I looked up at the heavens—my own set of glow-in-the-dark stars affixed to my ceiling. I stared at them every night before falling asleep. They burned bright green when lights first went off, before slowly fading into the night. To my left, the biggest star of them all sat on my nightstand. I had intentionally left it off the ceiling—as if giving me the chance to claim that I had caught a shooting star.

My mom and three siblings slept in one room, so I could have my privacy and study time in the other. A poor Mexican kid, scrawny, with a challenged sense of fashion, I began to struggle with my grades, as I dedicated every free moment to ministry. Although I was a full-time student, I worked almost full-time, traveling to Mexico every weekend—all without a car. I would arrive home around 11 p.m., grab dinner with mom, say goodnight, do some homework, and then practice guitar. I'd get up at 6 a.m., grab breakfast, and leave before my siblings got up. Days would go by without me seeing them.

The hands on the clock had passed number three, and yet I remained wide-eyed and pensive. I swung my legs off the bed and got down on my knees. I looked out the window and sought His face in the night clouds. My hands up in the air, I begged for His attention. Culture defined that I should marry a nice girl, have 2.5 children, find a good job, work hard for a promotion, and live a good life that would please Him—but I knew that wouldn't be enough for me. I was giving everything I had for the Lord, but I still felt I was missing something.

"I don't want to be like any other servant," I prayed, "I want to experience the fullness of Your love, of Your power. I don't want to only be shaking on the ground, I want to see the ground shake because of Your glory." And I said what I'd been thinking about for days, what I knew would be a shot off the board, "I want to be like Moses."

The prophet had gone from surviving in a basket down the river to bringing forth deliverance to his people during the Exodus from Egypt. He stood in the face of destiny and saw the hand of God move in history-defining miraculous ways—thunderstruck when God talked to him. The waters, lightning, and the masses would bend by his relationship with Yahweh. After what I'd been through, I could want nothing else.

I felt my insides sizzling. I was on the verge of some possibility, but I couldn't point a finger on it. I remained still but my soul tossed and turned. I saw those green stars above me shine bright and gleeful. I turned to my left, and there it was—my shooting star.

And it was then that I had a revelation. Everything I was doing at church and with the Foursquare was really good, and was really bright, but maybe I had to do something that was off the path of things that are good and bright. How about something awesome and radiant? I wanted to be that shooting star that trailed off the path—like Moses.

A movie began playing in my mind, with flashbacks of those whom I've known to fit outside the average. The sermons and callings with the Foursquare, the growth I'd had at Siete Olivos, the time serving with the gringos, the . . . wait, the time serving with the gringos? Guys and girls like me who come and go, who . . .

Wait a minute . . . "Like me."

It was my night of salvation all over again. I saw them alight from their dusty white vans. I saw them preach and testify. I saw them with their braided or buzzed hair, baggy pants, and parachute skirts. And once a week, I saw them wear a themed shirt with the logo of a cross formed from the cracking of a rock. Although all the participating Americans I had met were in high school, how come the shirt always said Azusa Pacific *University?*

Azusa . . . Pacific . . . University . . . Wait.

All I knew was that it was in Los Angeles somewhere—a college that somehow brings high schoolers to Mexico. It sends missionaries.

What if . . . ?

I turned to my left and there the star was, glowing bright, trying to tell me something. Like so many other nights, I reached over and grabbed it. I caressed it in my hands. Flipped it over and over. I brought it over to my lips. I closed my eyes and dreamt, awake.

I jumped out of bed as if bitten by a critter, flipped the light switch on, and dropped my rear on the desk chair. The computer couldn't spring to life soon enough. That dial-up sound took longer than usual, I swear. I opened Netscape. I knew most schools would have their initials and the extension ".edu" as their web address. I entered www.apu.edu.

And there it was. I clicked and clicked, read page after page, and saw picture after picture. On my screen the images glowed like an unbelievable oasis of goodness flowing with milk and honey. After struggling to demonstrate my faith and to live among the unfaithful and hedonistic, this was a sanctuary for Christians, where everybody was a Christian, everybody did Christian things, and everybody traveled around the world making more Christians. It was the closest thing I had ever seen to a heaven on earth.

I heard birds outside my window and realized the sun had started to greet the new day. I had school in a bit and I hadn't slept at all, but I felt more awake than ever. What's the worst that could happen? I had to. I slid the mouse over to the corner icon. "Request info." I looked up to the stars, the morning gleam covering and submerging them like a foamy wave. I clenched my star with both hands. I cracked open my grasp to take a little peek, and in the darkness I saw a bright glow which fought the darkness around it.

I'm a first-generation immigrant, on my way to being my family's first college graduate, and I'm thinking of attending an expensive private school. I typed my address, clicked submit, and softly whispered those words, "I will be a shooting star."

Mexico Outreach

Pastor Héctor called me at 7 a.m. on a Tuesday morning. "Hello?" He tells me that, as it turns out, he had been talking with some people from APU for a few months now. He had been helping them contact the Mexican immigration office to process the entrance of all those students who would visit during Spring Break. He said he was meeting with a couple of their representatives at 10 a.m. at a restaurant in Mexicali, and asked if I'd like to join them since I was going to be attending the campus next September. I said, "Of course." I skipped class, dressed professionally, and hurried across the border.

I showed up a few minutes early. I did not see Pastor Héctor, who I assumed was running late, so I started scouting for people who looked out of place. I quickly spotted a sweet old lady with hair resembling a tall white beehive, standing with a humble, balding man in his fifties who looked uncomfortable in his suit. "Excuse me, are you guys from Azusa Pacific University?"

I learned that the woman, Amelia, had started the ministry in the late 1960s when she met Carolyn Koons, a professor from Azusa Pacific, who wanted to take students across the border on short-term missions. That was the first time I had heard of "short-term missions." Amelia visited every single church, not receiving a cent, and made contacts for the American churches to visit. Eddy, the man, had been working for the Mexico Outreach department at Azusa Pacific for the greater part of his life, since his student days. As the only bilingual person in the office, he served as the de facto mediator. I learned that Azusa Pacific had many departments that involved students in ministry, all supervised by Carolyn. Mexico Outreach is the department in charge of the Mexicali Easter program. Each year only about 200 of the participants are APU students; the rest of the 9,000 participants or so come from high school groups all across the United States and Canada. The majority of them would visit Mexicali during Spring Break, with the rest visiting Ensenada at different times of the year, though especially in summer.

Now it all started to make sense.

I told them how I had been accepted to the school, though I had never set foot on the campus, and it was all because of the program they called Mexico Outreach. They had a smile that glowed with pride as they heard their ministry validated in such a way. They didn't get to hear stories like this very often.

I offered to help by visiting the Mexican Department of Immigration to inquire about the steps and procedures for students to visit legally. I quickly learned about a policy Mexico had implemented to document every American student who wanted to visit the country—a step taken in retaliation to similar U.S. policies. Even for the local immigration officials, the exact steps remained unclear, as they pulled documents and fliers out trying to make sense of the new laws they had received from Mexico City.

Since I was helping Mexico Outreach, I contacted the church in Cupertino and asked if I'd be able to stay with them while they camped. They immediately agreed. I was beyond excited. I'd get to stay with the missionaries I used to adore, while I volunteered with the school that brought them here.

When Easter of 1999 arrived, over 5,000 young people and their leaders from Washington, British Columbia, Illinois, California, Alberta, Manitoba, Arizona, Oregon, Michigan, Nebraska, and other states and provinces gathered for a camp/concert/mission trip experience at one of three campsites in Mexicali. Out in the middle of nowhere, rural farming communities hosted what I would call a Christian Woodstock. Hundreds of tents, vans, coolers, supply boxes, laughter, and chaos. Several canopies with Mexican vendors lined up at the entrance selling blankets, tacos, bracelets, necklaces, rings, glasses, shirts, and other cheap and pirated products. Washing stations stood in front of the kitchen. Bug zappers hung above us. An information center held registration forms, wristbands, themes shirts, and sweaters. A stage in the corner with thousands of beach chairs in front of it anchored the setting, while a semi-trailer with a large banner hanging from it served as a backdrop. The theme on the banner read: "This Changes Everything."

Students with red shirts and walkie-talkies, Team Ezra, stood at the gates as security. Students with blue shirts, Team Luke, gathered at the church next door as the medical/first aid team. Students and adults in green shirts, Team Nehemiah, staffed the kitchen and set up camp on the grounds.

At 7:00 p.m., long lines of people showing their colorful wristbands lined up for warm meals and fruit punch. At 8:00 p.m., the first guitar strums started, and Peter Neumann, the noble worship leader, led us in an array of Christian camp tunes that had us stomping, clapping, and waving, connecting with the power of the night. Ridge Burns stood tall as a long-time speaker, challenging the crowd, "We are not in the U.S. anymore. It is time to serve."

The night air buzzed and hummed, with thousands of excited young souls thrilled by the experience and expectant about what God was about to do.

Dodging a Bullet

When Sunday came, I showed up at El Taber as a member of the American team. Weird. The local kids arrived, we had a service, we had our greetings, we walked around inviting kids, and then we headed back to camp. But it was that "headed back" part that caught me off guard. It was very odd to see what happened behind the curtain.

The gringos laughed at jokes just like we did. They compared high school stories just like we did. The guys and girls we idolized as missionaries were actually humans who farted, burped, and argued just like we did. Their life in Mexico was not nearly as glamorous as we had envisioned. The food in their coolers was basic—peanut butter and jelly, or ham and cheese sandwiches. Those who showered did so in ugly, old, run-down public facilities in downtown Mexicali. They slept in dusty tents whose walls slapped them merciless on the face on windy nights. And they took dumps in stinky porta-potties lined up in the middle of camp where everyone could see you enter, hear when you went, and experience with you what it felt like to serve God in a foreign land.

I learned the girls wore those parachute skirts, which I mocked, because APU asked them to be very conservative and cover as much of their bodies as possible while in Mexico, supposedly to fit in. The guys purchased pants at second-hand stores because leaders told them they'd get ruined. They'd stuff them in bags and pull them out in the morning, wrinkled and smelly. They wore braids or buzzed their hair so they wouldn't have to worry about combing it in the mirrorless camp. And most of the vans where white because that's how they came from the rental agency.

Hearing their conversations I realized they were not as affluent as we had perceived them to be. Many of them came from families who struggled to make ends meet and even had to hold fundraisers—washing cars and selling baked goods—to raise money for the trip. Some came from divided and dysfunctional homes. Some shared how they were no strangers to bullying and ridicule for their looks, shape, or social status. Though the tone of their skin and language was different from ours, they bled, cried, and hoped, just like we did.

I also learned that many of them didn't really come for the "missionary" experience—very few of them actually considered themselves missionaries as such. Many came because it was what everybody was doing—some because they liked someone on the team. After a leader described their "servant's heart" for "sacrificing their Spring Break to serve in the dirt of Mexico," many admitted they wouldn't have had anything else to do other than play video games. Leaders knew that many students took the trip as a vacation, but they brought them anyways hoping that God would perform a miracle, as He had done many times before during this camp experience.

Given these revelations, I recalled my last conversation with Joel, when I phoned him. Maybe he wasn't telling me he had given up. Maybe he was just trying to warn me of a reality I hadn't yet understood.

Still, I kept concentrating on the mission at hand.

I figured Monday would be another average day. We packed the supplies, picked up our coolers from the kitchen with the day's lunch, and headed toward our "ministry site" for our *missionarizing*. Halfway through the day I got a call from Brother Alejandro, who in his day job as a lawyer had been advising Pastor Héctor, Eddy, and Amelia on matters related to the immigration deal. I discovered it would not be an average day after all when he told me, "They said that if we are not down at the immigration office at 6:00 p.m. to resolve this issue, they will deport every single one of you by 6:00 a.m."

My eyeballs almost popped out of their sockets. I asked Andy, the leader of the American church group, to take me back to camp.

As it turns out, a picture of an American girl wearing an Azusa Pacific University T-shirt handing out a Christian brochure to a Mexican girl had showed up on the cover of a local newspaper—the title, "Christians Are Proselytizing in Mexicali." Part of the article read, "Christians confuse children with their dogma."

The director of immigration, whom I believed to be a secret fellow Christian, confessed to us that the Catholic bishop of Mexicali had gotten on the phone and raised hell to some important people about our presence in the city. News got to Mexico City, and a sentence had been served. He and I spent some time going through materials searching for articles in current law that could help our situation. Although I missed dinner and chapel, I got word that the thousands of students back at camp had been on their knees during chapel praying for a positive outcome to our negotiations. The situation couldn't get more tense, but it could get much worse, and I felt as though the responsibility fell on me to make sure it didn't. God help me.

Reading through the documents, we found a clause that allowed people coming for philanthropic purposes to enter the country for a limited amount of time. The director talked to someone in Mexico City and asked for clemency for us this time around, since we were new to these recent laws, they weren't made clear to us beforehand, and we were there with no ill will. Mexico City agreed, with the condition that paperwork with evidence of our service be presented first thing in the morning.

Back at camp, we held an emergency meeting in Carolyn's RV with the leaders of each campsite and the Mexico Outreach staff. I learned that this was not the ministry's first altercation with the Mexican government, which was suspicious of the thousands of gringos pitching tents in the middle of Mexicali Valley cornfields every year. At one point, the government had sent military helicopters to fly over the cornfields to learn of the students' exact whereabouts and spy on their activities. The Health Department also surprised the ministry with inspections to test its food, water, and facilities. And now we had articles in the newspaper and threats of deportation. It seemed there was an ongoing plot to stop the ministry and kick it back across the border.

Everyone at the RV, except Peter Neumann, was old enough to have been my parent. Even though I had answers, I felt so small. "Please keep it together," I thought to myself. I talked to Ridge about the possibility of him getting arrested for preaching during chapel without a "preacher's visa"; to Carolyn about the steps the government could take to come and escort us back to the border; to Glenn, the new Mexico Outreach director, about what we needed to do in the future to avoid this kind of trouble; and to Eddy about what we could do temporarily this year so we could continue our ministry and bring the least amount of stress to those students already here.

Oh man, talk about a moment of truth.

Though it was around midnight, we got on the loudspeaker and asked that the leader of each one of the dozens of churches camping to please meet us at the church next door. We prepared forms where each church wrote down all the kinds of service projects they were doing that week: painting, construction, donations, etc. The reality was that this Christian community was heavily involved in service, spending thousands upon thousands of dollars in benefiting the poverty-stricken areas they served—further, most of the supplies were locally purchased, giving a boost to the local economy. The group's prison ministry coordinator and I stayed up most of the night typing these forms and getting them ready for submission in the morning.

Come 6:00 a.m., we were back at the Mexican Immigration Office. They reviewed the materials and accepted the deal. We had dodged a bullet. But we knew the threat wasn't over.

Glenn came to me after, shook my hand, and said, "Good job. I hear you are coming to APU for school. When are you coming up there next? We have to talk about getting you a job in our office."

At various times I had been close, very close, to giving up, but God had turned everything around and made a miracle of deliverance. I knew my efforts couldn't stop there.

When I finally headed north, my stomach was filled with butterflies. The months of Xs on my wall calendar had finally reached the circled day. It was happening. I rented a van, packed a few belongings, said goodbye to my family and the small apartment we lived in, and headed to an unknown world of possibility—to the Promised Land.

9

MORE THAN WORDS

"There is so much deep contradiction in my soul. Such deep longing for God—so deep that it is painful—a suffering continual—and yet not wanted by God—repulsed—empty—no faith—no love—no zeal. Souls hold no attraction—Heaven means nothing—to me it looks like an empty place—the thought of it means nothing to me and yet this torturing longing for God. Pray for me please that I keep smiling at Him in spite of everything. For I am only His—so He has every right over me.
I am perfectly happy to be nobody even to God . . ."
—Mother Teresa, *Come Be My Light*

Journal Entry: Saturday, September 16, 2000
"Llevo 2 semanas en APU." I've been at APU for 2 weeks. I got here Saturday, September 2, unpacked. I thought that after I said bye to Ruby and my sister (who drove me here) on Monday it'd be when nostalgia would kick in, but it didn't. I still don't feel it.

I've been through a lot of need already—especially hunger. I remember the other day I was really hungry. I have a five meal plan. At one of the eating areas you can get a sandwich, a cookie, and a piece of fruit when you swipe your card. I spent all my money on books and supplies and I won't get my first paycheck until the end of the month. I'm eating my sandwich for lunch, and the cookie and fruit for the two other meals. After a few days of that, your body doesn't feel good. I was sitting at my desk, I opened the little bag and pulled the cookie out to have dinner. I placed the cookie on my lips and felt it tremble. I was immediately filled with fear. I was broke. What had I gotten myself into? Did I jump in here through a wave of emotion and now it would cost me big time? There is no way I can make it. I cried. I felt miserable. But I decided that I would not be in defeat. I decided that I would have faith and believe God would supply even though I can't see it.

I got up and headed to the cafeteria to swipe my card for what would've been the next day's meals.

My mom sent me $100 to help me out. But fearing the money would get lost in the mail as it does in Mexico, she sent it as a money order. I couldn't cash it anywhere. I felt disappointed and hungry, but I laughed after.

I walked all the way to Wells Fargo and I deposited it. But I wasn't able to take the money out till Tuesday. So I walked to West Campus and I returned my French book. When I have money again I'll have to buy it again. But I bought bread, ham, cheese and water. I am happy.

Thanks, my God. I am being tested, I know. But I will remain firm because I know that you brought me here.

I love you,

Fernando

Mano Hermana

Pastor Héctor left me with a great idea before I departed for APU. "Those *Azusas* aren't doing things right," he said. "If they want to make a real impact, they can't be doing little service projects here and there. They have to all show up at one place and do something big that gets a lot of attention. Boom! A thousand people show up for a project and people would have to see the difference." I immediately understood the potential, but I had some reservations. First, Mexico Outreach was not primarily a community-service program. Participants were Christian missionaries who did community service as an expression of their faith and as part of their missionary work. Second, I had an overwhelming sense of the amount of logistical work, not to mention cost, that would have to take place before that happened. People in Mexico, the United States, and Canada would have to get on board, be trained, financed, and synchronized. I had seen how divided relations were, and some cultural Kumbaya wasn't gonna happen overnight. But a seed was planted—an inception.

Every once in a while Eddy or Glenn would entertain my idea of starting a new intentionally organized community-service program involving all the churches that came down with us. After all, community service was not new to them. Linda, the ministry coordinator, became an advocate for my cause and said that even though I reported to Eddy, I could help her in the area of coordinating church relations with our pastors in Mexicali. Doing this, I could begin to move pieces and eventually make my dream of such a program come true.

I accepted Linda's invitation.

In time, with Amelia's help, we started a pastor's committee and divided the Mexicali Valley into areas they would help us coordinate. Linda was not bilingual in any way and suffered from a severe case of stage fright. This provided the opportunity for me to become the spokesperson for Azusa Pacific University in Mexico. An opportunity that I took and ran with.

I was soon speaking at pastor conferences and eventually became a sort of "leader of pastors"—a young adult (who could've been any of their sons) who spoke with confidence and authority. I talked about big ideas and tangible steps to achieve greater things. I challenged them to avoid a language of mediocrity and accepted nothing less than punctuality and the highest standards. I would not accept excuses based on culture such as "Mexican time" or "Mexican shortcuts." We would do things right and praise God with excellence—the only alternative to that was the door. I gained their respect—and, dare I say, instilled a bit of good fear—and eventually became the main unifying voice for the hundreds of Mexican churches that APU partnered with in Mexicali.

At the same time that I was mobilizing churches, I was moving the pieces for my pet project. We were still very fearful of relations with the government. I was advised that maybe the best strategy was to stay at arms length and not engage officials, but I responded that maybe Mexico Outreach hadn't done things the right way in the past, the Mexican way, such as shaking hands and sharing meals with the appropriate people. I believed it was a better strategy to be proactive rather than eternally reactive.

After ongoing lobbying, Eddy and Glenn agreed to sign up each team for a four-hour community service slot, gave me a tiny starting budget for supplies, and left me to find a way to pull it off.

My first step was to make a phone call to Desarrollo Integral de la Familia (DIF)—Mexico's Department of Social Services. In Mexico's tradition, the current head of office's wife runs this department—specifically, the president's wife at the national level, the governor's wife at the state level, and the mayor's wife at the local level. When I called the Mexicali office, the receptionist asked me who was calling. "Fernando Alcántar de Azusa Pacific University,"

I said. I was pleasantly surprised when they remembered hearing about us in the news. They asked for my title. I didn't have one. "Ccccoordinator of . . . Mexico Relations." I wondered what Eddy would think about the promotion I had just given myself. I was able to reach DIF's president, Macristy, as she was warmly nicknamed. After I explained who we were, and some of my ideas, she said she would set up a meeting to connect me with the people I needed to speak with.

I showed up that day nervous as heck. I had let my facial hair grow out a bit to try to add some age and maturity to my baby face. I wore dress slacks and a tie and had a nervous jitter inside, but outside I showed a solid confidence. I entered the room and faced the four *delegados*, the mayor's representatives for the four areas in the Mexicali Valley where we had campsites (that year we had started a fourth one—a college camp). They seemed a bit shaken up about being summoned to this office, but mostly they were surprised that they had been called into a meeting led by a kid.

Macristy seemed surprised as well by my lack of years (something rare in a hierarchical, seniority-driven, leadership culture like Mexico's), but she kindly introduced me and gave a synopsis of my idea before exiting the room. I stayed there with a reluctant audience that had more questions than answers.

My time as a Christian preacher, actor, and missionary had taught me to engage people with charm, but this time I had much greater pressure to excel than normal. Slowly but surely I began to draw them in to the idea, but they had their own pressures and concerns and thus remained hesitant. They later told me that we were considered a "threat" by many in the media and the Catholic Church. Though they admitted they weren't yet ready to trust Azusa Pacific University, they would give Fernando a chance.

I decided to give the program a name that would give us a fresh start, be easy to understand, and inspire involvement. And that is how *Mano Hermana* (Sisterly Hand) was born.

Full of Faith

After realizing the magnitude of mobilizing thousands of people into a service project in a foreign country, I talked to some close APU friends into joining me in the maiden voyage.

Trying to have us fit in with the existing APU culture, I asked that we get a name for our team so we would feel connected and part of the family. I encountered strong resistance, and even mockery, from the majority of the staff since Team Ezra, Team Nehemiah, and Team Luke had existed pretty much since the early days of Mexico Outreach. They charged me with being a wannabe and trying to be ahead of my game. But I had a vision that this could grow into something bigger than me and my time, something long-lasting. I didn't want it to be known simply as the "community-service" team. I wanted it to be a *missionary* team.

I tried to think of a character in the Bible who was known for being filled in the Spirit of the Lord and who also dedicated his life to service. I searched and searched and that's how I found ". . . *Stephen, a man full of God's grace and power, (who) performed great wonders and signs among the people*" (Acts 6:8).

According to history, Stephen eventually became the first martyr of the Christian era. At the time, the apostles needed help with service while they concentrated on evangelizing. They didn't choose someone who was unskilled and worthless; rather, they chose someone who was full of faith and of the Holy Spirit. This is how Team Stephen was birthed. By its second year, the team had earned its own shirt, just like the other teams—ours was golden.

The process of moving the pieces and bringing people on board was not an easy one. I spent countless weekends working out of the trunk of a car—computer, flyers, gifts, maps, clothing for every occasion, and a whole lot of determination. I met people from the Police Department, Public Works, Mexicali Zoo, Parks and Recreation, and schools, and traveled to all corners of Mexicali and the Mexicali Valley forming alliances. I remember repeatedly walking into meetings and hearing the disturbing sound of, "Oh." "What happened?" I'd ask. "Nothing. I just didn't expect you to be this young" was always the reply.

We had thousands of people painting schools, fixing up parks (including the zoo), and cleaning up major roads, among other projects. To be honest, I don't know how we didn't set a place on fire, cause a major traffic wreck, or have someone end up in the hospital with a serious injury in that first year. We were college kids trying to pull off purchasing materials, handling chemicals and inventories, navigating dozens of vans in congested streets, and controlling hundreds of participants at once with nothing but our voices. All while making everything look positive and in control when the TV and newspaper cameras arrived.

Though I was technically running highly important elements of the ministry, I was still a student, then officially part-time, and hence was low on seniority. The full-time staff had company credit cards and office phones, slept in an air-conditioned RV, and had a title to be taken seriously. Still, as I was the one handling immigration issues and media inquiries, I bought a local phone and used my cash advance to load it with minutes. Running this shindig from a tent under the unforgiving heat, I was pulled in every direction. It was easy for people to simply say, "Call Fernando."

After the next Mexicali election, when a new mayor came into office, we entered what I call the "golden days of partnership." The new mayor and his wife became our greatest allies in government. They were unchangingly Catholic, but had a soft spot for people who wholeheartedly wanted to help the needy. A couple of years later she admitted to me that she had gotten some grief from leaders in the Catholic Church for working with us, but that she decided to set that aside and continue our flourishing partnership. In addition, I learned through someone else in government that it was the Catholic Church's accusations that had also caused the military helicopter and health searches.

At one point I received a call from the new mayor's wife while at camp. I had been, for a long time, fed up with the apparent dependence that had been developed by people in Mexicali on our giving presence. People—local officials included—were used to us coming and running all service projects, providing all the supplies, all the labor, and then leaving and doing it again the following year. A cartoon had appeared in one of the local newspapers. It had an image of a Mexican man from a low social class lying on a hammock, with a dream bubble that had the image of people (assumed to be Americans) sweeping the street with the caption, "So this is the American dream? How nice." An article had been written criticizing the government's lack of involvement in community service to the city. She had called to ask me to defend the government from such accusations. I told her that I was having a press conference later in the day, that the media would certainly ask me about the city's involvement, and that my religion prohibited me from lying and that I would have to speak the truth about the lack of participation from public officials. She asked me to wait a moment and that she'd call me right back.

She called a few minutes later and asked me to head to the mayor's office.

When I got there, I was quickly led to a conference room. I felt a bit nervous, but damn was I determined. When the doors opened I found a large conference table surrounded by the heads of all of the city departments that were involved with improvements and security. It was Spring Break, it was a Sunday, they were heading out on vacation, and now they were asked to come meet me and receive instructions on how they were going to do everything to "serve Fernando this week." They weren't in the best of spirits to begin with, but I made a point of saying that they wouldn't be serving me, but that together we would be serving the city. This was a partnership, and we were only visitors; people had to see that their leaders were the most involved. Needless to say, any resource I needed was a phone call away: police escorts, trees for planting, machinery, equipment, advertising, contacts, etc.

The response from the media was great, too—front page articles, in color. We used to be called a "threat," and now we were praised as "the other side of the spring breaker," and "an example to the world in service to the community."

I had the power to mobilize agencies of government and had special privileges to move police, supplies, and other resources with a phone call. Big businesses like Home Depot offered a 20 percent discount to any team or person who would mention my name. Anyone who wanted to enter the zoo for free throughout the year only had to say, "I'm here with Fernando Alcántar." I stood on stage and handled major press conferences with reporters from newspapers, television, and radio from both the United States and Mexico. I became a regular image on the six o'clock news during the two weeks of Spring Break. Reporters would give me their personal number so I could keep them abreast of our doings. We were highlighted in DIF's State of the City, where I was an honored guest sitting at the mayor's table. I supervised the "historic visit" of Mexicali's mayor, his wife, and their entourage to APU's campus. When I spoke at camp, I'd receive standing ovations. When I'd call a church in the United States, the youth pastors would say that kids reacted as if a "rock star" had called, "Is this Fernando?!" Things were flying high. People praised me as a "prophet" and as a miracle story of what God could do. My testimony was heralded as "inspiring." Everyone loved the persona of the poster boy for God's wonders. But . . .

. . . while outside I was all faith and fireworks, inside I was hiding a different story, sometimes even from myself. I had questions. Questions still about this faith thing. But enamored with purpose and service, I kept them private on the pages of my journal, hoping they'd never be read by those who believed in me.

Journal Entry: Tuesday, September 7, 2004
How to begin?
I am still recovering from the deepest and darkest valley I've been in since I started my Christian walk. Maybe not the saddest, but surely the darkest. The faithless-est. I believed with all my heart there was no God.

There is no proof and He won't show any. There is nothing I've seen or felt that I can't explain psychologically. I still pray to Him but it is not the same. I want to know. I want to know Him.

I guess I have to move on. I'm still not sure if I decided to stay for Him or for my lifestyle. I pray. I sing. I talk. I challenge. I serve. He knows I'm trying. I don't want to feel like this. I have many dreams, for ministry, not even for my own life.

For the last few weeks God has turned me inside out. Complete surrender. Every single night going to bed sobbing. Burning inside. Giving up everything. Love, relationships, friends, family, money, sex, life and any other area that could be important to a man. I've felt so low and so little. I'm nothing. I just want my life to have meaning.

I don't want God just to exist 'cause I need Him to.

I feel that God grew me out of my box. I need to run wild. Let me go! God, I will pack up my things right now. I need permission from God. See, is it me just confusing fire? I don't get Him. I don't. I don't want to be God but if He's with me something's gotta make sense. I don't want to be faithless. I choose to believe. I don't want to be wrong @ this. What if He never shows Himself? I would have deceived a lot of people and that would be a lot worse than just fooling myself.

I want God to exist. I don't just want to know Him. I want to touch Him. I never have. I don't want to just feel Him, I want to see Him, to hear Him. I can't say I ever have. I want to hug him.

Angels, look @ me in the eye. Show me truth. Show me life. Bring me meaning. Let me join you and swim in love. Hike in faith. Fly in freedom. Peace. I was going to say fire, but I don't want emotions. I want passion, but that will be a byproduct of purpose. I want God, not feelings. I don't want to be happy, I want joy. I do want happy moments. Is like saying I want sex. I do. But I want a good relationship. Deep, honest, based on God. I want You! Please, show Yourself to me. You are all I want. What else can I give you? What else can I do? I don't know how much longer I can hold on.

I love you, Lord.

The Work of His Hands

The ministry kept growing. I began sending teams to serve at government-run agencies to assist in places like orphanages, rehab centers, shelters for battered women, shelters for the mentally handicapped, shelters for the elderly, and hospices; and I started new ministries, such as providing aid to children with special needs and holding a values conference. We had teams coming down to build houses. We had an annual summer camp in Ensenada for hundreds of children, and I later started a new one in Mexicali.

But though results were great, all the running around, lobbying, stressing, and skipping of meals and sleep took a toll on my body and mind.

Every single year, and I mean every single year, I would walk to some end of camp by myself and swear that this was it. There was no way that I could do it anymore. I was misunderstood, undervalued, overstretched, and underpaid. Not to mention that I had developed a recurring ulcer and hospital visits due in large part to all the stress.

I was very conflicted.

The narrative of Jesus Christ captivated me. He had saved me from death, in body and soul. He had suffered way more than I had. So what if I was up to my neck in debt? So what if I was still single and alone? So what if I kept getting sick? So what if I didn't have a social life because I spent every moment doing ministry? So what if APU was not honoring my labor? So what if . . . ?

During one of those end of weeks in Mexicali, I walked away from everyone and went to tell God I was quitting. I had found myself again, AGAIN, in that place where I had to rely on the better-rested camp crowd to sing the words my exhausted lungs could not.

At a distance, I heard the crowd sing "Shout to the Lord."

I had always been delighted by the poetic and exalting nature of the chorus, ". . . *all the earth, let us sing.*" Up to then, I had never really responded to the line about singing for ". . . *the work of Your hands.*" But in that moment, I finally understood—it was the work of "*His*" hands." It hadn't been me. After all, that's what we Christians always say: if something goes well, it is never us, it is always God; if something goes wrong, of course it wasn't God, it was us.

I stood on that dirt field with my weak hands raised high and wept as I declared that it was His work. *He* had done all of this. The endless hours of planning, working, cleaning, traveling, fund-raising, recruiting, everything—it was all *His* work. He had orchestrated everything, moved every piece, and we had been mere spectators. We were so little and so insignificant and should be proud and thankful that He had let us be witnesses to His work and pieces in His master plan.

To this day I remember the slogan that adorned my shirts, letters, and speeches that heralded the unchanging depth that inhabited—and still inhabits—the core of my conviction to serve humanity: More Than Words.

10

TO THE ENDS OF THE EARTH

*"But you shall receive power when the Holy Spirit has come upon you;
and you shall be my witnesses in Jerusalem, and in all Judea and Samaria,
and to the end of the earth."*

— Acts 1:8

Jordan

Ever since I participated in that summer camp right after my conversion to Christianity, I dreamt of fulfilling its theme, *"Filled with Power . . . until the Ends of the Earth."* In my mind I pictured myself talking to people who had never heard the name of Jesus, enduring persecution, and serving in the most impoverished areas of the world—but to be honest, I wasn't completely sure it would ever come true.

That changed a few weeks after I started my job with Mexico Outreach and I received a list of the following summer's short-term mission trips sponsored by APU's Office of World Missions. I scrolled down the list, and, even though there were very exotic places on it, my eyes immediately came to a stop on one line—Jordan. For years I had participated in those Foursquare conferences where they had us fall in love with the Holy Land, the Middle East, and the Jews (not the ones from Charay). I was excited to serve the Arab community, but the words on the description— *"tour of the Holy Land"*— really sealed the deal for me. I'd be serving the Lord, and I'd be visiting the place where it all began. Where do I sign up?

But oh, a bigger question came up: how would I pay for it? I knew very few people I could send support letters to, and I was not connected with a local church yet, which meant that even though I was a struggling student, funds would have to come mostly out of my pocket. I applied, interviewed, and got accepted on the spot. I used the remainder of a scholarship as a down payment and deposited parts of my check from Mexico Outreach every couple of weeks to finance the trip.

At the time I thought that would probably be my one chance in life to travel overseas. People with my background make it to Disneyland and back on a good day, but don't ever dream of visiting places you'd see on cable TV. But I decided I would go all in on this opportunity, even if I lost it all. I didn't want to be the guy who almost did.

Our leader was a Jordanian student studying at APU who was talked into taking a group of students to serve during the summer camp season. Being able to send a team to the Middle East was a rare opportunity APU couldn't pass on—it was their first time doing so.

Summer camps are a great tradition and the most powerful evangelizing tool Christians organizations have—which result in about 80 percent of all new converts. Often forced to operate underground in various parts of the world, they energize and bring together the Christian community. Though religions other than Islam are practiced in Jordan, including Christianity, it is illegal to proselytize there. This means you can't go knocking on doors and telling people to come to Jesus, or you'd surely regret it. But if parents signed a waiver, and their kids came to our camp, then they were fair game.

Arriving in Amman seemed like an experience taken from *Lawrence of Arabia*. The weather was hot and dry. Sand ran wild through the paved streets. All buildings were covered in a tan rock (even McDonald's). Mosques blasted the call to pray every few hours, leading people to stop what they were doing, kneel, and pray. Older men wore checkered scarves. Many women wore black, full-body robes—many covering even their eyes. The smell of falafel flew in through the car window, and the language seemed to have an excess of deep "hhhh" sounds in its words.

We traveled around to amazing sites like Petra, enjoyed delicious shawarmas on the side of the road, and engaged in deep cultural conversations with the locals around the hooka (though we tried to avoid talking about American politics). But we weren't allowed to go out on our own, so we spent a lot of time baking in the heat and growing in frustration waiting for the next camp to start, the next trip to begin, or for the next meal to arrive. Fingers would tap and tempers would rise.

Journal Entry: Monday, June 18, 2001, 10:45 p.m.
Jet lag, no problem? Yeah, right! I woke up at 4:30 a.m. Sooo hungry.
I did not go back to sleep. I went out for a walk and I wondered why

people were not out yet. I took pictures and listened to the diskman.

We went to camp for the first time, I liked it. The college students were still there. I thought it would be fun to be there with them but then I had an eye opener. It wasn't culture shock, but I felt so weird and uncomfortable to see so many people and not understand one word of what they're saying. I finally understood in my own flesh what the gringos that I've translated for in the past have felt. I'm so used to having everything under control. I was the one who made fun of the Mexicans in English, and of the Americans in Spanish, and today I didn't even want to go buy chips being afraid of looking like an idiot from the U.S. who doesn't understand a thing. I didn't want people to laugh at me like I've seen Americans laugh at Mexicans and Mexicans laugh at Americans in the past. Like I've said before, it is a good experience to be out of my comfort zone and I know that I will be fulfilling my duties as a translator in the future with more respect and pride.

At night we had a dinner with missionaries from all over the place: Germany, Norway, Jordan, Korean-Americans, Americans and me, Mexican. The craziest part of the day was the food, something called Mansaf. A giant tortilla, covered with rice and lamb, soaked with goat-milk yogurt.

They started explaining how to eat it and I really thought they were kidding. All eight of us ate from the same plate. You had to place your left hand on your back (since that's the one you use to wipe your rear). You would pour yogurt onto an area of rice so it gets really soggy. With your right hand you had to pull a piece off the lamb, stick it in the rice, and then make a ball of it with the lamb at the center.

So here we are molding this ball of soggy rice in our hand from the place where we are all sticking our hands into and then popping it in our mouths. I almost threw up. At first I thought, NO WAY! But I managed to eat only two. If things continue like this I'm just gonna starve to death.

Dear Lord, grant me the wisdom to communicate with these people in a way which needs no words. I've seen it happen throughout the years and now You've opened my eyes to a whole new world. Thank you for preparing me for my ministry in Camp Gilead.

I love you. Good night. In your Holy Name, Jesus. Amen.

Camp Gilead

It was hard not to feel at home at camp. I was born under the blazing sun of

Mexicali, so I was used to this weather. I had spent weeks at a time helping manage camps for Mexico Outreach, so the scenery was familiar. And Arab culture shared many attributes with Latin culture, not to mention physical similarities. Meaning, if it hadn't been for my bleached hair, I would have been the only member of my team who didn't stick out like a sore thumb. That said, that hair did help me connect with the kids I was serving.

"Eminem! Eminem!" they cried out. They wanted to take pictures with me, and loved engaging in conversation. I was picking up Arabic pretty fast, and their English wasn't half bad. They followed me around and treated me with great love and respect. *"Habibi,"* they called me—my dear one.

During the high school camp we received a very special group of kids. Down the hill they lived a very controlled life. Up with us they wanted to get their fun's worth. They smuggled alcohol in their bags and were annoyingly loud and disruptive during meetings. The camp leadership had their hands full with them and tried to keep them separated from the rest.

But I had other plans.

I sat with them at activities during the day, and I would sneak into their tents at night. The leaders first objected, but when the kids promised to keep their voices down if I stayed, they changed their minds. We talked for hours exchanging stories. They learned about my transition from Mexico into the United States, and from Catholic to atheist to Christian. I learned they lived under a microscope, and why they were crying out for attention.

I learned about their endurance through persecution, and how they grow up feeling different because of their Christian faith. I learned that in their region, if a father converted to any religion, the entire family would be forced to convert to the new belief system—no questions asked. That's how many of them became Christian. I learned that some families had to move every three months, because once the rest of the family found out they had left Islam and converted to Christianity, they would threaten to burn their house down with them inside. I learned that many of them had to be homeschooled because when the teachers in public school found out that the family had decided to follow Jesus, they would automatically receive failing grades as a repercussion. I learned about the jokes they'd get for being different, the harassment they experienced for not following the norm, and the frustration they'd endured at a very young age from such isolation.

We treasured every minute we spent with each other.

Unfortunately, the camp staff didn't feel the same way. They decided these kids were taking too much attention from the rest of the campers.

I came out of the bathroom carrying my toiletry bag and towel one morning and saw a van begin to back out with all of them on board. I stood there shocked and silent. They were being sent home.

When the kids saw me they started shouting, "We gotta say bye to Fernie! We gotta say bye to Fernie! Stop the van! Stop the van!" Reluctantly, the driver stopped the van since the kids had already opened the doors and begun to jump out. The camp director stood in their way, his arms stretched to the sides as the dozen or so of them darted around him and surrounded me with hugs and thank yous. At a distance I saw his puzzled and disapproving look. But what could I have done? I loved these kids and thought they were the ones who needed Jesus' love more than anyone. But I was a visitor and it was not my call.

Once they left, the director asked to have a word with me. I thought he'd be mad at me—but again, what did he want me to do? He asked me what I thought about the call to send them back. I simply said, "It was not my decision to make. My opinion really doesn't matter." I was obviously hiding my disapproval. He shook his head and said, "I just don't understand how is it possible that a Mexican guy from the United States, who doesn't speak Arabic, can have so much influence over a group of Arab kids—more than the Arab leaders." I remained silent, though the answer in my heart was loud and clear, "Love doesn't speak any particular language."

And every camp was filled with its own share of memories. I'd have parents show up at the next camp because they said they had to meet this "Fernie" their kids couldn't shut up about.

Due to some political unrest, we were not allowed to enter Israel—which broke my heart. But the great experiences I had with Jordanians made up for it big time. Visiting the Middle East was a growing, leg stretching, and amazingly heartwarming experience that connected me to my religious roots in the Holy Land. Jordan was a great starting point in my dream to be a missionary. I wanted to be used by God to my full potential, wherever the greatest need was.

I've heard it said, "Be careful what you ask for."

Cambodia

In 2002, the following year, I signed up to participate in a short-term mission trip to India to serve at Mother Teresa's Home for the Dying, Missions of Charity. I felt that experience would stretch me even further, and I wanted to continue to be molded to serve the greatest needs in the world, even in the darkest of places. We fundraised, learned about the culture, and bonded as a team, but two days before departure, Pakistan began firing a series of test missiles. India fired a test missle of its own in apparent response. Given the rising tensions between the two nuclear-armed states, the United States immediately warned against travel to the area and our trip was put on hold.

A team already serving in Kolkata was immediately put on alert. Brian from the Office of World Missions, who was visiting our team in Cambodia, arranged for our India teams to transfer their ministries there. Phnom Penh, the capital, hosted a branch of Missions of Charity. In addition, the current Cambodia team had made some connections with local missionaries with ideas of other places where we could serve.

In one day we watched *The Killing Fields*, read a few Internet pages about Cambodia's history, wept internally over the loss of the dream we had been preparing for all semester, and got ready for a new mission we pushed ourselves to call "God's indirect plan." We couldn't allow ourselves to believe God was somehow caught off guard or surprised by any of this.

I struggled deeply with what we witnessed in Cambodia: the heartbreaking poverty, the children playing in the mud with flies over their heads, wives who knew their husbands frequented prostitutes, the out-of-control AIDS epidemic, agonizing malnutrition, and the knowledge that about one in four people had lost someone to the great and murderous dictatorship of Pol Pot almost thirty years earlier (1975–1979). Up to 2.5 million people, out of a population of 8 million, were tortured and executed for suspected ties with the former government and were dumped into mass graves around the country—many of those still unearthed. Doctors, teachers, and educated people were murdered in order to prevent a presumed coup d'état. Even children who raised their hands when asked who wanted to be a teacher were taken outside by regime soldiers never to be seen again. Mothers had their babies pulled from their arms and slammed against trees, or thrown up in the air to be used as target practice, in order to intimidate the already weak.

Walking into that place felt like walking into a black and white movie of historic tragedy. I felt I could smell the blood of innocence soaked into the muggy air, see the trembling ghosts of the suffering weeping on their hollowed death spots, and hear the shrieking shouts for mercy ignored by the vile.

How does a nation lift itself up when its legs have been cut from under them? Where does God fit in this picture of slaughter and dehumanization? Where?

I had many questions and prayed, as I had done many times before, that answers would soon come.

Journal Entry: Tuesday, June 4, 2002

How to describe the smell of Cambodia? I thought of this question as we walked back from Central Market today. People begging for money. Bargain after bargain. Kids hanging off Schoon's forearms saying, "a dollar to let go" as they followed us four blocks. The kids pinching Schoon and Greg for they are not used to seeing fat people. Not finding shirts with long enough sleeves for they have no tall people. Erin almost ran over by a moto. Craziness of traffic going in every direction. Shirtless men along the side of the road, looking and throwing kisses at our girls. The scent of food, dirt, humidity, sweat, mud, smog, and I don't know what else. Hundreds of motos taking over and switching lanes. Cars turning left, merging onto the left lane against opposing traffic, and then moving to the correct lane on the right. The feeling of insecurity that begins to create frustration in us.

I finally smelled Cambodia and stopped feeling as if we were living @ the American embassy.

But even though I've smelled the scent of Cambodia, I know there is so much more to feel, to sense. I will do that with the passing of days. This is the beginning. I give a step, God gives the path.

Watay

Surrounded by flooded bamboo fields, we entered a walled compound of white rooms with decaying lives. It had a school for impoverished children, a pharmacy, and a building with a room for men and one for women who were infected with tuberculosis. It also had the most heartbreaking two-story building, which housed a room for men and a room for women on the bottom floor and two rooms on the top floor for children—all of whom had HIV and full-blown AIDS. Welcome to Missions of Charity.

My experience with Mexico Outreach had given me a reputation of being a sort of Christian Peter Pan, if you will—someone with a child's soul trapped in a man's body. Several of my friends had called me a "baby whisperer" due to the "hypnotizing" effect I had with children and babies. I love children and they love me.

When we walked up the stairs in the AIDS ward, the children ran toward us with cheer, despite the visible open blisters on their young skin. Most of them were under six years of age, wore light, worn-out clothing, and had a smile that could light up Asia. I expected my reaction to be the same as back in the West, filled with joy and welcoming enthusiasm, but I did what I expected least after such a long-awaited dream—I froze.

Everyone else immediately began to pick the kids up, hug them, and greet them. But I was paralyzed by fear and ignorance, unprepared for what I should do in a situation like this. I had heard that if I had a small scratch on my body, and if they had an open wound, that it'd be the end of my story if I touched them—done, I'd be dead. I stepped back as my shame and guilt grew within me. How could this be happening to me? This is not the Fernando from Mexico. This is not the Fernando from Jordan. This is not me.

They all walked away and pulled the rest of the kids into one of the rooms and continued checking the facilities. Still in a daze, I stayed behind and pondered what was wrong with me. Defeated, I walked out onto a bridge that projected from the porch on the second floor to a tower. Maybe some fresh air would help. I sat down and rested against the rail. It was hot and humid, a typical Cambodian afternoon, but a soft breeze was blowing from the east. I got mad at the wind for treating me nicely when I least deserved it. If anything, I deserved lightning. I questioned my entire vocation as a missionary, regretting the sacrifices I had made in fundraising and apologizing to God for being a coward.

I then looked to my right, and there she was, a little girl leaning on a doorframe, as if frozen in time. Less than three-feet tall, with tattered clothes, a tiny index finger on her lips, and a terrible haircut, she witnessed my baffled little self with her ever so soft gaze. She analyzed me as if trying to figure out what I was made of. Her eyes would not let go of me.

Okay, this is it. How much spiritual humiliation could I withstand if even this little Cambodian girl had pity on my sorry brown ass?

She put her finger down, separated herself from the doorframe, and headed toward me. With very gentle confidence, she lifted my left arm, softly crawled onto my lap, rested her head on my right arm, pulled my left arm down, and covered her fragile body with it. She then turned and looked at me straight in the eye—and I was done. Stick a fork in me. This little girl grabbed my soul, took it out for a spin, and gave it back to me on a platter. Fear, shock, doubt—all gone. I was in, I was accepted, and I couldn't care less about what could happen. I was only capable of one thing, finding out how I could love in the most useful and real way. This is the reason for my existence, I knew, to hold and to serve little treasures like her.

Watay, my new little friend, had recently been brought to live at the hospice. Both her parents had been patients there at one point. After not making an appearance for a long period of time, the sisters decided to go check on them. Upon arrival at Watay's home, they noticed a terrible rotting smell coming from inside. After knocking down the bamboo and straw door, they found Watay playing with the decomposing bodies of her parents, who lay flat on the ground. Having been uncared for for quite some time, she suffered from various infections. On her head hair had grown into wounded skin. They thus had to remove skin from her scalp to remove the ingrown hairs and prevent further infection, causing her "terrible haircut."

This little girl had just shown me that I was indeed not in Kansas anymore.

Journal Entry: Monday, June 10, 2002
I've never been so physically drained and challenged. Today I was ready to say, in fact I probably did, "Jesus, I'm ready. I'm coming Home." Heat is EXTREME, humidity is like I've never experienced before. I felt like boiling water was underneath my skin running through my veins. Between noon and three pm is the worst time. Everything turned yellow and started spinning before I hit the ground. Some people thought I was also a patient. I was, and still am, sweating like a pig. Water comes out as fast as it goes in. I really don't know if I'll make it till Thursday.

We got up at 5 am, took the Boat of Hope, and here we are. This village is like taken out of a National Geographic video, next to the river, with its own temple and all. The shacks are a story above ground for flood precaution. The floor is bamboo tied together; I can see underneath us through the cracks. I can hear the geckos crying, the crickets singing, people chasing snakes, frogs; and something right now was crawling my way, probably a lizard.

The clinics are alright, even though I felt pretty useless. I brought my guitar and all 'cause I was told I was going with the kids and when we got there, I had to stay to be the "prayer male." I couldn't communicate, and when Ellen was praying for the ladies I saw many of them roll their eyes. Laura, our leader, was inspiring with a story about prayer and God's revelation. I prayed for that, that they somehow see God, either through healing, or a vision, and be a living testimony of God's power and mercy.

Today I told God, "Thanks for the joke." I was very uncomfortable, and felt useless. My greatest fear for the trip came true. The heat made things worse. Later, with the kids' ministry, I felt better emotionally, but not physically. I couldn't breathe. Even tonight, I know I won't sleep, I just feel it will be hell. I can't move. I don't want any part of my body to touch any other part of my body—it doubles the temperature and increases the sweat. I've been drinking so much water, yet I don't pee that much. It's all sweat!

We had prayer @ the boat. They love singing and it was great to see the stars, the water, the lighting at a distance. A good ending to a day like this. The breeze was good.

God, I ask for my health. Tomorrow we take a horse cart ride, and I will need you. There are no cushions but plenty of potholes and it feels like my bone will cut through my butt cheeks. I pray that we will be useful even with our cultural, and language limitations.

I love you. Night.

Play

For the sake of strategy, Sister Superior split us up into groups that would rotate each day among all the rooms and wards. She noticed that I had developed a special bonding with the patients through my guitar. She asked if I wanted to make it my duty to play for the patients. I'd be the only one allowed to go from ward to ward as I pleased. That didn't seem like a tangible contribution to some on my team who were packing pills in little plastic bags, or cleaning wounds on patients' genitalia, but she said there were different kinds of gifts for caring and healing. She said that music was a powerful gift found in the Bible—reminding that David sang for King Saul and alleviated his pain. I was more than okay with the idea. In fact, I loved it! It gave me a way to ease into the whole bodily fluids thing, while at the same time allowing me to wander around and meet everyone and to connect with them on a personal level. Some team members got jealous and a bit upset that I'd have this "special privilege," but I'd be lying if I said I didn't love this job. Air guitar became the "international symbol for Fernando," or so my team said.

Patients would anxiously wait for my arrival. I developed blister upon blister on my fingertips, but I felt that if there ever was a reason for why I learned to play guitar, it was this. I would be called in times of sadness, such as when we found an empty bed in the morning (meaning someone had gone home, whether down the street or up to heaven), and to help brighten the mood of those suffering from pain or fever. In this regard, I believed my guitar was just as valuable as a stethoscope or gauze. And to be honest, considering some of the patients' conditions, sometimes a smile was the best thing we could bring.

But not all experiences were gloomy. Thank goodness. We actually had many laughs and good times. But we always walked around with a feeling of expectation, waiting for that pin to pop the balloon. Most times, though, regardless of anticipation, death would catch us off guard.

I was having a great time one particular day. "Grandpa" was being his usual self, laughing and pretending he could play my guitar when in reality he was raking the strings with no rhythm. The ladies had walked into the guys' area to join in the musical hysteria. The nuns heard the commotion and joined in as well. A lady brought her hand to her mouth during laughter to cover her decaying teeth, but nobody really cared. Grandpa sure loved being the center of attention and loved having me around. "Bad grandpa. Bad grandpa," I'd say while slapping his wrist very softly. The crowd erupted in cheer and laughter. Shirtless and hairless, showing off his bony physique, he raised his feet up in the air with a big toothless smile. All of us in the TB ward, patients and nuns, began cracking up, having forgotten for a moment the sense of impending doom, rotten smells, and Third World realities.

Erin, the youngest member of our team, showed up behind me. Catching her breath, she said, "Fernie, grab your guitar and come with me!" "What happened?" I asked. "Hurry up!" she pressed. I took the guitar back from grandpa and rushed behind her. We entered the women's AIDS ward and walked to a patient lying on the middle bed in the back row. She must've been in her early twenties, but her present state looked like a weathered-out version of some future, older self. She had salt and pepper, damaged hair that was moist due to sweat. Her pupils had abandoned her eyes, leaving behind an empty and desolate white. I witnessed skin and bones, tightened lips revealing gnashing teeth, and veins popping off her porous skin. Her body trembled vigorously while she tightly held on to a large crucifix resting on her bosom. Her face pointed away from us, and it was obvious that her soul would shortly head in the same direction.

"What do you want me to do?" I asked as I stood there frozen, inept. Only one word came out of her mouth. Erin didn't need to say much else.

"Play."

I softly raised my guitar, placed my fingers on the strings, and tried to think of a melody that might make a dent against the claws of darkness squeezing her soul. I couldn't. But I did think of a song that, though she wouldn't understand it, seemed fitting for someone forced to endure an unwilling farewell to air. I cleared my throat, wiped a tear off my face, and brought my fingertips to the second, third, and fourth strings on the second fret, and played the worship and praise song "Breathe."

As if hearing an echo from a faraway land of a voice she used to know, she squinted before control began to slowly crawl back into her being. I hesitated to continue, slightly shocked, but kept playing and singing. Her face began to turn toward us. Her pupils momentarily began to focus on this world. Her trembling body gained some composure. Peace seemed to gradually flow back into her soul. The crucifix got a rest from her firm grip. Very slowly she turned her head toward us in search of the sound's source, stopping when she saw me. She stared straight into my eyes, without a blink, her mouth still open. My hands froze and my song became a gasp. I couldn't stay there much longer. My jaw began to tremble and my heart signaled I would soon become an emotional wreck. This is not what anybody needed to see right now.

I walked quickly toward the exit, veered past the doorframe, and rested against the wall, holding my guitar close to my chest. My heartbeat was out of control. I stared out into the distance with a million thoughts and emotions going through my mind and heart. Erin came looking for me a moment later and found me puzzled and restless. "What happened?" I asked. Two words left me lost in time and even more bewildered about the meaning of life.

"She's gone."

For weeks, months, years I kept processing my experiences in the mission field. I loved that we could bring a little piece of God's love into areas of the earth devastated by evil and hopelessness. But I always had this question, "Why does God let people suffer like this as He waits for us to show up?"

I'd play card games with my team, I'd show up late for meals, and I'd debrief each night, but I was a zombie who moved day by day without finding rest for my soul. My journal was the only witness to my questions.

The experiences I had while serving in Mexico, Jordan, Cambodia, and later Chile and Kenya still haunt me from time to time. My pen trembled each night as I tried to make sense of the darkness existing inside people. I am capable of love, you are capable of love, they are capable of love, but after so many trips of unexplained godlessness, I had become dim and desperate. Still, I kept hoping, just as many faithful do, that light would make an entrance, any second now, and help me make some sense of this abominable chaos.

In the meantime, I would continue to equip myself, and equip every other willing young person I could find, to go to the ends of the earth and do what God had empowered us to do with our gifts in a world in need—play.

11

CRACK ON THE WINDSHIELD

"The world does not consist of 100 percent Christians and 100 percent non-Christians. There are people (a great many of them) who are slowly ceasing to be Christians but who still call themselves by that name: some of them are clergymen. There are other people who are slowly becoming Christians though they do not yet call themselves so."

—C. S. Lewis

Journal Entry: Circa 2006
Worship?
We can worship and only hope. We can praise Him and only dream. Overwhelming hearts. Minds heavy with weight. Clouded souls. Sheltered moments. Defenses protecting an instinct that cries from within. Depths of unspoken truth; caves of mystery fulfilled. Silence louder than words and noise quieter than dreams. Look around you for the natural place, of pure incense and holy souls, untainted love and heartfelt emotions. Can you hear my honesty? I can't speak. Can you notice my arms waving? I'm sitting still. Can you notice me? I'm nowhere to be found.

Talk to me when I don't speak. I'll give my life away so freely. If you would only reach out and pick me up in my time of redeeming solitude. Painted in blues, dressed in reds, naked in whites, and desiring inspiring greens. Worship . . . if I could only have such a desire, such a goal, such unreachable peak. Confused by the chords, embraced by the sounds. Echoes of turmoil and busy paths. Choices and dead ends. Where is my choice and my reward?

Speak to me Being of Light. Part the clouds and part the sea. Stop the sun and stop the storm. Bring forth the dead. Bring forth the loaves. My words will multiply. My drawing will shine and illuminate their lives. My voice will touch and my coins will bless. Even my feet will reach. But where is my response?

Will you draw unimaginable pictures created in my time especially for me? Will Your voice like thunder shake me from my sin and temptation? Will Your words be written on the walls of my doubt and indecision? Will Your feet reach me and Your arms hug me? Will Your ears listen, and will Your eyes violate my privacy and enter the secrets of my life, break through the windows of my soul? You don't need a key. You don't need an invitation. You don't need a reason or an excuse. I need to worship You and if I were only to be the luckiest bastard on the face of the earth, well, Fatherless I wouldn't be, and Dad would take me out to play ball.

How can I worship You enough for You to love me in MY time; to have a tree just made for me? I want none of that! I don't need a sea to part, a sun to stand still. I don't need to walk on water and fire to fall from the sky. Keep the fish. Keep the wine. Lucky them that feared the flies, had their tables knocked over—sadly, even those who cried, "Crucify!"' They heard Your voice. "Forgive them," You said. "Blessed are those," You said. "Come and follow," You said. And You said, and You said, and You said. Where did our ears go blind? Where did our skin lose sensibility? Goosebumps, a memory; and sound waves a myth.

When did we stop deserving the words from Dad?

Come back from work now! Pick me up and tickle me. Tell me that You missed me all day. It's been a long day and I need Your guidance and Your validation. Tell me that I'm like You and that I have Your birthmarks, Your sense of humor, Your temper, Your gifts, Your build, Your eyes, Your ears. How can I worship You enough to have You put down the little plane models and the thinner and the paint, or to have You teach me how?

For one word I'd spare my life. One word to validate my life and give it meaning, purpose. What big of a price, of a need. For one word Lord Jesus, God, Holy Spirit . . . I'd worship You.

Ensenada

After my experiences in Jordan in 2001 and Cambodia in 2002, I pressed to up my involvement in the mission field. I wanted to be a real missionary. The Middle East had been a very intense psychological introduction to such work in a place known for persecution and rooted anti-Christian sentiment.

Cambodia was both a physical and emotional challenge in a place with a dark history of massacre, sickness, and hopelessness that shook me to the core. For 2003, I knew I was ready to take the next step. I had led mission trips with the Foursquare denomination in Mexico, but nothing like the big budget, big production, big picture trips Azusa Pacific University would put together.

After conversations with a friend from the on-campus Latino club, we decided to colead a team to her motherland, Chile. We would be partnering with YWAM (Youth With A Mission—a popular agency for international, youth-oriented, short-term missions) to serve a marginalized native population at the ends of the earth in Chulín, a tiny island off the Chilean shore. We picked some dates, put together a budget, turned in our paperwork, made advertisements, and got ready for interviews. At the end we had a very unique, flamboyant, and multicultural group of people we'd take with us to make an impact in South America—but not before an impact would be made on us.

On February 14, 2003, we went on a training mission trip to Ensenada, Mexico. APU's Office of World Missions took the approximately two hundred students who would be participating in short-term mission trips that summer, including ours, to Rancho El Refugio (then Mexico Outreach's Ensenada Campus). The trip had almost been cancelled due to a large storm hitting Mexico's Pacific shore. Since I had a commercial driver's license, I was entrusted with driving the fifteen-passenger van that would carry both the Chile and Kenya teams.

Once we got there, we set up tents in whatever dry ground we could find. Each team—Team Chile, Team Kenya, Team India, Team South Africa, Team Guatemala, Team Thailand, Team China, and all the rest—did their own thing that first night to bond before our day of service the next day. My coleader, Stephanie, and I pulled out an array of Valentine-themed goodies and shared notes of encouragement. We bonded fairly quickly and seemed to be setting a standard in camaraderie and loudness among the other teams. While doing service the next day, we laughed, we communicated, we got closer, and we learned about each other's personal gifts.

Though most teams headed straight across the border on Sunday as originally planned, we talked to the Kenya team and we all agreed instead to take a quick side trip to La Bufadora—one of the biggest blowholes in the world that is now a popular tourist spot with a diversity of vendors. We knew we would have a sweet time.

After we finished walking around, admiring the coastal rock spit out a fountain of water, and getting our shopping done, we headed back to the van as planned. Everyone had great smiles on their faces. Everyone took their seats. I turned on the engine and asked everyone to put their seat belts on (not everyone did). It'd be a long drive toward the border, but the sense of community and brotherhood we had achieved seemed priceless.

We headed out of the parking area in great spirits, but soon thereafter, that would all change.

Maybe fifteen minutes into the return drive, coming around a curve, I felt a pull on the back of the van. In real time it took me only a second to turn my head back to see what was happening. But that second took minutes in my memory. My brain sped up, trying to catch every detail I could to protect ourselves. I saw the back of the van being pulled in a different direction. I saw a look of surprise in those seated at the very back. Then I saw the beauty of the ocean, which used to be to my right, now to my back. Then I saw the look of panic in those seated in the middle seats. Then I saw the cliff that led to the ocean, which we would plummet onto if gravity was allowed to take its course. Then I saw Will, my copilot and friend, spread his hands out, clueless as to what was going on. But within that second, I knew.

The slim shoulder on the road had become soft with the recent heavy storm and given in to the weight of the van. The back right wheel had sunk in, pulling the van partly off the road. I felt the back wheels spinning and sliding on the side of the road, refusing to go down the cliff. What should I do? As I felt the van slide back further, I slammed the gas pedal. I thought of those faces I had just seen smile not too long ago, their arms around each other's shoulders, and I was not going down without a fight.

I felt one wheel gain traction as it got back on the road. When the second one gained ground, the van got a great surge of speed. Our heads jolted back. The van now moved uncontrollably down the middle of the road, swerving from left to right. Thankfully no other cars were around. I removed my foot from the gas and held on to the wheel as best as I could. The heavy back of the van had complete control over the vehicle's movements and stubbornly ignored my command. My hands stayed firm on the wheel, but the back of the van kept sliding from left to right. After a few seconds of frightful struggle, the van veered hard to the left, went off the road, and hit an embankment.

The next thing I see is the inside of the van filled with billowing dust and floating shattered glass. It got dark, then light, dark, then light, dark, then light again. With the heavy tail end of the van going up in the air, we rolled over once, twice, and then a third time before finally turning a quarter more and landing on our right side.

All sound escaped the world and time seemed to slow down. And then— buzzing, flashes of reality.

I saw my hands hanging and then shake as if I'd woken from a bad dream. My body was suspended in midair by my seat belt. Sound started to return. I reached for my seat belt but it refused to let me go. I realized the engine was still running and I feared an explosion. I reached for the keys, and they refused to turn off. Fear infiltrated my veins. I tried to reach for Will, who was below me. He wasn't moving. My stretched-out hands weren't able to reach him. I grew even more anxious. I reached again for the seat belt and commanded, "Let me go!" My body dropped and I immediately went into survival mode. I stood up, broke what glass was left off the side window, and pulled my body up and out.

My memory to this day remains patchy. I remember the first couple minutes, followed by a black still, then bits and pieces. People recall that mine were the first hands they saw pulling people out. But after helping some of them out, I went into a state of shock. My body began to shake. Guilt and blame infiltrated my soul. "Pull them all out!" I commanded to those few already out of the van as I headed for the street. With my hands stretched out, I stepped in front of traffic, asked people if they had cell phones, asked them to call for help. Once people pulled out their phones, looking for reception, I headed back.

It was chaos.

Will got out somehow and was walking toward me. I then saw him drop to the ground in pain as he said, "I can't move." I knelt in front of him, touched his chest, and grew terrified when his white shirt became soaked in red. Then I realized that the blood staining his shirt was coming from my own trembling hand. When I got up to ask for help, I saw Heidi, the leader of the Kenya team, fall to the ground in the same manner Will had, her body numb. Pain for my loved ones overcame me, but I managed somehow to keep functioning.

At some point I had to try to get the keys out, because I still feared an explosion. I jumped on the left side of the van, cleared some glass, reached in, and finally managed to stop the engine. With that small mission complete, I jumped down and returned to mayhem.

I turned to my left and saw a girl from the Kenya team walk toward me asking for guidance. I could do little but watch as the reddish-black flesh on her cheekbone grew the size of a tennis ball right in front of me. She fell on her knees. I shouted at Derek, another friend on my team, to stay with her.

By the look on his confused and stunned face, I could tell the words didn't register. I slammed my hands together and shouted this time while pointing at the girl, "Take care of her!" He understood and knelt by her side, placing a hand on her shoulder.

I eventually got on my own cellphone, called Brian, and left a voicemail hoping he'd hear it as soon as he crossed the border and got U.S. phone reception. I also called Alvin and Rosa, our missionaries in residence at El Refugio, to please come help. The anguish in my voice was later described as "someone who did not sound like Fernando."

I turned to the van and I saw people pulling Joy's red-soaked body out—blood squirting from her skull. She was sitting in the back corner where the van had landed first. Her body was convulsing.

I lost it.

"What is going on?!" "Why did this have to happen?!" I started to walk away from the van, screaming at my stretched-out hands, the ones which had been holding the wheel. I blamed them. Stephanie tried to unsuccessfully calm me down. She saw there was no bringing me back, at least not immediately, from the arms of despair. "Listen. What do you need me to do?" She asked.

The last thing I see after being placed in the backseat of a Mexican police car is members of my team, including Stephanie, standing hopelessly on the other side of the window, and Will, Heidi, and Joy being pushed into the back of ambulances on stretchers. In Mexico, in contrast to American law, you are guilty until proven innocent.

Still trembling with anxiety and filled with incertitude, I was taken to a police station down the hill. My personal belongings, including belt and shoelaces, were taken from me to prevent self-inflicted harm—though, ironically, no one ever thought about caring for my recent and evident injuries. I was placed in a cold, dark, humid, lonesome jail cell with a square hole on the ground in the corner for a bathroom.

Over the station's radio I heard of an accident and how "two are paralyzed" and "the girl is dead." My brain and my heart fell down to my stomach. I lost balance and control over my legs. My tears felt like acid, burning my skin on their path to the ground. My eyes were emptied of light. I brought my right hand to my gut and forced out a gasp of hopelessness. For five infernal hours I prayed and felt my insides wrestle, wishing I had died instead of someone else.

Part of me had.

I sat on the floor against the wall, hugging my legs, my face buried between my knees, drenching my filthy pants. Finally, I looked up and saw a face who suffered for me, a familiar face, a Christian Mexican assemblyman who had been helping us in Ensenada with some connections. He silently reached out his hands through the bars and welcomed me as I ran into his arms. I wept and asked about my team. "They are okay," he said. "But I heard . . ." He told me that there had been other accidents due to the conditions. The storm had damaged the roads pretty badly. He said that my friends were being taken care of at the hospital—that Will and Heidi were having problems with movement, and that Joy remained unconscious due to her skull being cracked in three parts.

Though a little life slightly began to crawl back into my body with this news, it was quickly battled back by demoralizing guilt.

Soon after that, I was handcuffed to the back of a small police pickup and transferred to a second jail further into town. Once there, I was handcuffed to a chair in the waiting area. Police and wanderers observed and pitied this shaggy, dirty, bloody boy trembling in his seat with a gaze lost in oblivion.

After some time I was, once again, handcuffed to the back of a truck in the breezy, cold night. Still in bloody clothes, I was transferred to yet a third jail.

I was placed in a cell that I shared with a man who was lying on the dirty ground, his broken legs wrapped with wooden sticks and gauze. He had suffered a car accident while running from the cops and, like me, instead of being taken to a hospital, was placed in jail with the same filthy, smelly clothes he was wearing during the incident. His wife was a Christian woman who had suffered through his life of debauchery. Through my sharing and testimony he said he'd turn ways for the holy. I thought my time in the shade would be worth it if he gained eternal life.

After ten hours of being dragged from jail to jail, I was finally guided to a bathroom so I could clean myself up for the first time. "But why?" I asked.

I opened the door ready to face my destiny. When I reached the front desk I saw Alvin and Rosa waiting for me with others, including the assemblyman. They had moved heaven and earth to get me out, even called the U.S. embassy. If I had stayed overnight, since Monday was a holiday and offices were closed, I would have been transferred to the main prison where real danger would've fallen on someone like me. They saw that I had been through hell and saved their words, loving me with a compassionate look. They laid a hand on my shoulder, hugged me, and quietly guided me to the exit. As I was guided out of jail, I felt I was still dragging heavy chains on my hands and feet: chains of guilt and shame. How would I ever face everyone who by now must truly hate me (as they should)?

The door opened to a loud cheer of celebration.

What?!

Twelve people packed in a tiny atrium hugged me, rubbed my shoulders, and left me shocked and feeling undeserving.

Why don't they hate me? Don't they realize what just happened?

They insisted to be there when I was released. My biggest surprise came when Will made room through the crowd to hug me, cast around his neck and all. "Where is Heidi?" Heidi was unable to walk and was waiting in the van (she spent some time in a wheel chair after the accident). Joy was still at the hospital. She had woken up and immediately signed a waiver absolving me of culpability so I could be released.

Brian heard my message when he crossed the border, sent most people back to campus, and cleared a van to return and pick us up. But since Brian returned with someone else, there was no room for me, and I had to stay back and wait for someone to return the next day to pick me up.

There were a lot of lonely, painful, silent tears that night as I waited at Rancho El Refugio.

The next day Carolyn Koons picked me up. We drove by the hospital and were delighted to hear that they had placed temporary staples on Joy's skull so we could transport her to a hospital in the United States. She was happy to see me and expressed she was very sorry for what I had gone through.

Excuse me?! What *I* had gone through? Why don't you hate me?

We received her release papers with instructions, got her in the van, and headed across the border. Joy seemed awkwardly calm and talkative. When we arrived at the hospital in the United States, her parents greeted us at the entrance to the ER. I had to get out to open the van door and thought quickly about how I would withstand the punishment of hate they'd rightfully apply to me. If someone was going to hate me, it surely had to be them. Her dad rushed toward me as if he'd been waiting for this moment for quite a while. I wondered if he'd push me against the van as he demanded an explanation, or if he'd just shout at me and spit in my face. He then grabbed me by the shoulders and pulled me toward him, embracing me with vigor and warmth. "We were so worried for you! Our church small group has been praying for you since yesterday," he said.

No, this is the part where you hate me, where you tell me I'm worthless, where you blame me for the pain I have caused. You hugged me before you hugged your own daughter, for crying out loud! "I can only imagine what you've been through," he continues, "I am so sorry."

My soul was paralyzed. What kind of crazy, irrational, godly love is this?

When we got back to campus we were greeted by instant popularity. A coworker welcomed me at the office door the next day with the phrase, "Fernando, you're a hotter topic than *Joe Millionaire*" (a then-popular reality TV show). The campus pastor had mentioned us in chapel. Professors had led prayers for us at the beginning of class. The school offered all available resources to help us. But no amount of therapy, support, or even tears could fully mend what had happened very deep within.

Jon Wallace, APU's president, called me into his office. I was ready to start cleaning out my desk, but he had a welcoming demeanor about him. He just wanted to know that I was okay and to hear from me what had happened. He calmed me down and reassured me that he'd have no concern with having me drive another group of students the very next day, if I felt comfortable with it. He asked me what I needed. I talked mostly about what our two teams needed. We had survived, but we weren't exactly okay. Many of us experienced grief and post-traumatic stress in our own particular way, and we were trying to move on with our lives.

After several conversations with both the Chile and Kenya teams, the administration further tried to reassure me that the accident was not my fault. The school had also done its own research. I learned that whenever they typed the words "15-passenger van" in a search engine, tons of results showed up with the words, "Death. Death. Death." "If anything, you were a hero," I was told—a four-letter word I wasn't able to digest. Not only that, but members of my team said they wouldn't hesitate for a second to have me drive them anywhere again. The next day, in fact, I did drive several team members to go see Joy in the hospital, who was even more alert and kind than before.

What was it about this Christian community that was fixated on forgiveness, compassion, and putting the needs of others before one's own? "It must be Christ," I thought.

People said that if this accident had taken place while in the United States, it would have made national headlines. APU began to clear their inventory of 15-passenger vans after that, as many colleges in the nation did, due to other similar terrible events and experiences. A problem lay in the van's very design. When loaded with passengers, its center of gravity shifts up and toward the back, making them incredibly difficult to control in situations like ours.

But once the dust settled a bit, fierce reality came crashing down to our feet, especially mine—we were at war with the Enemy. We all tried to reason this catastrophe in our own particular ways. But to me, it was evident that the Devil felt threatened by this movement of love. He was taking no prisoners. He just wanted casualties. Seeing the magnitude of the reality of spiritual warfare, I became filled with conviction about how to better train our missionary troops, and how to inspire further zest. The Mexico Outreach leadership eventually felt overwhelmed by my sometimes overpowering drive. I felt like a true soldier, camouflaged, and ready for battle.

I was able to compel people into action with a short speech. I was able to broker impossible partnerships with secular groups. I was able to raise the standard and continue to find a new something, with a few someones, to serve somewhere. The imminent reality of death, of attack, had me on overdrive. Survival and achievement developed in me a commanding presence that catapulted me as an icon of godly service to both the faithful and the faithless.

I also realized eventually that in the process of saving the world, I was losing myself. I was tired, weathered, and running on passion fumes. And in order to get more passion, I needed a new challenge. And whenever I found a new challenge, I'd find a new battle. And whenever I found a new battle, I blamed the Enemy. And whenever I found the Enemy, I'd have to ask for God's help. And every time I had to ask for God's help, I'd have to wonder where He was. And every time I'd have to wonder where He was, I'd have to come up with an answer. And every time I had to come up with an answer, I had to confront the questions all over again. Every time I was confronted by questions, I'd go back to square one and get high on passion so I didn't have to deal with the questions. I always found a new something, with a few new someones, to serve somewhere. And that is all fine. But I would eventually have to grab my balls tightly, raise my eyes and a fist to the sky, and refuse to leave unanswered.

And there it was.

Right after our van lost control and went off road into that embankment. And right before the tail end went up in the air, I saw it. I can press the PAUSE button and freeze the image sitting in that van. I can reach over and see it with the light of day still behind it. Before the rain of shattered glass, the humming of screams, and smashing sound of metal—there was a crack. A crack on the windshield appeared before me just before all hell broke loose. It was an instant, but it signaled the impending wreckage that would follow.

Press PLAY.

I had lived among death for over five weeks the previous year in Cambodia. I held children who had been abandoned, hurt, and tormented by their own parents; children who were born with a death sentence in their veins. I met women who had been used and disposed of as rags; men who had lost their humanity at the arms of rage; a nation that had lost its soul by the corrupting power of greed.

I had lived among Arabs in Jordan and heard their stories of persecution, need, and ongoing fear. I broke bread with families who had been divided by religious beliefs. I wept to stories of lives that had been devalued and ended by those proudly representing a Higher Power.

I had lived in Mexico and witnessed the claws of poverty striking children, hungry, roofless on a cold desert night. I saw the innocent be inflicted with cruelty by the merciless thirst of adult indulgence. I shook with families deteriorated by the fruits of debauchery and the extinction of dreams.

Where was God in all that?

I understand that we, as "children of God," have been commanded to "go ye therefore" and be "His hands and feet." I cried about it many times in chapel at APU, in conferences with the Foursquare denomination, and in services at churches where I led. I wanted to be those hands and feet. But when I stepped onto the battlefield I realized that this was not a new battle. There is no way that God would've been waiting all this time, letting people die, be tortured, suffer, just so some college students would raise money and go help for a few weeks to provide needs they are incapable of fulfilling. The immensity of the international austerity is so vastly overwhelming that the selective and delayed engagement of a living God has to be questioned! Where the hell are You God?! People are being torn to pieces as we speak— and they have been for centuries.

When we had that rollover accident, I figured it was the Devil trying to prevent us, me, from doing God's work. He was upset that we had gone to Cambodia, and he was upset that I'd go to Chile, back to Jordan, Kenya, Mexico, and so on. I believed the Army of the Lord was having some great victories and that Light was eradicating Darkness. But very, very deep inside I heard a crack on my own glass. I first ignored it and covered it with something sweet and intoxicating—passion.

You know that taste. You've felt it too.

I had learned my lesson previously: "If something good happens it was God. If something bad happens it was us." So because of that, and since I kept going deeper into the hole of desperation, need, and sadness, I kept drinking that liquor so I could avoid thinking about the rationale for such monstrosity—godlessness. I kept sweet-talking myself with the traditional Christian stories that "evil exists to highlight the good," that "it is OUR duty to eliminate evil," that "the Devil is King of the World for now but soon would be defeated," or that "God wants to use us to tell of His great power."

I kept patching up that crack with a new plan to save the world, to mentor students to make a difference, to mobilize tens of thousands to fight hell on earth with a new ministry that would bring glory to God. And the more I dug in, the more shit I found. But it didn't make sense. Why is there so much godlessness when we keep bringing God in? And how is it possible that an All-Powerful God would be limited by the limitations of the humans He created and could destroy at any moment? It's madness to believe that He'd let people be tortured by human hands or natural disaster because He is "waiting" for the right time or the right person. Excuse me?! "The right time?" "The right person?" Are we saying that people in pain are pussies for not holding on a decade longer before succumbing to the grave? Are we saying that God is not powerful enough, or even worse yet, not willing enough, to have done something in hundreds or thousands of years to "orchestrate" goodness?

I was mad as hell.

But I couldn't let go—not yet. God's promises, ministries, communities, were doing something. I kept shoving passion down my throat and seeking new challenges hoping that if I believed more, sacrificed more, bled more, then God would use me to alleviate suffering. That had to be it, because nothing else worked. It wasn't Him, it was me. If only I was torn to pieces like Jesus, then He'd be able to use me to make the changes that were needed. It was my fault, it was your fault, that God hadn't acted to save the people He'd "do anything for." And every single time I was confronted with this harsh reality, I did what most of us have done, what probably you continue to do: I took it as a life lesson, sought emotion through comfort-worship, put problems aside to process in some near future when things were going better, and classified any current results as representing God's indirect involvement.

12

WHEN DEATH PAID A VISIT

*"It takes ten times as long to put yourself back together
as it does to fall apart."*
—Finnick Odair, in *Mockingjay*

In the Blink of an Eye

Healing from my questions was an ongoing process of praying, serving, and getting distracted—sometimes all at the same time. And what better way of doing this than by serving in youth ministry? Few things in life have ever given me so much joy and purpose as working with high school kids. That, and a strong desire to pull my hair out—a sentiment every youth worker has. We're masochists.

I tried to be very creative with my kids, inside and outside of the classroom. One of the first activities I did with a group I used to lead for Harvest Rock Church, a Pentecostal church in Pasadena, was to go on a hike to a waterfall in Ramona Falls near Escondido, California. We talked about the outing for a few weeks. When the day finally came, we ended up with a small group of eight travelers: three pairs of brothers between the ages of fourteen and seventeen, unique as they come; Gelfe (*Gel-fee*), a Filipino immigrant, also a volunteer leader; and myself.

On that Sunday morning on August 27, 2006, we attended the first service at Harvest Rock so we could leave as early as possible. We packed water, snacks, and attitudes. We hopped in two vehicles and headed south on the 5 toward San Diego. I had only been to the waterfall once, but I was confident I could find the way.

It was a hot day with no breeze. We parked the cars at the end of a residential neighborhood. The kids got out of the car, unamazed and highly critical of the terrain before them. Suddenly, one of the kids rushed to the sidewalk, followed by his buddies. "What are you doing? . . . Oh." He pulls his bright blue shorts down, along with his underwear, takes a squat, and drops a fresh turd on the searing sidewalk. Gelfe rushes back to his car and comes out with some toilet paper, gives a segment to the boy, uses some of it to pick up the souvenir, and throws it onto the fields on the other side of a wooden fence. "Um, guys, that's the kind of stuff Gelfe and I can get arrested for," I said. "Please don't do it again."

It'd be an hour and a half hike thorough hills, around boulders, and across ravines. At the end there'd be a nice waterfall pouring into a pond. There'd be rocks where we could jump off and backflip into the water.

About a third of the way there, Gelfe and I started hearing the "are we there yet?" rants. We stopped for a quick break in an area with an assortment of boulders, a perfect place for a rest and a photo op. In teenage-jock lingo this meant it was a perfect time for a gun show. They started posing, flexing, and grunting as they took turns taking pictures.

One of the kids decided to give the biggest boulder, a forty-foot rock behind us, a try. Since bouldering is one of my most cherished hobbies, I decided to try to tackle it too. Unable to figure out a way up the boulder, he soon gave up and stepped back down as I continued to the top. By this point the others decided my bouldering was not worth waiting for and began to rejoin the path to the waterfall. Gelfe and one of the kids, Robert, stayed behind to wait for me. Gelfe took a picture as I stood proudly on top while Robert stood on a small boulder to my left.

The boulder was easy to climb up, for sure. But as with many boulders, it felt considerably different on the way down. I held on to a small protrusion of rock with my right hand and quickly began to look for a new hold. I inserted my left hand into a crevice and made a fist so I could use it as a handhold. My feet dangled in midair as I sought for a place to rest them. I had reached a curve on the rock below me, so I knew I had run out of options for safely stepping down on that side. Agitated and tense, I decided to go back up and find another route down the other side. My skinny arms were pretty stretched out by now and my position challenged my upper body strength. Fear began to creep in, but I was unwilling to let it show.

I tried to make one more effort to pull myself up and reach the foothold I needed to regain balance, rest, and recover my strength. As I pulled my body up, the rock I was holding on to with my right hand separated from the boulder. A trail of red powder landed on my face, leaving me momentarily blind as I hung thirty-five feet up in the air with nothing but my left fist stuck in a crevice. My feet dangled as my right hand desperately scratched the boulder, seeking any kind of traction. The skin on my left hand became irritated and started to hurt badly—I knew it had started to peel off. I began to consider how I would fall and realized, there was no good scenario—at this height it would hurt a lot no matter how I fell. The breeze had picked up and was now unforgiving and blowing harder, making it more difficult to balance my body. Fear crawled deeper inside of me. I didn't have another option. I knew it now. I would have to let go.

On average, a human eye takes between 300 and 400 milliseconds to complete a single blink. That's roughly between three-tenths and four-tenths of a second. And that's exactly how long the rest of my experience lasted. I'm looking at my fist inside the crevice. I see the rocky ground below me. I see the path ahead covered in trees. I see the clear afternoon sky above me. I see the boulder's surface three inches from my face. And I blink.

I open my eyes a fraction of a second later and feel disoriented. The trees, the boulder, the strong wind, have all disappeared.

Where am I? Why is it so quiet?

It doesn't feel outdoors.

It seems like I'm inside.

That's a wall.

That's a ceiling.

Those are blinds on the window.

A window.

It feels like I'm lying down.

Why is one of my eyes covered? Am I only seeing out of one eye (the right eye)?

That seems like a foot. That foot is heavily bandaged. Why is it bandaged?

Am I on a bed? It feels like I'm on a bed.

That's a curtain (on the left side). Why would there be a curtain? Is it dividing the room?

Wait, is this a hospital? It feels like it might be a hospital.

Those people look sad, like they are hurting for someone. Are they crying?

I think someone is in the hospital.

I think someone got hurt.

Did that girl just pass out from looking at me?

Wait, I think that is *my* foot.

Is this me in the hospital?

Did I get hurt?

Oh my God, I think I fell off that cliff!

Out of nowhere, like a slithering snake, trembling pain started to creep in through my fingertips, my veins, my arms, my muscles—sooner rather than later I existed in an agonizing and painful present that felt as if it had no end. I couldn't remember anything from the previous twenty-four hours, but I could imagine that I had fallen, and that it was pretty bad.

I didn't have to imagine it actually, the results were right there.

Both my legs were wrapped in bandages. My left eye seemed wrapped shut. My veins had needles in them, connected to tubes, connected to bags and machines. A catheter inside me led to a clear bag, filled with yellow urine, hanging at the end of my bed. I couldn't move my legs. My arms barely lifted. It hurt to turn my neck, even to open my mouth. And I gasped when someone removed my blanket; most of my skin was now in different shades of purple, black, green, and blue. The only parts of my body I remember still having a natural skin color were my fingertips.

People didn't seem surprised that I had opened my eye. Apparently I had drifted in and out of consciousness the past twenty-four hours, but my brain only then decided I was ready to take in my current predicament.

I spent a month at the hospital between surgeries and nightmares. And then a month at a rehab center where I'd learn, like a baby, how to stand, wobble, and eventually to walk again.

It wasn't until I left this place, on a wheelchair and with crutches in the trunk, that I started learning and understanding what happened that fateful day. I spent hours, days, weeks, months, asking question after question to every witness. I had to process my own experience through their eyes because my brain was protecting me from additional turmoil, blocking off all memories of the incident. As I began to duct tape the quotes, the tales, the stories, the "Oh, I remember that . . ." moments, and the documents from the hospital, I froze chilled by the realization of the incredible trauma my body had endured. But also the trauma my soul would have to digest and process before any kind of healing seemed anywhere near possible.

In a fast-forward review of my last memories, all I remember is that the wind was blowing, the rock I was holding on to came off the boulder, red dust fell in my eyes, skin peeled off my hand wedged in the crevice, my feet dangled, I desperately scratched the boulder hoping for salvation, and I blinked.

PAUSE.

Still screen.

PLAY.

Once I added in the missing pieces, I learned my body fell like a pencil, straight to the ground. My left heel hit first, shattering immediately on impact. My ankle broke, destroying the cartilage that connected with my leg. My left femur encountered a pointy rock, breaking it into three parts. As if a second joint had been artificially created in my mid-thigh, my leg cracked, bending upward—in other words, my left foot was sent wrapped around my neck. My right leg struck a rock below, ripping off layers of skin from my calf and thigh, leaving vulnerable my blue veins, red muscles, and white fat. Another pointy rock struck my face, causing damage of its own. My left eye socket shattered, leaving my eyeball slightly poking out of my face. My jaw broke off, hanging loose. Eight teeth in my mouth broke. A bottom tooth struck my upper lip, leaving a raw piece of flesh hanging off and bleeding. I received a bad concussion from slamming the back of my head against the ground. The general trauma my body received left muscles, ligaments, and skin torn and bleeding at the mercy of time.

Gelfe and Robert rushed to my aid. Gelfe then sent Robert to go after the rest. They thought it was a bad joke until they saw my bloody, mangled body trapped between the rocks. Fortunately, Gelfe worked with X-ray equipment in a Pasadena ER—experience that proved helpful.

With no cellphone reception, three kids ran in opposing directions as if each chasing the corner of a triangle. By the time the third one reached 9-1-1, the dispatcher said notice had been received. Back at the boulder, the group tried to find a way to pull my body out of its rocky entrapment, causing the least amount of additional pain and damage—it seemed impossible. Fearing I might bleed to death, Gelfe prayed and questioned if he should break off my left leg at the top and wrap a tourniquet around the stump to stop the blood flow. This would mean I would lose the leg. He didn't do it. A gush of blood coming from my left eye socket covered my face and dripped off the hands of those in my aid. They asked, since this was the most visible wound, if that's where it hurt. Each time I replied, in a very distressful growling sound because of a detached jaw, "No. My leg. My leg hurts." I would come in and out of consciousness always repeating the same words, including, "What happened?" At times I'd breathe out strongly, driving chills through their bones. They grabbed my head and cried out, "Don't leave us, Fernie! Don't leave us!" "We love you, Fernie! Please don't leave us!"

About an hour later a helicopter showed up. Five of the kids ran waving their hands in the nearby open field while my head rested on Daniel's lap. The responders in the helicopter appeared to have seen them, yet they flew away, leaving the kids shocked and scared. A second helicopter showed up later and flew down to meet us, but it too had to leave because they didn't have the equipment to lift me up. The kids were enraged in disbelief. A third helicopter finally lifted my body and flew me to Escondido, where I received the necessary medical help.

It took two hours from the moment they made the call till a helicopter finally took me away.

At the hospital, doctors dislocated my left hipbone and cut into the leg, so they could literally sledgehammer a titanium rod through my femur all the way to the knee. They inserted a titanium plate and ten screws into my left foot hoping that I'd still be able to walk. They inserted three smaller titanium plates into my face: one holding my eyeball in place, one helping my nostril stay open, and one giving the shape of a cheekbone. They reattached my jaw, but left the flesh hanging off my lip for another week. Not including the original trauma, the surgery procedures themselves would be enough to leave me feeling beaten and destroyed for months.

I was told that before surgery I kept going in and out of consciousness, that I was even able to leave a drug-hazed message, both on my mom's voicemail and at work. "Hey guys, I hope you are doing good. So, I wanted to let you know that I had a little accident, so I am not sure if I'll be able to make it to work tomorrow. I'll be there as soon as I can. I hope you are doing well. Byyyyyyye."

But truth is, in the postsurgery stage, no amount of drugs seemed to alleviate the pain. I lost sense of when it was daytime and when it was nighttime. All I knew was that the wounds hurt, and that they hurt bad.

If You Love Me
I was at a game night with a couple of friends several months later. They were trying to distract me and welcome me back into the world of the living. A round of Settlers of Catan, cheeseburgers, and beer should do the trick. The wife of one of my friends innocently brought up the issue of my recovery and asked, "How painful was it? Did it hurt a lot?" The others all gasped and froze. Everyone's eyes wandered around; they raised their shoulders and lowered their heads, but eventually quietly focused on me. I hadn't yet thought of a particular way to explain it. I looked into the distance, remembered my time in the hospital and rehab center, and thought of an analogy that might help

me explain to them how it felt. "Imagine you are at a bonfire, at a camp. For some strange reason you put your hands over the fire. You become fearful when you smell the hair on your arms singeing. You see it and you feel it, but you can't remove them from the fire. You start to smell your skin burning, yet you keep them over the fire. You feel how your first layer of skin starts to melt off. Yet, you can't remove them—they are bound in that space above the fire. You become terrified because you can now see your blood vessels, the fat inside your arms melt off your muscles, and then your flesh starts to reveal your bones. You tremble at the sight overpowered by pain, but you . . . can't . . . remove them . . . from the fire. Though there were breaks every now and then, that's often the kind of pain I felt every TWO SECONDS . . . for minutes, hours, days, weeks."

Her eyes widened, a piece of marshmallow held at the entrance of her mouth. I didn't mean to shock them. The memories were still very vivid.

Back in recovery I couldn't sleep much. I might manage two hours before being awakened by a bolt of lightning that made my veins pop out and my soul leave my body. All I could do was clench the sheets and send my head back in teeth-gnashing torture.

I remember a particular night at the hospital as if it was yesterday. An idea had haunted me for days. Finally, I looked out to the night sky through the gray hospital blinds and spoke to the full moon as if it were the eye of God. For days, I hadn't spoken much, trying to find ways to have this thought escape me. But how could it? It was in every breathing, aching moment. My right hand came out from under the sheets, shaking and weak. I looked at the moon. And though my lips shivered, my heart spoke with the memories of bones shattering, blood gushing, and sleepless endless nights of torment, when I begged to pass out so I wouldn't feel any longer. If these words would leave my lips, if my breath would utter them, if valor would reign over fear, then I had to make sure every fiber in me, from my head to my toes, would most truthfully mean them. And there, from the most inner corner of my soul, I felt them gliding through every room of my being as if asking for consensus and preparing for farewell. By the time they reached my mouth, I tell you, I had never meant words more than the ones I uttered at that very moment in that lonely, gloomy, dry hospital bed. I looked up to His eye, reached out my trembling hand, pleading mercy, and, with quiet power, I prayed, "Jesus . . . if you love me . . . please, let—me—die."

I looked out the window for days and, still alive, sadly witnessed the moon move past its stage of full glory.

My doctors told my friends and family that it would take up to nine months to a year for me to get back on my feet and be able to join the world again. And that when I did, chances were I'd never be the guy I once was. That option seemed impossible to me. Each hour that I spent motionless on that bed, my muscles became even more atrophied. Each day that I spent locked up in that room, the world moved toward the future while leaving me behind, my soul sinking deeper in a tomb of the past, collecting dust, spiderwebs, and broken dreams.

It took me two months, not nine months, let alone a year. Two months for me to get back on my feet with the use of a wheelchair, crutches, and eventually a cane. But they weren't easy months.

Even once I was out of the hospital, my recovery was far from over. I was seeing up to eleven doctors, with thirteen hospital visits a week, for almost a year. I even had to return to the ER from time to time. Each time they reminded me of all the things I was never going to be able to do again: "You'll never be able to run again." "You'll never be able to jump again." "You'll never be able to play soccer again." "You'll never be able to climb mountains again." "You'll never be able to walk barefoot again." Over and over, piece by piece, they kept taking my life away from me and leaving nothing but an empty shell.

Journal Entry: Monday, October 9, 2006

I almost died again. I have proof the world is against me. God doesn't like me. I will always serve God. First of all I have no other choice. And that is the only thing he wants of me: service, glory. He doesn't need my love or something like that. Even after all the mistreatment and neglect he has given me, I have tried to love him. Why? Because He is my God and I will always be with him. What can I do so he can love me the way I am, even though he didn't choose me from my birth? I try and I try. Even people love me, but He doesn't.

Empty sermons filled with wishful thinking. They don't know God.

Open your eyes! He kills thousands! Lets suffering happen in massive scales! All for his glory. HOW? I have to serve Him. I try to love Him. Hard. But how can anyone in their right mind approve it?

I am scared. Very scared. To dream. To believe. To ask. To pray. To learn more. To be hated more. How can I go on? I will, but man, with God against you even when you serve Him and love Him. Wow! I know I am stupid and I'm little, ugly, poor, I'm worth nothing but, well, I must be wrong, but I don't think it should be like that. There should be more people like Jesus. We don't need to have crucifixion in our minds all the time. I just want to help. I really need help from the Holy Spirit. And I even think it would give GOD MORE GLORY. But he doesn't like me.

So close to death its flavor damaged my lips. Titanium in my bones, in my face. The scar on my cheek. My disfigured eye. Who am I now? I am not even 30 yet. Will God hurt me more than this? Is it possible? I guess it is? How can I serve Him? Is He really good?

Well, no more venting. It's out. I hope I can move on. I don't know what or how, but I have to. Because I didn't die. I don't want to die yet. I prefer not to suffer like that again. NEVER!

I Forgive You

I had indeed tasted the rust of Death's knife in my mouth and there was no escaping its poison. Publicly, I moved forward in my ministry with Azusa Pacific University and Mexico Outreach—I had to, there was a lot on the line. But I am not talking about me. I am talking about the thousands of people who benefited each year because of the services we provided. But privately, the shadows became thicker and thicker as days went by.

The best that I could do to resolve this predicament, as illogical as it may sound at first, was to identify God as two personalities. Meaning, I would focus on Jesus as the good guy and Jehovah, his father, as the bad guy. Jesus was the loving friend who came and sacrificed himself for us and suffered under the will of the egotistical, worship-craving deity willing to sacrifice his son, and the rest of us for that matter, for his personal glory. By doing this I could still hold to an image of God that fit according to the lessons I'd had, and taught, about him—the image I had come to love and find comfort in for so many years. But I would also find room for my brain to make sense of all the evidence of godlessness and the senseless casualties of divine apathy.

I wrote, I prayed, I sang, but no amount of comfort worship could bring light into my torment of thought. On one of those nights of torment I came up with a new solution, which sounded ludicrous at first, but which allowed me to keep holding on to the cross—to forgive him. Everything in my life was attached to religion. It was my life and, because of that, I felt that my beliefs had to be real. God and I would have to have a little mano a mano if we were gonna remain an item.

I told him how upset I was about what he had allowed to happen in my life, and about what he had allowed to happen in the world under his watch.

Massacres, torture, starvation, cruelty—all just the beginning. With a real fear of being stricken by lightning just at the thought of it, I had to tell him, "You are a real son of a bitch."

No bolt of electricity jolted through my body, so I continued talking. "I have done everything you've asked of me and more. I have sacrificed my time, my money—I am broke for you. I have sacrificed my relationships—I am still single and lonely. I have sacrificed my health for you—I've had three ulcers because of the stress from Mexico Outreach and almost died out on the mission field. I have sacrificed everything for you and you keep showing signs of not giving a damn about me. Why?! And now this. What is this, a joke? You want to show me how powerful you are, and how insignificant I am, by beating the crap out of me—you interstellar bully?!"

People tried to reason with me about how it was a miracle that I had survived. I heard the stories about how my "Guardian Angel must've missed his watch," how "God must have a great purpose for your life," how "all things work together for the good," and, the always patronizing, how "God works in mysterious ways." Doctors and nurses supported such notions by saying they hadn't seen a case like mine—where someone survived the kind of trauma I suffered and then walked out of the hospital by his own power in such short amount of time. But with all due respect, they could shove their admiration up their asses. It was the most difficult challenge I had ever experienced. It was my sweat and tears, it was my blood, it was my effort.

Stories of an all-loving, all-powerful, all-knowing God became much harder to digest.

So what did I do? Of course, the same thing I had been doing since day one. I found some new passion to fight for. But before that, I raised my fist to the sky and told God, "I don't want to hold this grudge in my heart. I will not be like you. I choose to love, not to hurt. If I have the power to love, I will love. If I have the power to end or prevent suffering, I will. You may do what you want. And I don't want to carry this with me. You are God, and I am human, an insignificant human, and that is just the way it is. But you have fucked me over and over, and this time you've crossed the line in neglect and pain. I will do what you cannot do. Call me heretic. Call me blasphemous. Strike me with lightning. Destroy my body. How much more pain can you cause me, for crying out loud? You want to threaten my soul, my eternal soul? After this, how much more can you do to me? But if I will be alive, I will try to move on. And I tell you this, from the bottom of my heart, as someone who loves you, You . . . are . . . an asshole. But you know what, I say this also from the bottom of my heart, because I need to say it, regardless of who You are and how You feel . . . I forgive you."

I Love You and Good-Bye

There are three phases to a traumatic experience. Phase one is safety and stabilization. It is difficult to emotionally process the event. There is a sense of insecurity. It is a time for the body to heal and for the mind to learn to trust the world once again.

Any reminder of the event made me relive the event, something I passionately avoided. During this phase, I had unregulated bursts of emotion that people around me had difficulty understanding. Friends heard it. The Mexico Outreach staff heard it. God heard it.

Phase two is remembrance and mourning. Once the body is stronger, the mind and heart can start their healing process. It is a realization of, "Oh shit, it really did happen." We can now integrate the story of the trauma into our lives and stop pretending it's not there.

When I left APU, two years after the accident, I went on a ten-day vacation to visit a friend in Colorado Springs. It was a chance to get away and rest my mind and heart before I started my new job. It gave me the strength to be able to tell my story, for the first time, without breaking down.

When I returned from Colorado, a friend invited me to go on a hike to a waterfall in the Pasadena foothills. Sliding down a rock and into the water, unwillingly and very briefly, cracked open my memories and revealed, for the first time, a few flashbacks from that fateful day. I could see, from my right eye, crimson liquid gushing out of my left eye. I saw the panicked faces of those in my aid through a layer of red. I could hear voices, though I couldn't understand them. Feelings that were buried very deep within erupted unannounced while I wept and trembled like a child in my friend's arms.

Phase three is reconnection and integration. It is a new opportunity for hope. It's a chance to integrate the story into life and to take steps away from victimization and toward empowerment.

Eric, a close friend and the guy who first took me on that hike to Ramona Falls, came up with an interesting idea, "What if we go back to the place where you fell? It may help you bring back more memories and process everything you still need to process."

I was perplexed—scared mostly—but after some consideration I agreed to do it. Jeff, Eric's best friend and also a buddy of mine, said he'd love to go as well and be a part of this meaningful time with me. We went to bed and decided to rise early and head back to the epicenter of my blocked memories.

There was a sense of reverence when we got to the place. The path looked like it belonged in Middle Earth from *Lord of the Rings*. I pictured Frodo and Sam meeting us somewhere along the way. Hot yellow dirt, scattered rocks, forest at a distance, and the awe-inspiring curves of green-pasture mountains.

When we got to the boulder, I expected a million flashbacks to start hitting me all at once. Both Eric and Jeff stood right next to me as if preparing to catch me in my fall. But nothing. Not a single memory.

I began to analyze what might have happened through simple deduction. Where I stepped, where I stood, where I tried to come down—and there it was, where I fell.

But still, no memories.

We eventually continued our walk toward the waterfall. We played in the pond for a bit, and then headed back and crossed paths with the boulder again.

Eric encouraged me to blast it with four-letter words, "Curse at it. Scream at it. Just go at it and let it have it." I turned to it and thought about it. I opened my mouth—but nothing, nothing came out. It didn't feel right.

We started walking again, and about sixty feet away from it I suddenly stopped. "Guys, can you give me a minute?" I requested. "Of course. Do you want us to go with you?" Jeff asked. "No. It's okay. Thanks," I replied. Then Eric stepped forward, "I am coming with you." This seemed okay. He was in many ways a soulmate, and we walked quietly toward it.

"Stay here," I said, when we were about twenty feet way. Eric nodded, and I walked the rest of the way by myself.

I stood in front of the boulder and wondered if this was the time to annihilate it with my wrath, but something else happened instead. I felt an odd connection to it—as if it had shown me a different angle on her face that I hadn't been looking for.

I stepped forward and looked her straight in the eye. Unexpectedly, I did the dumbest, most pointless thing you can think of—I began talking to her, very softly at first. "You fucked me. I have been using you as an excuse to validate my anger and my pain. You have caused me the greatest agony I have ever experienced, and probably ever will. I've been trying to pretend either that it never happened, or that you are the reason for all my troubles. But to be honest, neither one of those actions is helping me move on. You exist. You are right here. And that day did take place. Those months of recovery were real. The pain was real. I hated it, but it is real. It wasn't a bad dream. It did happen, and I can't move on pretending otherwise. But I have also filled my heart with anger against you. And here you are, unmoving. You were here before, and you will be here after. And I've used you to validate my reckless emotions and my fury. I thought that by doing that I'd be able to reason with my demons and give meaning to my lack of balance and control. But it's not working. And I don't want to be angry anymore. And I don't want to be broken anymore. I need to let you go."

I got even closer to her now. So close that my breath stroked her face. I felt her show me her vulnerable side. I heard her apologize for the unintended catastrophe she had caused in my life. I saw her lower her face in shame. I stretched out my arms as wide as I could and embraced her with a hug that felt both natural and needed. My face rested on hers, and I continued to speak softly in her ear. "You know what, I can't go on pretending I'm okay. You are part of my life, and you will always be. It's impossible to rip you off of it, but it doesn't mean I have to carry you with me forever. So I will do this, I will talk to you this once, for the last time, and I will leave you and will probably never come back. But please know this, I am no longer angry at you. I forgive you. I forgive you for hurting me. I forgive you for fucking me. I forgive you for destroying everything in me and leaving me almost dead in body, and in spirit. I honestly do. And there is one more thing. Yeah, you know what . . ." I breathed out deeply, "I love you. Good or bad you are part of me, and you will always be."

I let go of her, then brought my hands to her face, gently held it, leaned forward, kissed her softly, and said my last words. "Thank you. I love you. And good-bye, forever."

I walked away from her and haven't gone back since. But I left a different man. The pain I felt began to cease. The anger I felt began to dissolve. The burden I felt began to lighten up—the feeling of imminent death that used to lurk around every corner I turned evaporated. I used to smell its rotten scent in the air, taste its bloody residue on my lips, and see its shadow hovering over my dreams. But now, each step I took away from the rock was a step toward light and redemption. Each choice that I'd make away from fear and hopelessness was a change toward happiness and joy. Each risk that I'd take to prove my heart was still beating away from death was an opportunity to fill myself with an anchoring awe that led me back to life.

My relationship with another rock in my life, I feared, might sooner or later share the same fate.

Part III: Back from the Cross

"I do not feel obliged to believe that the same God who has endowed us with sense, reason, and intellect has intended us to forgo their use."
—Galileo Galilei, *Letter to the Grand Duchess Christina*

13

CHURCHING THE WORLD

*"If one wishes to form a true estimate of the full grandeur of religion,
one must keep in mind what it undertakes to do for men.
It gives them information about the source and origin of the universe,
it assures them of protection and final happiness amid the changing
vicissitudes of life, and it guides their thoughts and motions
by means of precepts which are backed by the whole force of its authority."*
—Sigmund Freud, *New Introductory Lectures on Psychoanalysis*

Pandora's Box
The United Methodist Church is the largest mainline Protestant denomination, the second largest Protestant church, and the third largest Christian denomination in the country. And on September 2, 2008, I began my work as its first, and probably only, Director of Leadership Development for Young People for the California-Pacific Conference of The UMC.

"Cal-Pac," as people nicknamed this conference, has its headquarters, or conference center, in Pasadena, California. This regional body oversees about 400 churches across Southern California, Hawaii, Guam, and Saipan, with a population of about 83,000 members. Cal-Pac is known as the UMC's most diverse conference in the United States, with large sectors of Polynesians, Blacks, Hispanics, Koreans, Japanese, and other minorities with beautiful voices.

During the June 2008 Cal-Pac annual conference, participants voted and approved a series of "Leadership Initiatives." Initiative #1 was to create the Center for Leadership Excellence (CLE), which would be a world-class, cross-denominational, leadership-training institution that would serve as a beacon of hope and an example of service—a gift to the world. An executive director would be hired to lead this institute. Initiative #2 was to hire a director who would lead initiatives for the mobilization of young leaders for the transformation of the world. That's where I come in ("Initiative 2" was a nickname I had during my first few months). Initiative #3 was to form a committee that would advise the CLE on how to move forward, in coordination with the Conference, and create breathtaking, God-honoring leadership programs.

I learned during my second interview that the executive director for the CLE had recently been elected bishop at a different conference. Meaning there was really no direction, no budget, no planning, and no vision for the center. Even so, I accepted the job, and there I was. Two conference staffers were entrusted with advising me—the "new kid on the block"—while I got my bearings.

At this point I attended a nondenominational church. But for United Methodists, tradition is a fundamental part of their identity. "Born and raised United Methodist" is a trait people bragged about as if it was the highlight of their resume. New youth leaders in United Methodist churches without such a history were not considered United Methodist. Fresh into my second week at the conference center, one of the other directors made a statement that made my challenge real from the get-go: "You gotta know that people around the Conference are gonna hate you on the spot, just because you are not a United Methodist. You know that, right?"

Indeed, I was the highest-ranking non–United Methodist in the Conference, and also the youngest director at the conference center, making my hire a very controversial one. I quickly understood the understated hard-core identity United Methodists had with regard to their name and history. Though my colleague's words surprised me, I was confident that, having worked with many denominations through Mexico Outreach, I'd be able to bridge the gap.

I was assigned an assistant to help me move things along. Frances had worked there for nineteen years, so I thought, "Great. Experience." When I met Frances I realized that, at sixty-five, she was the oldest assistant in the conference center. I quickly learned she had many virtues. One of them was that she had a great understanding of the Conference's history. She knew the big annual events and their dates and the names of key players I should reach out to, and she had ideas about how I should start moving the pieces.

At one point I asked her for a list of youth and young adult leaders in the Conference. If I was going to influence youth ministries, I had to know who my commanders were. She then started pulling, one after another, blurred faxed copies of ancient rosters that had been collecting dust in drawers. I immediately understood that I was not only going to start from scratch, but that I was also going to start without key ingredients. So first things first, I knew I had to update our technology and our record keeping.

I had been using Apple products for a while thanks to my time with Mexico Outreach. Our office had been the only fully Mac-oriented office on the APU campus. I had become very comfortable with Pages, Keynote, and iMovie, among other software. I also knew that Apple had been making its way into pop culture as an icon of breakthrough technology, revolutionary designs, and radical coolness. For all of the above reasons, I asked for a Mac when I was asked what kind of computer I'd like.

Little did I know I had just opened Pandora's box.

I was immediately told no, because "the rest of the office is PC." I kept making the case that, with Apple, you didn't have to worry about files not transferring from one operating system to the other, and that Word and Excel transferred perfectly through email. I then learned the office still used WordPerfect. Now, I knew WordPerfect and loved it when it came out, but I couldn't believe the conference center was *still* using one of those early versions.

I said, "I'm sorry, but you are literally asking me to reform your systems and make yourselves more appealing to a younger generations, but at the same time you want me to use software that most people outside this building have not even heard of, let alone use?"

The answer was blunt but honest, "Well, yes."

One of the IT guys stopped me in the hallway to ask, "Do you have any idea what you started here?" I was speechless. I was accused by several conference staffers of starting a "revolt" and a "controversy." People would bring their emotions out with high-pitched voices and ask me, "Why do you want to be different than the way we are?"

I heard a phrase that became very familiar to my ears, "This is the way we've always done things."

This "revolutionary" request of getting an Apple laptop was perceived as so drastic, it made it all the way to the bishop! By asking to have a Mac instead of a PC, you would've thought that I had requested that the denomination move away from Wesleyan doctrine and toward Calvinism—an act of heresy.

I'm thinking, "No way can we be so stuck in tradition. No. It can't be."

I even started to believe somebody was playing a prank on me. I mean, we're trying to have a "world-class" institute here, right? But I'm given typewriter technology, no record of who works with young people, no clear sources for funding, no real staff, and no idea of what direction to take— except a pat on the back and a "good luck!" And I knew things would get even more interesting once I started talking to youth leaders out in the field.

The Center for Leadership Excellence was originally supposed to be a separate institution from the United Methodist Church. That's how they sold it to me. But I quickly realized that the UMC had a lot of expectations from the CLE as well, often on a personal level. Frances gave me some wise advice. She told me the denomination is very hierarchical and very political. "They all want Jesus to tell them what to do," she said. Then, lowering her voice, she added, "But there are certain people who God tells directly what others should do."

If I wanted to make any changes, I was gonna have to meet some people, make friends, and get to see what was happening out in the churches firsthand. Frances' first recommendation was for me to sit in meetings with the Conference Council on Young Adults and the Conference Council for Youth Ministries. The councils were supposed to have two representatives from each of the eight districts: Hawaii District (which included all the Hawaiian islands, Guam, and Saipan), Santa Barbara District, Long Beach District, Los Angeles District, Pasadena District, Riverside District, Santa Ana District, and San Diego District.

At the first meeting I attended, which included both youth and adults, representatives from half or more of the districts were missing. I learned that a consultant handpicked most of the representatives present, but there were also independent minds selected by the district advisers. Seated as a guest, I witnessed a polarized argument of hot tempers, strong opinions, and high tones, where opposing sides argued about the proper role of youth in the church. One side, composed mostly of youth, claimed youth should have a more significant role in leadership involvement. The other side, composed mostly of adults, said youth should act as learning spectators due to their lack of experience. The message was clear: "It's not that we are telling you what to do, it's that we know how things are and we want to protect you. Trust us, it's better if you do it this way." The youth, in turn, demanded that they be taken seriously. That their age did not mean they didn't have intelligence. That their voice should matter. They stated that, if they had an opinion different from the Conference, they were going to share it. Observing veins popping on foreheads, people standing and shouting, and fists slamming on the table, I knew my work would be tougher than I had originally imagined.

I left that meeting puzzled. 1 Timothy 4:12 reads, *"Don't let anyone look down on you because you are young, but set an example for the believers in speech, in conduct, in love, in faith and in purity."* I have claimed that right myself innumerable times. Young people are not puppets. The least they can do is speak up. If anything, I wanted to guarantee that right.

I decided I had to start having conversations with some key leaders in the Conference and get a better feel about what the hell was going on out there when nobody was watching. I visited some leaders at their churches and was visited by others in my office. And on that seat across from my desk I saw tears of pain roll down frustrated faces, one after the other.

I then arranged for roundtables in each of the eight districts and welcomed every youth and young adult leader to come meet with me and have an honest conversation. They all shared similar experiences. From one end of the Conference to the other, voices said, "We're struggling here but our church is unwilling to adapt." They would tell me how hard it was at the local church level for the youth worker, and how they felt abandoned by their conference.

I learned of how afraid youth leaders were to speak up to their superiors for fear of losing their positions. Many said they were treated as "glorified babysitters," and their superiors would not grant them full-time status, even though they worked forty to sixty hours a week, in order to save on wages and benefits. They were not given enough resources, often paying for necessities out of their own pockets. They were not allowed to sit in church councils, or to have a vote on decision making. The youth leaders believed kids were being tolerated until they became adults, at which time they would finally be welcomed into the church.

I'm thinking, "Bloody hell! Kids are not the church of tomorrow, they are the church of today. No wonder UMC churches are losing young people by the legions. It's because they really never let them in in the first place."

I also met with leaders of the ethnic caucuses. Hispanics, Blacks, Koreans, Polynesians, Japanese, Filipinos, they all had a bone to pick with the Conference as well. I heard about how they stayed on the sidelines, having given up on the majority white caucus that gave them mostly nominal token positions. Every time they went to an event or meeting, they felt they were in a white church, in a white style, that presented white ideas. Members of the ethnic minorities shared they would open up prayer or play music, but other than that, they were always nicely stored in the souvenir closet and brought out only to show off during big events—*look how diverse we are.*

Every group I met with that worked with young people—about seven groups or so—all had the same thing to say. They had all tried to work with the other groups, but it became impossible for them to do so. So even though they all had the same limited number of kids to work with, with the same limited resources, they were going to do their own individual thing. They had given up on the others, and that's the way it was going to stay.

I certainly had my work cut out for me.

Was it my responsibility to solve this issue? On paper, no. I was not supposed to be the United Methodist supervisor for youth and young adult ministries. But I realized that before I worked on adding additional floors, windows, and picture frames on the walls, I was going to have to work on the foundation. And I did not let myself forget, I left my ministry at APU and came here because I wanted to transform the church from the inside out.

As I had to remind myself again, no wonder they say, "Be careful what you ask for."

The diagnosis was: the church had no quality publications (digital or print); groups that worked with young people weren't communicating with each other; there was no clear funding for youth ministries; groups felt isolated; staff was unequipped; there was enormous resistance to change; there was a deep-rooted apathy and conformity from those who'd been there for a while; and deep frustrations that accumulated through time forced people either to give up trying or to leave the UMC altogether. "I'm a recovering United Methodist" is a term I heard often outside those circles. All of these elements created an environment that seemed unhealthy and unbeatable. And I learned that, though some churches had supportive pastors, this feeling was echoed by numerous youth leaders in local congregations who felt unsupported, underfunded, unequipped, overworked, and misunderstood.

I faced an uphill battle. I remember walking down the hallway by the bishop's office and heading downstairs. Halfway down, maybe just because it was the nearest place, I sat on the stairs and leaned my head against the wall and thought to myself, "I don't know if I can do this."

I was overwhelmed.

When I asked about budgets, one of my advisers pulled out a number of spreadsheets with accounts and amounts of money that were, in one way or another, directed for ministries with youth and young adults. Most of this money did not have a designated supervisor. And I'm like, "Say what?" He said that most of these resources had been allocated years ago and the committees responsible had either vanished or leadership had left, and through the passing of time these accounts remained on the books in Methodist limbo. Once a year, the consultant would show up with the accounts for current events with all balances in the red. They'd start transferring money from other accounts into these to bring them back to black, and then leave things as they were until the next year and do it all over again.

I was stunned.

"Are you kidding me?" I said. "This is how you are running finances for the Conference, like pulling money from under the mattress?!" I was pissed. But I also understood that this was a cultural problem, more than a particular individual's fault. People respected the structure, the tradition. Out of their best intentions they approved initiatives and budgets, and later moved on to the next thing without setting a follow-through plan. It is part of the system and bureaucracy of "Big Religion."

This was consistent with the ongoing outrage over funds the churches are required to give to the Conference—known as *apportionments* ("taxes" paid to the Conference by the churches). The Conference leaders run programs of their own, but since they have no tithing members, how much they do depends on how much money they get from the churches. But the churches' claim is, "Why do we have to give more money for the Conference leaders to do service, when we can do the service ourselves?" Hearing stories of misplaced, misused, and forgotten apportionment dollars only added to the fire.

My adviser then asked whether I would like to take control of the accounts and try to manage them. I said, "I don't *want* to, but someone has to." This was inconceivable.

And that is how I, unintentionally, started to become the de facto overseer of youth and young adult ministries for the Conference.

Many steps followed after that.

My conviction to right the situation within Cal-Pac grew, and I made a commitment to those leaders who had stepped up and joined me in a movement of change. I would be their advocate and take their voices to those places where they would not normally be heard. I couldn't do less than believe in them. I had never met such a group of sacrificial, loving, passionate, dedicated individuals who were willing to lay everything on the line to serve young souls who they believed, as I did, were our future. Working with them, being able to call them my friends, continues to be one of the great honors of my life.

And thus began a revolution, a movement.

I changed the image of the Center for Leadership Excellence and gave it a contemporary look with a new logo and an edgy feel to everything that had its name. I began designing, with my Apple laptop, publications that were relevant, creative, and pleasant to the eye. I designed an e-magazine that became the most popular method of communication for the Conference. We moved away from the ancient blurred faxed rosters and developed the largest database of people in youth and young adult ministries ever in Cal-Pac. We moved from abandoned Internet subpages that nobody knew how to find, to a full website that contained all information about everything related to Cal-Pac youth and young adults. Our social network presence, such as on Facebook, YouTube, Flickr, and Twitter, received three times more visitors than our grown-up counterparts. Most importantly, participation tripled! We created brand new programs for the districts and for etching caucuses, along with partnerships with other departments. Our pool of volunteers became larger and more diverse. And the number of students in leadership soared, something for which I was most proud. The best compliment I received during my time with the UMC was, "You've developed the most empowered and engaged group of young leaders we've ever seen."

My department was setting the pace for all other departments in the Conference in terms of quality, energy, acceptance, pride, and, above all, trust. Wherever I went, people kept talking about the good things they were seeing. They loved the programs, they loved the inclusion, they loved the publications, and half of them loved Fernando—which, as I was earlier told, would be a great challenge. The other half always felt threatened by the radical changes of a non–United Methodist, doing non–United Methodist things, to improve their United Methodist ways.

The Full Grandeur of Religion

As part of my diagnosis, I also deduced that people were leaving or not joining the UMC because it had taken large steps to modify traditional theology. The UMC, like many other mainline denominations, is known for being considerably more liberal and open to diverse interpretations of scripture.

To give an overly simplified explanation, when it comes to a relationship with a creator, conservative churches typically have a more emotional connection with God, and a more feelings-based analysis of biblical teaching. A "love God more" approach. The liberal church, on the other hand, will have a more intellectual connection with The Almighty, and a more academic-based analysis of rules and laws. A "know God more" approach. When it comes to God's relationship with humanity, conservative theology will see it from the angle found in John 15:15, *"If you love me, keep my commandments."* You show love by obeying the rules: "Rules must be there for a reason, let's analyze that reason." Liberal theology, on the other hand, will see it from the angle in Mark 2, where people break through a roof to lower a paralytic man so Jesus could heal him. You show love by breaking the rules: "The person is more important than the rules, let's focus on the person."

These "left brain vs. right brain" divisions have occured throughout humanity's history, across almost every type of human endeavor, such as politics, entertainment, philosophy, and culture. Why would religions be any different if they are also made up of humans?

Over the years, the UMC (especially in Cal-Pac) had effectively filtered out its more conservative members, especially in leadership. Its interpretations of scripture had led to controversial and polarizing decisions, including accepting divorce, having women in leadership, interpreting the Bible nonliterally, being pro-choice on abortion, having multiple paths to salvation, calling God "Our Mother," tolerating sex outside of marriage, and espousing the ever-so-hotly debated "God made them gay" theology.

Based on my read, this socio-political-religious-cultural transformation toward what I considered extreme liberalism had slowly but surely created a morphed and, dare I say, mutated version of Jesus Christ. If raised outside of the confines of the UMC, the traditional American believer would struggle to identify with the church's progressive version of Christianity.

Many accused the UMC of becoming an inbred (and many would say incestuous) community of believers who created their own theology, their own Jesus, their own culture, and their own technology. "There is a reason why we are were called 'Methodists,'" I was told—their very name first started as a derogatory term for their systematic methods of worship.

Being a United Methodist, just as being part of any other kind of religious (or political) group, provides its members with a sense of stability, family, history, vision, and, most importantly, identity. Regardless of how dysfunctional the system may be, it is always a safe place to land. It provides answers, support, and a way to contribute to a big picture. Again, isn't that part of the natural human experience?

Out with the New
About a year and a half into my term with the UMC, a new high-ranking administrator was hired—Athaliah.

During our first meeting, Athaliah said something to me that day that she would repeat at least five other times over the next two years. In essence, she told me, "You are not a United Methodist, and to be totally honest with you, if I had been on the hiring committee when you were interviewed for your position, I would have not hired a non–United Methodist. I understand you are very qualified, and that you have done some good things, but I just feel that if we are the United Methodist Church, and we are doing United Methodist leadership, we should have chosen a United Methodist."

I had achieved a public presence and a plethora of positive results in a considerably short amount of time. Each day, I came in early, left late, and drove all over the Conference mobilizing the pieces to accomplish what we had dreamt about. And in a few seconds she had managed to devalue my sacrifice, qualifications, and efforts. As I recall, she did add that she meant "nothing personal" and that we should "do our best to work together" and "try to do great things for the denomination."

Athaliah represented a feeling that was shared by many in the UMC. United Methodism was a powerful tradition that should be promoted and celebrated, perhaps with new external designs, ribbons, and balloons, but not tampered with at the core. Though I preached United Methodism, she knew I attended a non–United Methodist Church, and I believe she was afraid of two things: one, that my efforts would succeed and people would become attracted to non–United Methodist ways and eventually seek other churches; and two, that my efforts would succeed and that the United Methodist Church would adopt non–United Methodist ways.

Soon after I began to receive complaints from people out in the field. Youth leaders and young people expressed a fear about the direction the Conference was taking by hiring her. I kept asking for them to give her time to get acclimated. But from my standpoint, their concerns weren't unjustified. In at least one of our meetings, Athaliah theorized why my programs were flourishing while she was having trouble putting together programs of her own. I recall her offering three reasons. First, she did not have access to the budgets I had earlier gained access to. Second, the fact that she is a woman prevented her from having real power in a world of men (perhaps, but the bishop and a large number of Conference leaders were women). And third, she expressed her belief that I was better accepted in the Conference than her because "being attractive has a lot to do with how people perceive leadership." As I recall, she added, "And you are very attractive, so naturally people see that and they see you as a better leader." At this point I was just flat-out insulted.

I wanted to storm out of her office and never come back. But I had my hands tied and could do nothing but hold my tongue and swallow my pride.

Finally, after two years of pulling back and forth, she asked me to come to her office and said that, due to the dire economic crisis, they had decided to eliminate my position. True or not, I knew this would allow her to take over all my budgets and programs, which I had earlier heard she was taking credit for in meetings when I was not present.

On my last day, holding tears back, I told her that I was very grateful for the opportunity and that, in addition to the valuable job experience, I had gained a great network of friends. I also told her that I had made myself available at any time to leaders in the Conference if they ever needed a speaker, a seminar presenter, or an adviser for any of the programs that I had developed, any of the ones that were in process, or any new ones that they might develop in the future. Her response left me cold to the bone. "I will make sure that does not happen!" I remember her saying, before adding, "Those roles are reserved for people who are part of the church. And you are not a United Methodist, so you are not part of the church."

I wasn't sure how much deeper she could cut.

But I also realized her views were part and parcel of Big Religion bureaucracy. The identity of the entire structure and all within it stands on this one axis, and protecting that axis and annihilating the enemy is a way to validate the entire enterprise's existence. For that, I felt more pity than anger toward her. At least now I would be free.

Since I left the office that day, I haven't looked back. I do not feel hatred toward her or the UMC for their decisions. But I do feel a sense of sadness for witnessing goodwill trumped by ideology. When a new bishop came along who was described as more energized and more open to change, several leaders were faded out, including Athaliah. At the time I got calls from people who said I should apply to be her replacement, but I was in a different place theologically and professionally by then. Still, I kept many of my dear friendships with those faithful servants I am honored to have known. I am proud of the many young souls I saw grow into leaders of character. And I am proud of developing programs that to this day continue to open doors to the potential of human beings who dare to dream.

But this is a call to anyone who is part of a denomination, society, or institution who puts their group's identity before that of natural human development: no matter how proud, how great, or how ancient your history is, it should never serve as a boundary to the natural evolution of human potential. We are masters of our own destiny. We are explorers of the deepest mysteries. And we are bound by nothing other than our own will.

14

THE VALLEY OF THE SHADOW OF DEATH

"Death's got an Invisibility Cloak?" Harry interrupted again.
"So he can sneak up on people," said Ron. "Sometimes he gets bored of
running at them, flapping his arms and shrieking. . ."
—J. K. Rowling, *Harry Potter and the Deathly Hallows*

The Phone Call

The summer of 2009 had been the best of my life! And the upcoming summer of 2010 was promising to be my second best. I had moved past the shadows of boulders, hospitals, and fears. I had backpacked in Europe, run with the bulls in Pamplona, swum with sharks, hiked a volcano, skydived off a plane, and bungee jumped off a bridge. In addition, working for the UMC had allowed me to grow my leadership skills and confidence. I had free reign to start new programs, bring people together, empower youth, and apply transformational change in the paradises of Southern California and Hawaii. Life was good. Booya!

It was a typical mid-March day. A Tuesday. About 2:30 p.m.

I had gone to the gym, pumped some iron, showered, had lunch, and returned to the Cal-Pac Conference Center to continue working at a hundred miles per hour advancing the work of Christ.

My cellphone rings. Seeing "Mom" on the caller ID brought an instinctual smile to my face. But I was surprised. She knows I have a crazy schedule, and though we usually talk once a week, and certainly no later than every other week, we usually talk in the evenings or on the weekends when I'm not at work. It must be something special.

"Hi mom. How's it going?" I asked. "Hi. How are you? Are you at work?" She asked. "I am. What's going on?" I said. "Nothing," she answered. "It's just that I just got back from the doctor's office. And you're not going to believe whom I saw there." She had taken my little sister for a consultation. "Who did you see?" I followed. In the most nonchalant way, and with a certain degree of excitement, she answered, "Your grandmother."

Now, her mom lived in Charay, does not have a passport, and does not travel anymore due to Alzheimer's. I knew there could only be one other possible option. But it couldn't be. She never talks about that, much less brings it up with excitement. *"¿Quién?"* I asked as if static had prevented clarity. She quickly followed, *"La mamá de tu papá."* My father's mother.

Dead silence.

They say mothers always know. I know mine did. She had never brought this up before. And now, I couldn't say a word. But it wasn't just that I couldn't say anything. Something had shaken me. I can't tell you what it was. There was a sharp hum in my ear, soundless and thick. Maybe I gasped. But she knew. I was dizzy and couldn't continue, so she asked, "Are you okay?"

I honestly couldn't tell you.

According to her, she went to the doctor and my grandmother was there for a consultation. My grandmother recognized my mother as one of my father's friends from way back when, "Aren't you . . . ?" She was living in El Centro now. Her son, my uncle, hadn't shown up to pick her up yet so my mom offered to give her a ride home. I sat down and listened, wondering where this would go. And then my mom said the phrase that started it all, "So maybe one of these days, when you are here visiting, we could drive by her house, and she might be outside watering her plants, and you might be able to see her and she won't be able to see you."

Scythe.

I felt like I was living a real-life game of Jenga and the most inconspicuous little piece had just been pulled out. Then one after the other, in very slow motion, all the pieces begin to tumble down, smashing into the ground with force.

My mother, so innocently, had just told me that maybe I could see my grandmother, but she couldn't see me. My own grandmother didn't know I exist. Furthermore, I felt I was something to be ashamed of for existing. A dirty little secret.

She knew I couldn't continue the conversation, but she didn't know why. She said we'd talk later. "Okay," I agreed. I hung up the phone, gently set it down, and looked way, way, way out there into oblivion. For how long? I don't know. Damage assessment hadn't been done. The pieces were still tumbling down. Dust hadn't settled yet. But I knew something had shattered.

I went home that day and sank deep in my couch. Was I going to get over this after dinner? No, because come Friday and I was still haunted by the repercussions of that conversation. I didn't know what bothered me though, and why. "I mean, I'm 33 now," I told myself. "I'm a grown man." I had talked about these issues many times—it was part of my testimony. I had counseled young men who had grown up fatherless. Why was this still affecting me?

A couple of weeks went by and I continued to struggle to sleep, eat, and concentrate. The moon would stare at me through the window as I lay restless. Energy would be sucked out of me daily, for no apparent reason. Going to the gym became a burden. The mere thought of going out with friends taxed me. I relied on drive-thru for meals because I couldn't garner the will to mix ingredients. I wanted to cry all the time, but I didn't know why. I would crawl into a ball and couldn't tell that hours had gone by.

"What is happening to me?" I kept repeating.

Hurts, Hang-ups, and Habits

April. It had been a month since that phone call and I was becoming even more fearful that I was losing control over my own life, for no apparent reason.

The church I was then attending, Christ's Church of the Valley in San Dimas, California, gave a special presentation about a program it held on Monday evenings, "Celebrate Recovery." The program was based on a series of booklets by Rick Warren, author of the ever-so-popular *Purpose Driven Life*, meant to help those who are suffering and in need of healing from the "3 Hs" of hurts, hang-ups, and habits.

But how could I attend such a program? I was a Christian leader for crying out loud. I preached to thousands. I counseled people on this stuff. I led a denomination. I served as a missionary around the world. I mentored kids around the country. I had seen and performed miracles of healing, hadn't I? What would it say about God's absolute power if this *icon* of Christian leadership was seen bent over as if godless on a cold desert night?

But this was a big church, and I was one of the crowd, so I decided I would show up and check it out. I'd leave my Christian leadership background a secret—until necessary.

When I arrived I found a group of broken brothers and sisters who had succumbed to life's shadows, such as alcoholism, divorce, sexual abuse, codependency, domestic violence, drug addiction, and sexual addiction. We all met in the sanctuary and then organizers sent us into small groups where we'd deal with our issues together. I went with the "wild card" men's group, as we came to call it. When I joined the group, everyone's eyes fell on me. There I was in my metrosexual attire: Guess pants and shirt, bracelet and necklace, and funky hairdo. I looked ready to hit a nightclub, with no sign of being haunted by demons.

I sat around the circle, apprehensive about sharing my thoughts with a group of strangers. Most of these men were old enough to be my father.

We read the five meeting rules, along with Celebrate Recovery's 12 steps and 8 recovery principles—as we would each week week. This process would eventually seem redundant, but we understood the need for it. None of us minded repeating one part, though:

> GOD, *grant me the serenity*
> *To accept the things I cannot change,*
> *The courage to change the things I can,*
> *And the wisdom to know the difference.*

That first week, as introductions began, I looked around the circle and started to see the masks come off. Some were nervous, as I was, but seemed determined to get help. Divorce, infidelity, heroin addiction, cocaine, prison time—the list goes on, until it gets to me, "Ah . . . depression and anxiety." I'm looking at these men and I'm thinking I don't belong. I hadn't yet acted on my feelings. Their paths had led them here because of the scars of their choices. But of one thing I was sure, there wasn't a thing I could share in this group that would shock, surprise, or scare anyone in it. They'd seen it all, and lived it all.

So I shared.

"I once was strong. And I am now broken. It feels like Death, though dreaded, might be an ally who'd do me a favor if it'd just let me go now instead of postponing what seems sometimes inevitable. I don't know how long I can stand living under a cloud, in a valley of ghosts. I have this fear that I may soon become one of its shadows."

It did feel good to get those words off my chest.

After a few weeks of introductions and filtering out those who'd stay and those who wouldn't, we ordered our first Celebrate Recovery book (there'd be four of them, each with several lessons inside). We'd read a lesson during the week and answer the questions in the most brutally honest way possible, not holding anything back. Another Monday would come, another journal would be read. But I still couldn't find a lead into what I was really falling apart for. Not until question five in lesson three: *"How are your feelings for your heavenly Father and your earthly father alike? How do they differ?"*

Bingo.

This whole thing started with my mother's call on that Tuesday afternoon. With her revelation, she was able to challenge the core of my entire existence. If my life had no significance or reason at its origins, then no matter what I would accomplish in my life, no matter how lofty my achievements, I would find no solid ground on which I'd build my life back up.

"This Is Your Son"

May. It'd been two months and I was nowhere near the edge of the woods, but I had a lead on what direction to take next. And that path led back to my mother. I grabbed the phone and gave her a call. My birthday was coming up and I told her that I'd be coming over to celebrate with her and my siblings. She was surprised. It had been many years since I had spent a birthday with them. My birthday usually landed around Memorial Day, when I'd take advantage of the three-day weekend to go on a road trip with friends.

We had a low-key celebration. We had dinner and cake for me and my brother (who was born twelve years and two days after me). After we were done, I asked mom if she wanted to go for a walk. I told her that I'd been thinking about a few things of late (I did not bring up my depression), and I told her that I'd like to get in touch with my father to ask him a few things. She was surprised and asked why. "I just want to ask him a few things," I repeated. I then asked her if she would please help me find a way to get ahold of him. I figured maybe she'd know some old friends who knew someone who might know his current whereabouts. She then says, "Well, as it happens, when I saw your grandmother at the doctor's office, she gave me his contact information in case I wanted to reach him. I have it back in my purse."

I was both pleasantly surprised, and a tat scared. I was expecting this to take a couple of weeks, maybe months. And now his information was right in front of me. "What will I say to him?"

I returned home with my tail between my legs. Every day I'd take that piece of paper out, stare at it, and put it back down. Monday. Tuesday. Wednesday. Almost on Thursday. I'd punch in a few numbers—8–0–5–9— then put the phone down. What could I say? How would I say it? What if he doesn't answer? Worst of all, what if he answers the phone? What if he rejects me and tells me right there and then that he wished I had never been born. What would I do then? I played the movie all the way to the end and I knew it would not end well. I was already experiencing severe depression and I knew where it would end. With the credits rolling up the screen.

Saturday. I'm at home. I walk around the duplex with the piece of paper in one hand and the phone in the other. I have to do this. I'm gonna do it one day or another, right? The numbers are all in. Do I hit send? I haven't been able to so far. Oh God, I'm scared.

SEND.

"*Hola. Buenas tardes,*" a female voice picks up the phone. Do I hang up? Do I . . . ? Time is going by and I'm just standing there speechless. Why didn't I think this through? I thought he'd answer. "*Hola. Disculpe. ¿Se encuentra . . . ?*" I said. "Junior or Senior?" She asks. "Senior?" I guessed. He comes to the phone. "Sorry. Excuse me, are you . . . ?" "Yes," he replied. "*Yo soy Fernando Alcántar,*" I continued. He repeated my name as if trying to recollect something. Unsuccessful, he asked for more information. I added, "Fernando Alcántar. Son of Teresa Garcia." He immediately reacted, "Ooooooh, I lost track of you guys a long time ago."

We shared some quick updates as to our whereabouts. He said he was married and had four other sons living in Northern California. He worked in the agriculture industry and served as a deacon in the Assemblies of God Church—a Pentecostal denomination.

After a short conversation he offered to have a sit down with me next time he drove down to Imperial County to see his family. He said perhaps in the next three months.

The following Saturday he gave me a call. He said he was driving back from El Centro up the 210 freeway and asked if I wanted to grab a bite to eat. I had a scheduled meeting with the UMC. I immediately called one of my coordinators, explained in thirty seconds that I had an opportunity to meet my long-lost father, excused myself, and then headed out to meet him.

Right there in Monrovia at Acapulco restaurant, my life changed.

He got out of his truck and came to meet me. His wife stayed behind. We both wondered whether we would have any physical similarities. I am 6'4" and slim. He is shorter and thicker than me and carries himself with a humbler walk. I tried to spot any mannerisms or features similar to mine—anything that would cry out "this is my lineage."

At the table, when I had the balls to look up, I saw his face, his balding hair, and my past in his eyes. I realized that I craved not only knowing about my past, but also having a future, which scared me shitless. How do I answer his question, "How has it affected you to grow up without a father?"

A lava of emotion swelled up in my throat. I didn't know whether to shout, curse, or hit him across the face. Summoning my courage, I looked up and said, "Growing up without a father has been the hardest, most difficult thing I have ever experienced—directly or indirectly. Because you weren't around I didn't have someone to teach me how to be a man and who would've prevented people from taking advantage of me. Because you weren't around, mom had to always work to provide for me, and married a guy who tormented me and my sister. Because you weren't around I lived in a little town experiencing need and isolation. Because you weren't around I have suffered from low self-esteem, low self-worth, confusion, anger, and depression, and I have had to fight the biggest battles with the fewest rewards. Because you weren't around I have struggled to understand what love means to its fullest, even when it comes to the love of God."

I wanted to believe him when he said that we could start over again. I wanted to believe him when he said that we couldn't bring back the past, but that we could create a new future. I couldn't believe it when, come June, for the first time, I had someone to call to wish a happy Father's Day. And I couldn't believe it when he called again so that I could also have lunch with his wife. And I couldn't believe it when he said the reason he wanted to meet again was to ask me what I wanted to get out of meeting him, and if we could take a DNA test. And I couldn't believe it that the day we took the test, which proved that I was his son, was the last day I ever saw him.

Journal Entry: Saturday, March 19, 2011
Two days before Hawai'i and I want to end this. I want there to be a God just so I have someone to hate! Having an enemy like that would make sense why I am not happy. Why my desires are frapped and why my will is irrelevant?

When I die they'll remember me and they'll be shocked. They'll say I didn't come to God. They have to understand it was God acting as inexistent who did this. It is his fault. I am afraid of him, he has no love for anyone other than himself and his will. I have no life to speak of but the one I know of here on earth. Not all of us are good, but it exists. I tried to make a difference.

I'm broken. I'm done.

I Could Have Jumped
I was staying in a room on the seventh floor of a Waikiki hotel. I'd be speaking

at an event I had created for the UMC in the Hawaii District. I saw the beach from my balcony. I heard the loud sounds of the festivities a few blocks away. I saw the evening saying farewell to the sun on the horizon. I held on to the rail and squeezed it with both hands. Looking down seemed so tempting. So close. If I leaned over just a bit more, I would fall into eternal peace and end my living hell. I lean over. Anything that would alleviate this pain would certainly be worth it. I am not just having a bad season. I am not just under a cloud. I am anxious about everything without a reason. I am tired of sleepless nights. I am tired of feeling like my heart is skipping beats and about to explode. I am tired of trembling and wishing breath would stop fueling this internal fire of sadness, fear, and desperation. Nothing seems as sweet as would my impact against the ground below—right there on that clear spot. I would finally stop feeling.

Reluctantly and with little hope, I called my friend Tammy in California. Holding the rail with one hand and the phone in the other I asked, "Do you have time to talk?" She knew me well and immediately understood what was going on. Me eyes were set on the space below me—my insides trembling. She is a certified therapist and knew exactly what to do. With calm and delicate tenderness, she spent the next two hours getting me distracted, as we talked about trivial and random issues until the edge started to wear off.

I could have jumped.

I had been secretly battling depression and anxiety for a year now, with no end in sight. I was attending weekly meetings with a therapist, and monthly meetings with a psychiatrist for medication. I had gone through so many kinds of drugs—Zoloft, Lexapro, Abilify, Celexa, Wellbutrin, Anafranil, Diazepam, Lorazepam, Trazodone, Xanax—I was a walking pharmacy. But the best they could ever do was to keep trying something new. It seemed like I was always waiting two to four weeks for the new meds to kick in. And sometimes the medication would have the opposite of the intended effect and have me almost jump off a Hawaiian balcony. "But how do I survive the wait?" I kept asking my doctor. "It is a whole month we are talking about here." The answer was always a decrepit, "Let's hope for the best. Come back in four weeks and let's see how you're doing."

I stopped going to the gym and going out with friends. Retreats and camps were torture, even in Hawaii. It became almost impossible for me to hide what was happening inside of me. I would be hit with an intense fear that I was about to die—as if every vein in my body had been punctured— and I would make a quick exit. My heart pounded while I shook, lying on the ground, sweating, gasping for air. I bore witness to the agonizing reactions my body had, the twitches and palpitations, with absolutely no power to stop them. It always felt like a heart attack. All I could think of, all I desired, was to find a way to have it stop. And I would experience these panic attacks four or five times a day!

The best I could do to calm down and be able to sleep each night was to drink enough to get a buzz and numb myself. I started to spend a lot of money so I could experience the amazing relief of intoxication. The flames would slowly subdue as I reclined on my couch and thanked the heavens for the existence of this sweet scorpion's nectar we know as alcohol.

I understand why so many stars like Kurt Cobain, Michael Jackson, Whitney Houston, and Robin Williams have fallen under the spell of temporary numbness—because any break from involuntary insanity seems like a gift from God. Until, of course, eternal silence trumps one's strength.

Mayday

I slowly saw my power and my confidence erode with the sands of time. It became exhausting to put up a strong façade for others—I just didn't have it in me. I started avoiding crowds. They made me more anxious.

Afraid that I might lose it in public, I began to open up to people about the storms that I faced within. I realized I didn't have that many friends. Most people I knew had this idea of Fernando up on a pedestal—the one who had everything figured out and whose faith knew no limit. I felt I couldn't confide in them that I was descending from that pedestal with a mayday and a trail of smoke behind me.

But that fear of disclosure took a back seat when I plunged into a steep descent.

Maybe it was the new medication. Maybe I was just a bit antsier than usual. But right in my living room my soul began to detach from my body, leaving my muscles weak and tingling. I raised my arms and wondered if they would split in half. I became detached from my surroundings and stood in a dream, not knowing what was real and what wasn't. My heart pounded violently, hurting my chest, building pressure inside my brain. I lost control over my own body and chased after my own breath. No gasp, meditation, nor prayer alleviated what was certain to be my doom.

In desperation, I called my psychiatrist and told him what was happening—that I didn't think I'd make it long. He asked me to wait an hour and see if the symptoms subsided. If not, I should check myself into the hospital and tell them what I am thinking of doing. But wait an hour?! Did he not understand what I just said?

I wobbled my way to the bathroom, splashed water on my face, and begged sanity to return to me. I went back to the living room and, though I crash-landed on my couch, I believed I was still falling. The pressure inside kept accumulating and I knew that I had to find a way to release it or my body would explode—with blood splattering all over my furniture.

I walked to the kitchen and looked around for options. I grabbed my chef's knife and played with it. It didn't seem like a crazy idea. No. Madness would be to go on feeling like this. How many more of these attacks would I have to endure? "I just need this to end, right now!" I thought.

It felt so good to have that cold metal on my wrist, but bleeding out from there wouldn't be fast enough. How about my throat, or stomach? Let's not forget my arms and legs. The possibilities seemed endless and sweet. This could all end soon. I wouldn't feel pain anymore.

I thought of my family. I knew they'd be shocked at first, certainly sad. Eventually their pain would subside and they'd move on. People die all the time. But who would notify them? Who would manage the funeral and burial arrangements? I'd be a burden for a while, but it would go away too. I just needed to end this right now. Maybe they would eventually understand.

But maybe I could hold on this one last time. I knew the pain wasn't going away, but maybe I could hold on a little longer.

I grabbed the phone and asked a friend if he would come over. I didn't want to chat. I had reached the point of no return. I needed a ride to the hospital. He was having dinner and said he could be there in forty minutes. I didn't have that much time. I put the knife down and headed for the car. I would drive myself—with any luck I'd crash and finish this all up. I had a crazy rush the whole way. Phantoms flew in circles around my car.

I somehow made it to a Pasadena hospital emergency room. When I reached the front desk, I couldn't believe the words that came out of my mouth: "My psychiatrist asked me to come and check myself in because I want to kill myself."

The woman at the front desk asked me to sit down for a bit. I did as told. I then asked how long this would take. She said it'll take a few minutes. It took a bit longer. This was doing nothing for me. If my body was going to explode either in this waiting area or in my living room, I would rather it be the latter. I told her I was going to take off to get some fresh air. She told me to wait two minutes—that she'd try to have someone hurry up.

I was put on what they call a 5150 (fifty-one–fifty)—an involuntary psychiatric hold. Hospital personnel placed me on a wheelchair and led me to a room upstairs. I thought my head would explode after all. The world spun in circles as they pushed me down the corridor. The phantoms from the car had followed me inside. They placed me in a white room with padded walls and a single bed. They asked me to take my clothes off and gave me a white gown to wear. When they opened the door, I saw myself on a monitor. I looked up and saw the camera in the corner of the ceiling. I was to stay here until the psychiatrist could see me.

A couple of hours go by.

Eventually they transferred me to the psychiatric ward, which was divided into two main sections—one with the moderate cases, and one with the severe cases. I was placed in the latter until the psychiatrist could approve my transfer to the former. But since they took hours to process me, by the time I was ready to be transferred, the psychiatrist had left for the day.

Being in that place was almost as traumatic as what brought me there. Many patients were heavily sedated and lived permanently in a world that wasn't ours. The awake ones made noises, had tantrums, and released fluids on their clothing.

I spent that first night sharing a room with a guy who never moved but who had a daunting look on his face. I lay there restless, cold, and terrified about what my life had come down to.

Feeling better the next morning, I decided I would not let this place bring me down even more.

As I had breakfast out of plastic cups, I remembered the movie *Patch Adams*, in which Robin Williams plays a real-life doctor who helped mental-health patients heal through the power of laughter. I befriended the patients, even the ones who wouldn't respond. I tried to lead them in song and wore kitchen and hospital equipment as costumes to make them laugh. The environment had changed so dramatically in one morning that the nurses approached me to ask, "Are you sure you belong here?"

When the doctor finally showed up, he spoke with the nurses, read my files, and talked to my psychiatrist. He believed that I was having a negative reaction to my new medication. Though a 5150 requires a seventy-two-hour hold, he said he'd consider releasing me early with appropriate instructions for follow-up. Part of me wanted to stay in a safe place while I tried a new medication. I honestly felt I wasn't yet out of the woods. But the other part of me was really, really scared by what I had already seen.

When I got home, I asked several of my friends to come spend a night or two with me. This lasted for two weeks. When someone was with me, the pressure wasn't as abundant. I felt I had a bridge, a way out, and it allowed me to control my emotions in a better way. When a panic attack came, they would hold my hand, embrace me, and make sure we'd run its course together.

I knew I had survived a crash and burn, and I sure didn't want to go through another one ever again.

The phantoms of depression and anxiety are two deadly bastards that will hold on to your life, clinch on you with their teeth, and suck every ounce of sanity out of you like a leech on steroids that is possessed by the devil. So I prayed. I prayed so hard. "Please Jesus, I have lost myself. You said you'd be by my side. You said you'd be my healer. Have you not noticed that I have already gone off the edge, and then some? Where the hell are you?! Where?"

15

FRIENDS NO MORE

"A man that has friends must show himself friendly;
and there is a friend that sticks closer than a brother."
—Proverbs 18:24

The Honeymoon

When I heard the GOOD NEWS and was ANOINTED in those Foursquare conferences from 1996 to 2000, the speakers and leaders would approach me and congratulate me for having a "devout heart for The Lord." I didn't understand why that was something they should congratulate me for. "Isn't this the way everybody should behave?" I thought.

It didn't matter whether I sat in the front row (my usual spot), toward the back, or somewhere in the middle, I would raise my hands up in the air and softly caress His face, His spirit. I would sway my head from side to side, melting deeper and deeper into His presence. My mind would travel to the days when I hugged my boombox in my pitch-black room and begged my story to end. I thought of the tragedies I might have experienced if I had gone on living without Him. And I thought of the promises I had that would soon be fulfilled because He is "faithful and just." I couldn't help it. Tears would run down my face, one after the other, and, as long as the music allowed me, I would stay in those moments, both trembling and laughing, desiring nothing more than to hear His sweet, sweet voice—the voice of Jesus, my best friend.

I was captivated by this love—by His love. Everything seemed perfect. I assumed it was all real.

Denial

When I made my EXODUS into the PROMISED LAND in 2000, I faced the liberal behavior of some of my colleagues, the financial pressure of making it through the week, and the challenge of doing homework at two in the morning, because that was the only time I had free. In addition, my ministries were challenged by obstacles, my relationships seemed in decay, my family was at odds with one another, and my health was attacked by stress and exhaustion. At the same time, the world tempted me with vain promises of lust and greed. Through it all, however, He was always there for me in my secret place. I would close the doors, turn on the music, get on my knees or sometimes lie flat on the ground, raise my hands to the sky, and sing Him a prayer. The answer would not come immediately, but I always felt refreshed after a good cry in His arms.

But there were times that I needed more than a good cry. And I was told that God always answered. His answer sometimes was "yes," sometimes "no," and sometimes "wait." To be honest, I could never tell the difference. I just figured time would tell which one it was. But I so desperately wished to know so I could figure out what to do next. Frustration grew as I knelt powerless, waiting for the next sign.

When I preached with MORE THAN WORDS until 2008 to thousands of young people, to congregations, to politicians, to businessmen, and to the media, I believed I had to "fake it till I make it." I kept my frustration secret and kept preaching that prayer was the only way to achieve miracles that would leave us speechless and thankful.

I was in *denial*. I refused to accept my doubts, ignored the bad parts of my faith, and focused only on the good parts.

Anger

When I traveled TO THE ENDS OF THE EARTH during my APU years, I withstood the sour realities of divine absence. I couldn't understand how a loving God could allow the butchering of millions of innocent people in His name. People He said He loved. So I consumed the intoxicating nectars of passion, and the narcotic fumes of purpose, so I could retreat into happy land and ignore the obvious discrepancy between His words and His actions.

When there was a CRACK ON THE WINDSHIELD, I duct-taped my questions and shouted in secret so I wouldn't inconvenience the fragile state of those who challenged God's protection and omnipotence. I wanted to blame God. But since I couldn't, I blamed myself, I blamed you, I blamed all of us for the lack of God in the world.

I was *angry*. I didn't understand why, if something went well, it was always God, never us; but if something went bad, it was always us, never God.

Bargaining

WHEN DEATH PAID A VISIT in 2006, I protected my faith by developing a personal theory of God's vision and personality that would preserve my ideals of my good and faithful divine friend. I brokered a deal with myself that allowed me to recognize the irrationality of the God idea and call it like it was, but at the same time still allow me to stay in the club—Jehovah bad, but Jesus good.

When I was CHURCHING THE WORLD from 2008 to 2011, I ignored the cultural stronghold religion had on its minions and tried to focus on a bigger picture of reform and possibility. On one hand I saw the inevitable corruption of the religious system. On the other I saw the potential that religion could have when used for good—religion bad, but service good.

I was *bargaining*. I convinced myself that I could serve two masters and live with both Faith and Reason.

Depression

When I walked through THE VALLEY OF THE SHADOW OF DEATH from 2010 to 2011, I begged Him fervently to aid me in the midst of the terrifying state of losing myself—my prayers always landing on deaf ears.

Finding my biological father finally helped me understand something about my heavenly father. He had never abandoned me. He had just never been there. He had always been the sweet idea I treasured with hopes of a happy ending. There have been real people who have stepped into that fatherly role from time to time, which helped the idea of a heavenly one stay alive.

But the real guy, His story, is just something found in old documents.

I became *depressed*. I had finally crashed. And I cried. A lot. I didn't have it in me to fight this reality any longer. Once I lost my identity, I had no idea who I was, or whom I would be.

Acceptance

Cody is a kid I used to mentor, also one of the kids who chased after the helicopter out in the open field when I fell off that cliff. He was raised in a Christian household, had endured more than people endure in two lifetimes, and had maintained a persistence with regard to faith. "Why are you leaving the faith?" I asked him at the gym one day. His answer left me frozen.

I had a déjà vu moment. An eerie sensation. Something that connected this conversation with one I had with another seventeen-year-old fifteen years earlier. Instead of a bandana around his head there was a stylish hairdo. Instead of a loose shirt and baggy pants there was a tank top and gym shorts. Instead of freckles on his face there was acne. Instead of a scrawny build there was a football jock. And instead of Spring Break '96 it was the summer of 2011. But still, the daybreak and twilight of my faith seemed to be connected by a pair of very gentle eyes.

Cody was leading the next workout, but my hands were up in the air, my eyes were anxious, and my stand was uneasy. But I wasn't done. I had a million more questions to ask him, and he could tell. He put his hands in front of me as a sign of explanation, glanced away for a moment, and looked back at me with that tender look of his. He then uttered these words—words that to this day remain tattooed in my memory, *"It's kinda like when you have a relationship with a friend. You can only spend so much time investing in that relationship until you ask yourself, 'When is he going to invest in it too?'"* He blinked once, patted me on the shoulder, and headed to workout.

That's when it hit me. Damn it. The reason why my anxiety kept rising instead of decreasing is because I kept waiting for this guy, someone I'd read lots about, heard lots about, preached lots about, and loved lots about . . . even though I had never heard directly from him.

My favorite verse in the Bible has always been Proverbs 18:24, *"A man that has friends must show himself friendly; and there is a friend that sticks closer than a brother."* I had done my part. If you were my friend, you would have been my friend. Not through sermons. Not through songs. Not through poems. Not "indirectly." If you were my friend, you would have been my friend—plain and simple. I will no longer wait for an idea, I decided. I will rely on me. I will rely on people who are here with me, who shake my hand, embrace me, support me, give me a ride, put food in my mouth, scold me, and look me in the eye. I will no longer feed a fantasy. Just as no amount of belief make Santa Claus or the Tooth Fairy real, I knew that believing just a little bit longer would not give me everlasting life.

I finally *accepted*. I have been your faithful friend. And you have been in stories, sermons, and hopes, but not in real life. It is way overdue. Jesus, my dear fantasy, we are friends no more.

Journal Entry: Posted on Facebook, November 20, 2009
The Friend I Miss
Like an old friend I used to have, I miss him. He was there when I was wide-eyed and knew not the world. When my smiles were instinct and

my fear was unfounded. He was there. Like an old friend, we stepped into the caves of life and found adventure and not regret. We found awe and feared not love. I miss him.

I sit alone on my couch and I miss my shadow. I have no questions of what could be, because it happened. The blowing off of a candle. Hostage of reason. Stricken by fate. And I saw it happen. Thirty feet up in the air as distance got shorter. Tenderness fell to the ground and came up the Other. I looked under the rocks. I've searched up on the clouds. I miss him.

The picture of his bloody tears won't leave me. Arm up in the air as he asks for help. Frozen by my own fear. Paralyzed by my inadequacy. I knew not that World would have its way, that Complacency would simply stare, that Indifference would pray and walk away.

And sometimes while I sleep I hear the chant. A whisper I wish was louder of a lament I wish was softer. Does it blame me? I don't know. But it seeks an answer. We were friends and I don't know if we are no more. But I miss him.

Like an old friend I think of him and wonder how my life would've been different if he stuck around. Would I have dressed in black? Would I have avoided the criticism of the Unfallen? I throw the ball and expect a smile. I realize I have a grin and eyes are swollen. I wonder if the streets I've walked would have more hops and fewer steps back. I wonder if the clothes I've worn would have more stars and far less skulls. I wonder if I'd have a hope in my dream and no ink on my skin.

But the Unfallen know not of that historic height. They wonder why a skull on black. They see the dark that walks behind and not the light that was inside. Fallen truths bring a bitter taste to virgin ears. I can see them squint. I can see them shrug. They don't know whom I have lost, the shadow that won't come back, the baby smile that was stepped on. I know that warmth is now cold. I know that fear is now numb. I know his strength is now my void. And if I cry it matters not. They only know that I have blinked. And until now it won't make sense. My story's arms no longer embrace. I was promised flowers and I got thorns. I know now why I blankly gaze, shiver doubt and breathe out glaze, I've lost a friend.

Now I know I miss you, Innocence.

In Our Hands

Ricky calls me out of nowhere and invites me to go on a five-day cruise that leaves out of Long Beach with stops in Santa Catalina Island and Ensenada, Mexico. Though cheap considering the full package, I was not completely afloat financially and I wasn't sure how much longer I'd have my job with the United Methodists due to my dimming faith and issues with an administrator. But maybe because I was tired of battling depression, maybe because I had a memory of the crazy adventurer I used to be, or maybe because I was curious whether I could be friends with this guy, I accepted.

Ricky had recently separated from his wife, was sharing the raising of their two beautiful boys, and was wondering what he could do with his new-found freedom. He had been a good Christian boy who was now allowing himself to experiment with the pleasures the world had to offer. He had gotten comfortable with binge drinking, serial fornication, and a curiosity for discovering the adventures he never knew existed.

Danny, a dark-humored and short-fused Americanized Arab guy with a dry temperament would join us on the trip. He seemed to try hard to make people feel like he didn't care. "This guy is an asshole" I thought. For the life of me I couldn't figure out why he and Ricky were friends. But then again, I wasn't completely sure why we were.

Together we jumped off cliffs, went on night hikes, and got drunk off our senses whenever we had a chance. It was a whiplash effect from the reserved and abstinent life we used to live, fueled by the depression of recent separations, now targeted with intoxicating self-gratification. It was also an extension of a numbing silence we'd eventually break to let our personal stories of shadows come forward. It was smiles and frowns coexisting in peace.

When the day came in mid-September 2011, Danny's parents gave us a ride to the port. I listened to their conversation but couldn't make much of it. I was focusing too hard on controlling my anxiety. I feared an attack and wondered if, having nowhere else to go while on a ship, I'd be tempted to simply jump off. I inconspicuously pulled out my pills for depression and anxiety from the small pocket in my jeans, downed them with leftover Mountain Dew, and smiled as if nothing was up.

Trying to distract them and myself from what I was feeling, I came up with a silly idea. "Hey guys, what if for these five days we pretend we are someone else? We could pretend we are foreigners. I could pretend I'm from Spain since I speak Spanish, but it'd be fun to pretend I'm from France. I know some French and I've been to France. There is a French character on my favorite show, *The West Wing*, who is an asshole I could base it on." Both Ricky and Danny seemed caught off guard by the idea but entertained the possibility. They went back and forth, imitating the accents of Australia, Scotland, India, and Iraq, but otherwise didn't think much of it. I was a bit disappointed.

Once we boarded the ship, the Xanax took effect and I felt more sedated than anxious, causing me to worry I'd be a drag. During the first dinner on the cruise we met a group of four girls who would become our dining mates for the duration of the trip. Ricky and Danny immediately jumped into conversation with them, hoping at some point to crawl into their pants. I leaned my head on my fist, tucked away in the corner, and wondered how I could fake an excuse to get off this damn boat.

Toward the end of the meal they began to talk about current events. I hadn't said much more than hello up to this point, but I started to listen in. One of the girls mentioned how tough the economy had been recently. I was stuck on the ship for five days whether I liked it or not—so I jumped in the conversation and said, "Oh yeah! I saw on TV that it's been pretty bad."

If you lived anywhere in America and were at least somewhat conscious, you knew about the economic recession and the jobless crisis that started in late 2007. Startled by my sudden contribution, the girl took a pause, turned to me and asked, "Yeah. Um, where are you from?" I thought, "Oh my, this could be my chance. Should I? Who cares? It'd be something stupid that we'd get over." I pulled memories from my French class at APU, placed my tongue deep in my mouth so I could exaggerate my "Rs," and spoke in the best French accent I could without prior practice, *"Ah, je suis from France."* All four girls—and Ricky and Danny—perched on their seats a bit higher and stared at me. "Really?!"

What the hell. Sure, *"C'est vrai."*

I was a French TV producer named Jean Paul Rivière. I had met Ricky and Danny a few months back during a visit to Los Angeles and they invited me to join them on this cruise.

Though I had been totally unengaged in the conversation, my new nationality gave me an allure the girls couldn't get enough of. I thought, "Mmhh, I wonder if this could work for the rest of the cruise." I knew it was Michael Jackson night in the ship's nightclub. The Jean Paul extravaganza was about to be unleashed.

Before heading out of our room, we loaded up on vodka that we had smuggled in opaque bottles of mouthwash. When we walked into the club, I heard the accentuated bass beats of "Billie Jean" and thought, "This is my jam." I walked straight onto the dance floor, took my shoes off, threw them at Ricky, spun in place, and began my choreography. The crowd emptied the dance floor and bore witness to this 6'5" moonwalking Mexican MJ.

"Smooth Criminal" followed. Mercy.

The three of us were inseparable during the day, but come night, Ricky was a whore on the hunt, Danny was upping the ante at the poker tables, and I was leaving blood on the dance floor. The rest of the trip was a frenzy of group pictures; endless drunken celebrations with strangers; flirty, French-accented whispers in girls' ears; and the loud cheering of hundreds while I danced on the cruise's auditorium to the roar of, "Jean Paul! Jean Paul! Jean Paul!"

Everything had been fun and games until our stop at Santa Catalina Island.

Ricky and I left Danny sleeping at the beach and headed to the nearby hill for a quick round of bouldering. With the ocean at our backs, we looked up the 300-plus-foot cliff and questioned the idea. I wasn't sure this was the safest way to introduce Ricky to the sport. But he insisted, confident in his superpowers, saying it'd be a fun ride.

The first part of the climb was fairly easy. The inclination wasn't abrupt but rather increased gradually. He stayed about four feet below me and about ten feet to my left. The ground was solid, and we had plenty of rocks to hold on to. We kept talking on the way up. I kept giving advice and asked if he was doing okay.

Once we were past the halfway point, the difficulty level increased. The smiles on our faces turned into concentrated looks. I tried not to scare him, but I was beginning to wonder whether we should turn back.

Our hands began to shake slightly. Our muscles grew tense. All of a sudden we felt the earth beneath our fingertips move. The now sandy surface gave in to our weight, and we started to slowly slide down.

We turned toward each other with terror in our eyes, the ground slipping under our trembling and grasping fingers and feet.

We managed to stop our descent after a few feet and tried to climb back up, but every six inches we'd climb, we'd slide down three.

By this point, we were officially freaking out, but we tried our hardest not to lose it. I tried hard to push back flashbacks from falling off a boulder a few years earlier, but deep down I wondered, "Will this time be *it*?"

"Ricky, this just got really scary," I said. "Do you think we could go back?" Assessing the situation, we both agreed that, given our position, it would be impossible to attempt a descent without tumbling down to our deaths—so we just hung in there for a couple of minutes, holding on to the mountain, contemplating our next move.

"Ricky, I see a small boulder sticking out of the mountain to my right," I told him. "It might be solid. I could try to reach it. Do you think you could too?" In a soft and terrified tone he replied, "Honestly man, I am so scared right now that I can't even think. You should try it and see if it's possible for me to do it." I hated the idea of moving away from him. The boulder was about twelve feet to my right, but every foot felt like a mile while hanging off this cliff.

To make things worst, a deep crevice rested between me and the boulder. I looked to my left. I looked down. And I realized there was only one thing I could do. I reached over and held on to the edge of the crevice with my right hand, pushed my feet deeper into the mountain, reached over with my left hand, bent down a bit, and put all my concentration toward executing what would be a defining move. I eyed a rock and a dry root I could hold on to on the other side of the crevice, and I started a count inside my head: "One . . . Two . . . Three!"

With all my might, I pushed myself up in the air and over the crevice.

Landing on the other side, I immediately began to slide down. I pedaled with both hands and feet at full speed, trying to beat gravity at its game, desperately fighting the mountain, barely reaching the boulder. I gathered my nerves and pulled myself up. I then sat on the boulder and held on to it with both hands.

My heart raced as I sweated bullets.

"Are you okay?" Ricky asked softly. It took me a few seconds to control my breath. The boulder was only about a foot wide and a foot deep, but it seemed solid. "I don't know, man," I said. "You saw what I did. Do you think you could do it?"

In a desperate voice, he responded, "There is no way."

I looked above me at the sharp edge of the mountain, the ocean before me, and the beach where Danny slept way out in the distance. We were alone on this one.

My voice broke when I turned to Ricky and said, "Ricky, there is nothing I can do here. I'm gonna have to try to climb up the rest of the way to get help. I think I can do it from this end." He didn't even look my way when he said, "I'm too scared. I feel if I move one foot your way I am just gonna fall down. I think you should go ahead and get help. I can't move, Fern. I'm sorry. I'm so sorry."

My heart tore in half.

I looked above me. In my mind I traced what the most doable path would be. I detached my hands from the rock I was sitting on, and with my intestines begging me not to move, I threw myself onto the mountain and began to pedal my way up, sending tons of debris behind me. Without looking back and saving nothing, I went at it, swing by swing, and climbed the hundred feet or so up to the top.

Scraped and bloody, I had no time to gather myself and immediately ran toward the road. "Help! Help! Help!" I kept shouting, but no one answered. I ran back to the edge of the mountain and found Ricky pretty much at the same spot where I had left him. I turned to the beach and tried to locate Danny. "Danny! Danny! Call 9-1-1!" I shouted. The beachgoers all looked so tiny from up there. I thought I saw him stand and look our way, but I had no idea whether he heard me.

I paced back and forth looking for options. And I found none.

I looked down and saw Ricky again, I looked up to the sky, and I found myself at a crossroads—a moment of truth. So far everything had pointed me to an idea of a God whom we cry out to, but who never answers. People live and die every day with no direct correlation to their faith or prayers. Having faith and praying just makes them "feel better." Nonetheless, here I found myself in the perfect situation to throw myself on my knees, like every other desperate bastard, and hope that God would perform a miracle. But whether I prayed or not, I thought, I was about to see my friend fall to his death.

I had no intention of having a theological debate at that moment, but it found me. Do I really believe God is a loving, all-powerful being who lives above the clouds and wants to help us through our struggles? Or do I believe that the God story was created to give us hope out of the chaos we see in the world? I cannot be a hypocrite who believes that common sense, intelligence, and reason say there is no chance a Santa Claus in space exists, and then shout his name and run to his invisible arms with the hope of salvation every time it gets tough, even this tough, can I?

If I believed, then I believed. And if I didn't, then I didn't. So what's it gonna be?

I looked out into the distance, clenched my fists, and firmly made my decision, "Whatever happens, I'll at least keep my intelligence. Even if Ricky dies, there is just no possible way that this god is real!"

Though it took only a few seconds to say those words, I felt their rippling effect expand beyond that moment. The crack that began years ago had finally and irrevocably shattered my windshield—the small pieces cascading to the ground . . . and I felt peace.

But this situation was not over. My friend still literally hung on for dear life with his fingernails. I breathed out and went back to the edge of the mountain.

Ricky tried climbing up and soon went out of my sight. The route that he chose eventually changed to a steeper grade, and I saw him disappear under a dirt slope that would require him to reach over to advance further. He went quiet and I feared the worst. I kept calling his name with no reply.

"Oh my gosh!" I shouted when his head suddenly popped up above the slope, having launched himself upward. I quickly pulled my hands to my mouth as his hands fought for purchase; I did not want to break his concentration.

His stomach now lay at the edge of the slope, his hands grasping earth, his feet dangling in the air—but not for much longer. The dirt that formed the slope beneath him gave way and he began to slide down with it. "Oh, fuck! Fuck!" he shouted. I panicked and wondered whether I was about to see him fall to the bottom, his life becoming smaller and smaller until it ended in a mushroom cloud of dust.

With a primitive instinct he swung his hand toward a prickly pear cactus to his left and held on to the root for dear life, his feet swaying freely beneath him. He then did the same thing I did and began to desperately pedal his way up the mountain, launching boisterous debris behind him, until he reached a stable area about thirty feet short of the top.

He stopped to catch his breath.

From there I coached him as best as I could. He took excruciatingly small steps toward the top. He'd advance a foot, then slide—advance and slide. Once he finally got close, I told him to head toward a tree at the lip of the cliff. I figured its roots would be solidly fixed into the ground.

I wrapped my legs around the trunk of the tree and hung down with my arms stretched out to him. He was exhausted and sweating profusely. The sliding dirt was gaining ground on his upward strokes and I feared he didn't have enough strength to make it to the end. "Come on, Ricky. You can do it," I said. In a final push he threw his right arm up and grabbed my forearm. Deciding he'd have to take me down with him if he slipped, I pulled with all my might. He is several pounds heavier than me, and I thought he might pull my arm off. The veins in our arms and faces became alive and red. Our throats let out an exhaustive gasp, "Aagh!"

Almost at the top, he threw himself at me just as I gave a hard pull, and we fell embraced onto the ground, shaking vigorously and unwilling to let go.

We lay there until we gained our composure. We couldn't speak much.

Bruised, filthy, and scared, we started the walk down the mountain, this time following the road. When we reached Danny, he couldn't believe our story.

We hugged it out and went into the water to take the edge off.

The cruise adventures continued and the trip became a landmark filled with crucible moments. Being Jean Paul for a week allowed me to separate myself from Fernando. Jean Paul lived a compensating, exuberant fantasy of mischief and recklessness, while Fernando took some time off to heal. The pills I took on the way to Long Beach were the last ones I ever took for depression and anxiety, which began to wind down after the cruise. And most importantly, I stopped being held hostage to a belief that kept me in chains with false hopes. To put it plainly and simply, the moment I let go of Jesus was the moment I got control of my own life and began to heal from my depression.

It also defined my relationship with Ricky and Danny, who became my closest confidants. The three of us wore a mask to the outside world that projected strength and stability. In each other's presence, however, we were able to take our masks off to share our vulnerability, our doubts, and our humanity. The three of us created a safe place to make mistakes, to be accepted as we were, and to look after each other while we figured things out.

Back on solid ground I realized that I had been grieving faith for the last ten years in a slow, torturous process of *denial, anger, bargaining, depression,* and, finally, *acceptance* of what was always there—doubt. Though I consider myself a smart man, I had long ignored the call of Reason because I enjoyed loving Jesus so much. But loving and thinking should not be at odds. They no longer are—at least for me.

That cruise taught me I could almost lose my best friend, I could lose my sanity, and I could lose my health, but I would never consciously and intentionally lose my will to think. My life is in my hands and in the hands of those who love me, and their lives are in their hands and in mine. We are no longer in the hands of a mystical creature who only shows up through our feelings. Our lives—and our ability to love and to think freely—are in our own hands, and that is something we can really hold on to.

16

PURGATORY

*"... legitimate powers of government reach actions only, & not opinions,
I contemplate with sovereign reverence that act of the whole American
people which declared that their legislature should 'make no law respecting
an establishment of religion, or prohibiting the free exercise thereof,' thus
building a wall of separation between Church & State."*

—Thomas Jefferson, from his Letter to the Danbury Baptists

New Life

After I left the United Methodist Church, I had a clear vision of where I
wanted my vocation to be—higher education. I wanted to use the experience
I had and invest in developing new leaders. I saw leadership, civic engagement,
and diversity as tools worth expanding—a silver bullet to aid a world on fire.
I knew I could still be a missionary for causes I believed to be life changing.

And that is when I received a call from one of the least expected places,
Utah. I thought I had applied for a job at Utah State University in Logan,
but the call came from Price. I was confused. The College of Eastern Utah
had merged with USU in order to stay afloat financially. And that is how the
school became USU Eastern.

When I arrived on campus and drove around Price, I thought I had walked
into a ghost town. Price is a small, rural mining community with a little over
eight thousand people. Downtown has not been renovated in decades. Most
of the town feels like that as well. And I understood why. It is stuck in the
middle of a long and dreadful canyon, infested with deer, blocked often by
snow. It takes two hours to reach Salt Lake City via a highway considered one
of the most dangerous in the country. There are no planes, buses, or cabs; it
is very hard to get in and out of the town. The blood flow into town is very
limited and creates an idle, stagnant culture.

I thought to myself, "This place is straight out of *The Hunger Games*—District 12!" I wanted to give the school the benefit of the doubt, but I wasn't really excited about what I saw. Campus life was almost nonexistent. The facilities were antiquated. Students had been dropping out by the hundreds. And both the students and the employees remained bitter about the school's forced merger with USU and their loss of identity as CEU. I'd definitely have my work cut out for me if I wanted to be the school's director of student life.

Throughout my interviews, everything pointed me toward giving a most definite "no" were I offered the position—until I met the chancellor. He mentioned the hard task he was hired to do—to save the campus. He added that it would be great if someone like me, from Los Angeles, would come to a small town like Price and use big city skills to invest in local students. The results would be priceless for them. I also had a conversation with the student body president. Born and raised in Price, he wholeheartedly loved the town and the college, and he wanted everyone to see how great a place it was to live and learn.

The two of them inspired me.

When I got back to California, I had a tough conversation with myself. How many times had I preached that we should go to the ends of the earth, into the most devastated and forsaken places of the world, and bring new life? Why would I stop being a missionary now that I had found something tangible to improve people's lives? Leadership. Any effort in Price would be ten times more tangible than in a larger metropolis. So when I received a phone call from the chancellor offering me the job, I wanted to say "yes" on the spot. But when he mentioned the salary, which would be dramatically less than my previous one, I had to think about it overnight. I researched cost of living in the area and the numbers just didn't add up. I would be significantly lowering my quality of living. But I also realized it wouldn't be a "Fernando decision" if it didn't involve risk and an opportunity to make a positive difference, despite temporary discomfort.

The following day I emailed the chancellor accepting the position.

A few weeks later, in April 2012, my sister Carolina and I drove the 715 miles to Price, Utah, with as much as I could fit in my new Jeep (which I appropriately nicknamed Peeta). And we talked. For fourteen night hours, through mountains and deserts, we talked about how our lives had changed since those days in Port Hueneme. About the bedtime stories at night. About the log and climbing the wall. About the Christmas tree, the golden ornaments, the musical card, and the crazy family. About our mom's transformation. About Don's erratic behavior, our memories of fear, and how we had learned to cope. But most of all, we talked about how we had grown through adversity, learned through our many mistakes and our refusal to let destiny choose our lives for us.

After taking a nap, we walked to campus so I could sign my hiring papers. I gave her a tour of the campus and showed her where my office would be in the student center. Walking through the hallway, she saw something peculiar outside. "What is that?" she asked, pointing to a glass door. We rushed outside to see the last snow of the year. She had never seen snow fall. Her face lit up with a glow I hadn't seen in years. She stuck her tongue out trying to catch a flake, leaning forward every time she saw one.

I stood there watching her, feeling I was seeing that little kindergartner once again. Innocent, wide-eyed, and filled with dreams.

Two months later, Ricky, Danny, and I drove the rest of what I owned in the world in a large U-Haul. And we talked. For fourteen night hours, through mountains and deserts, we talked about how our lives had changed since that cruise. About how we were together during the day, and went our own ways at night. We talked about Jean Paul. We talked about hanging off a cliff. We talked about the girls, the poker, and the dancing. About late-night hikes, drunken parties, and impromptu adventures. But most of all, we talked about the things we had lost, letting go of the past, and moving on to the next chapter.

I couldn't believe that I was leaving everything behind to live in a totally different place, with totally different people. I was alone. And I was scared. But I used those feelings as motivation to focus all my energy into what I was doing, into what I loved, for as long as I would be there. I would try to serve and give with no regrets.

They hired me because they feared going extinct, they wanted something transformational, and it was not my intention to disappoint.

Mormons

Student leaders helped me unload things from my Jeep into the dorm I'd be staying in while I found a place to live. We followed with pizza and fellowship.

My sister then went to take a nap and most students left to go on about their day. The student body president and another student leader stayed behind for a chat. We talked about my travels, and my thoughts about moving to small-town Utah. They then asked something that seemed to be bugging them. The student body president was struggling to get the question out, so the other leader, a female student, helped him out, "He wants to know if you're gay."

I was initially taken aback.

"Ah? No," I replied. "I am what they call metrosexual."

"It is just uncommon for a guy in his thirties, handsome, that dresses well, to be single around here," the girl responded. "I don't know why he was so concerned about it," she later told me. Yet she said something else that surprised me almost as much, "I am actually happy they hired a non-Mormon. We could use some diversity around here."

I smiled along at that moment, but when I went to bed that night, I did wonder what I had just gotten myself into.

I learned the state of Utah was founded mostly by Mormon refugees who were escaping persecution. The founder of Mormonism, Joseph Smith, claimed he received a revelation from the angel Moroni in 1823 that told him where to find a book of golden plates, which he translated as the Book of Mormon, thus founding the Church of Jesus Christ of Latter-day Saints.

But that was not the only revelation he received from an angel. The most controversial revelation was that he would be destroyed if he didn't take multiple wives, as prior prophets had done in the Old Testament. He went on to wed up to forty women, including some who were already married and one as young as fourteen. In those early years, things were tense between Mormons and the United States government, which continually prosecuted polygamists and confiscated their assets. In 1890, the LDS Church finally decided to ban polygamy in order for the Utah territory to be accepted into the United States. The issue continues to be culturally linked to the religion.

Utah is the most religiously homogeneous state in the country. It is reported that over 62 percent of the population are members of the Mormon Church (they refer to themselves as LDS). Living there, though, I felt the percentage to be quite higher. Carbon County, where Price is located, is said to be one of the most "diverse" counties in the state, with a bit over half being LDS. Utah County next door is the state's most Mormon county, where about nine out of ten belong to the faith. Provo, head of the county, hosts Brigham Young University, the largest Mormon university in the world.

During the first few months I was there, I had several invitations to do stuff. People invited me to go check out beautiful natural spots like waterfalls and canyons. I was taken off-roading and shooting. I was invited out to eat. I couldn't believe how nice people were there. But I was also surprised how often the same question came up, "So, what do you think about Mormons?" It took a short conversation with my supervisor to understand what was happening. "They are trying to convert you," he said. "You'd be a great trophy in their cabinet."

At work, I felt like a minority. People talked openly about their Mormon events, about their Mormon festivities, and about their Mormon traditions. Student government meetings felt like a Mormon youth group planning team since every single member was LDS.

When I first suggested that we should have an espresso machine in our cafeteria, I was told, "We can't do that. The Mormon majority would feel offended." While I was there, the LDS Church passed a new revelation stating that it was no longer sinful to drink caffeine. A great cultural landmark in the state. BYU kept their anticaffeine policies, though, making it possible for a student to be sanctioned for walking around campus with a Starbucks cup.

As time went by, I started meeting non-Mormon people, and we shared our experiences of living in Utah. The first consensus was that even though the state is legally called Utah, in real life it is really "Mormon Utah." In Mormon Utah, the LDS Church controls most everything that takes place in the state. Further, most members of city councils are Mormon, and they enact laws that support "the community's culture," which is code for Mormon values.

Non-Mormon friends would say that "it is not as bad in the Salt Lake area." I kept asking, "Why does it have to be bad at all anywhere?" I was advised by countless non-Mormons to live under the radar, or in the closet, about my non-Mormon identity. As long as Mormons felt I could be converted at some point, I was told, they would continue to be nice to me. "But I don't want to be a Mormon," I said. "Yeah," they replied, "but make sure they don't know that, because they will turn against you the moment they feel they can't convert you. The Mormons are very vengeful, and they will rip you apart if they see you as a threat." I couldn't believe their words. I had been a Christian for a large part of my life, and though we wanted everyone to be Christian, and thought everyone else was going to hell, we never acted like the mafia, much less at a statewide level. "Just be careful," they added. "We've lived here longer than you. We've seen many people destroyed for not playing along."

Even Mormon students that moved to Mormon Utah from other states and countries said they felt uncomfortable there. They said that "back home being Mormon is just a religion. In Utah it is a culture."

To me, this much became clear, Utah is Mormon country, and all are expected to abide by LDS rules and values, Mormon or not.

One of my responsibilities as director of student life was to develop a leadership course for every student leader on campus: student government, resident advisers, service center representatives, and enrollment ambassadors. For half of the semester we focused on personal leadership development and understanding the power of influence. The second half of the course focused on ethics and decision making. In order to better relate to my audience, I chose a book I used at APU, written by an APU Christian professor, that compared Christian ethics to other ethical points of view. I feared this book would be too religious for a public school, but took a risk in order to better connect with the Mormon students, who made up about 90 percent of the class.

The reaction was not what I expected.

The majority of students, prior to their expected two-year proselytizing mission, had never stepped out of Mormon Utah, much less traveled to a different country. They have lived Mormon, breathed Mormon, dressed Mormon, talked Mormon, ate Mormon, slept Mormon, studied Mormon, and most certainly only dated Mormon. The moment I mentioned that we'd evaluate contemporary social issues using several different ethical lenses, only one of them being a religious lens, a red flag went up. The idea that there could be another point of view, other than the LDS point of view, was outrageous.

A student in the class, Saul, came to me and said he considered it a "waste of time," demanding to be allowed to drop the course. I told him I didn't make the rule that every student leader had to participate in the class; this rule was before my time. Saul wasn't looking for an explanation. I sensed that he just wanted to look me in the eye and have me know what he thought.

Other students, such as Esau, loved my lessons. In fact, Esau said he might want to come talk to me sometime, claiming I was one of his favorite teachers. I told him my office door was always open to him. When he later knocked on my door, he said he had been struggling with depression and he needed help. I made him aware that the counseling office offered free sessions for students. He said he trusted me and asked if I could be his mentor. I told him I would do my best to support him.

In the conversations we had he opened up about what he considered his "deepest, darkest secrets." With an unending flow of tears, he made confessions about troubling issues in his family. He was afraid and felt he had nowhere to go and had no one to talk to. On top of it all, he was struggling financially and wasn't sure if he'd be able to come back the following semester. As he revealed, it had gotten to the point that he had to choose between buying food and putting gas in his car. I was broken inside for him. I made a commitment to check on him regularly as he dealt with his family issues. I also tried to invite him out to eat once a week and had him take food home to help spare him some meal costs. I felt especially good about helping him because he was an exemplary student and human being.

Nevertheless, I learned that a few students had knocked on the dean of student's door to complain about how I was teaching things that were against their beliefs. "Is he teaching you to leave the LDS faith," he'd ask them. "Well, no," they'd reply, "but he is talking about them."

Upon hearing of these complaints, I almost dropped to the floor.

The main reason why I got my master's degree, and why I took this position, was because I would get to teach. I spent hours preparing the curriculum, going through books, and planning class. I was so excited to teach the young people I so passionately love and believe in. Yet my efforts were met with torches and pitchforks—not because I asked them to believe in something other than Mormonism, mind you. No. They objected simply because I acknowledged that opinions outside of Mormonism existed.

The dean of students suggested that maybe my LA curriculum were too advanced for Price students. I told him that was preposterous. I came here not to prepare Mormon leaders, nor Price leaders. I came here to empower *world* leaders. People who can speak excellence outside the school's walls. Wherever they served would be up to them.

The school ran a humiliating investigation. They reviewed the book, had someone sit in my class, and took a survey of what I said.

At the end of the term, to my surprise, the class received overwhelmingly positive reviews, and the school backed off. Some students even suggested everyone on campus should take the class. Even the president of the Mormon Institute across the street, a student in my class, said he'd recommend it to anyone.

I was perplexed.

Still, I continued to receive warnings from other non-Mormon staff and faculty. "You gotta be careful, Fernando. You started shaking things up and people don't like that around here." Someone even told me, "You are not Mormon. You are Californian. You are Latino. And you are metrosexual. They use people like you as target practice around here." I was told that zealot Mormon students had put a bullseye on me. The problem was not only that I was teaching about things that existed outside of Mormonism and treating them as normal. It was also that I was living an openly non-Mormon life. I was charismatic, many students loved me, and that scared them to death. I was told, "You cannot be open about not wanting to be Mormon, be successful and liked, and get away with it."

On occassion I cried myself to sleep, wondering if I had made the biggest mistake of my life. Most Mormons were so good and nice to me—some of the nicest people I had ever met. But I also knew that those who weren't nearly as nice acted with the protection of the LDS Church, of the majority, which would never take the side of a heathen outsider over one of their own.

Purified

I tried not to let my situation get to me even further, but truth is, it was hard not to feel lonely and isolated. I started seeking communities I could be a part of, but most were run by churches. I sought options with the Parks and Recreation Department, which proved fruitless. I then began to seek groups through websites such as Meetup.com, but the closest ones to Price were in Provo, eighty miles across the canyon. The first group I joined was a former-Mormons group. I would drive up every other Sunday morning to meet at a coffee shop. The looks I got from people for walking into a coffee shop, and on a Sunday—you'd think I was walking into a brothel.

I heard traumatizing accounts from those who had lived under what they called the "yoke of Mormonism" and about their isolating exit from "a brainwashing cult." Some had lost their jobs, some their friends, some even their families—all for leaving the LDS Church. Still, I enjoyed hearing their stories and learning from them, and later playing board games and having food with them. It helped soften the terrible isolation a freethinker can have in Mormon Utah. But it wasn't enough.

I was so invested in the college, and so excited about the new campus culture we were developing, that I convinced my little sister, Sharon, to transfer to USU Eastern in the spring. She brought a close friend with her. Coming from 120-plus-degree El Centro weather, they experienced a real shock when they arrived that winter.

These two familiar faces helped Price feel a little more like home.

I then began to sign up for relationship websites such as Plenty of Fish (POF.com) and Match.com. I knew it'd be hard to find a mate in this area, but I thought that at least I'd be able to find some new friends to hang out with. In the greatest irony, I found Kelly, my neighbor across the street, on POF. Kelly became my closest friend in Price—but I still had no luck finding a girlfriend. I did a Google search for the best dating sites on the Internet and found a list of the top ten. I was surprised to see Craigslist as the top one. I knew Craigslist as the place to sell and buy video games and appliances, not to find a relationship. Intrigued, I decided to check it out.

Under its personals category, Craigslist has options for *women seeking men* and *men seeking women*, along with options for *women seeking women*, *men seeking men*, and *casual encounters*. Though alone in my bedroom, I looked over my shoulder when I discovered this, as if fearing that someone would think I was interested in any of the latter three. Now that I had left religion behind, I was no longer threatened nor disgusted by homosexuality as I had been before, but I still considered it an uncomfortable and undesirable lifestyle.

I clicked on the *women seeking men* category and found only a handful of posts, most by self-described *BBWs*, which, as I came to learn, stood for big beautiful women, those "pleasingly plump." Out of curiosity, I clicked on the *men seeking women* link and found a list several pages long. I was stunned to see that most of the posts had pictures of men's genitalia and to-the-point offers for casual, fast, and kinky sex. I wondered if women actually replied to such messages. What had I been missing?

After replying to a few posts and posting one of my own, I realized that the majority of messages from women were actually automated programs trying to entice men to pay a fee to be able to talk to them further—a scam. Though I eventually found a couple of women who were real, the fear of Mormons finding out about their online activities made them quit all communication, and we never met.

It became really frustrating to find someone to connect with. Most girls were Mormon, only dated Mormons, and were married before twenty-one—to Mormons.

Horny and sexually repressed, but mostly curious, I decided to explore what I saw as the more "controversial" categories. I thought about how I would explain it if someone found out that I had clicked on them—as an accident for sure, maybe as research . . . At first I was taken aback and disgusted by the graphic posts men made for other men. I couldn't understand the lingo either. What is a *top*, a *bottom,* and a *versatile*? What's a *twink*, a *bear*, a *swimmer*, *HWP*? Who can *host* and who can *travel*? Judging by the requests, a lot of guys in Utah apparently had a thirst for *RMs* (returned missionaries).

This was a whole new culture I was very unfamiliar with.

After seeing so many posts from closeted Mormons, I couldn't help but wonder if every Mormon Utahan was secretly gay. Part of me squirmed at the comments and pictures, but somehow I couldn't deny that I had an internal curiosity that asked to know more.

I also read some posts that were very personal. It was obvious that most wanted—and needed—sex; it made sense, we are all human. But some men shared they were seeking guys who wanted to explore what this lifestyle was like, maybe in a relationship, even if it had to be locked in the closet to avoid Mormon persecution. I found myself drawn into the stories, the feelings, the desires, and the struggles of these humans living in a cultural stronghold and realized I wasn't much different from them.

Still, at night's end, before I turned off the computer, I deleted the cookies and search history from my browser, and I repented for exploring such a despicable site. I swore that I'd never look at it again.

Weeks went by. Programs at USU Eastern began to kick off. Attendance at them began to increase dramatically. We had events almost every day. I was often busy nine to midnight, sometimes even on Saturdays. I certainly kept my mind occupied. But there were nights, when I got home at a regular time, that I kept looking over to my laptop, wondering what new posts might have been made on Craigslist.

I felt both tempted and guilty.

I'd go online to check the news and toy with the idea of visiting the site. I'd try to think of ways to rationalize why I should check it out. "If I am not gay, and I have no desire to be gay, why would I check it out?"

Whatever the reason I chose, I went back to the site. I spent hours going through all the posts, getting myself acquainted with the themes, the lingo, the culture, the stories. There were definitely more propositions for quick sex than for dating. I was especially drawn to those site users who said they were new to it, those who were exploring. I wondered if I was one of them.

I knew I had been tempted before, *curious* for sure, but there was no way I was gay, I thought. I mean, I was passionately drawn to girls. The way they feel in my arms on the dance floor, my head resting in their smooth hair, my hands caressing the shape of their body—they excited me. My first crushes were girls. I thought of marrying a couple of them. And while it was true that I'd thought that some guys were incredibly attractive and handsome, that was just me being fair about beauty in general, right? And while it was also true that sometimes I'd felt a connection with close buds, that was just because I have a very intentional way of showing love that most men don't have, right?

"Is there a chance I might be bisexual?" I had thought about the idea before, but under the doctrine of Christianity, I had always pushed my thoughts and feelings deep into the darkest corners of my subconscious. I had told myself that as long as I was attracted to girls 51 percent, and to guys 49 percent, that 1 percent would make all the difference and I'd be okay. I would not sin against God and burn in hell.

Growing up in a machismo-based culture like Mexico's, I grew up believing it was acceptable to use derogatory terms for homosexuals such as "*joto*" (*ho-to*)—fag. "There is nothing manly about being used like a woman," I was told. The Foursquare church taught us that AIDS is God's punishment for homosexuality—an abomination. When I attended APU I was taught in my abnormal psychology class that homosexuality is a mental disorder caused by sin that we had committed, or sin that was committed against us. When I worked for the UMC I learned that many believed that acceptance of homosexuality might be the issue that again divided the denomination in half. And I now lived in a state where followers of its predominant religion, Mormonism, had donated millions of dollars in support of California's Proposition 8, a measure approved by voters that made same-sex marriage illegal in the state—a measure that I myself had passionately supported for all of the above reasons.

I was definitely past ambivalence and fear now. How far past that? I didn't know. I hadn't asked.

I tossed and turned in bed for days with an intense fear of what I might be. I had images of most of the gay men I knew—flamboyant and feminine with rainbows coming out of their ears and butterflies flying out of their asses. I didn't want to be like that. I didn't want to speak in a soft, high-pitched tone, or push my chest forward to compensate for a lack of breasts, and I most definitely didn't want to take a dick up my ass. I didn't want to judge anyone, but with all the cultural and religious baggage in the back of my mind, I thought, "I just don't want to be gay!"

With no one to talk to, I was terrified to the point of tears. Loneliness felt deafening and my doubts hollowed my core. "Fernando, what if you get married, have kids, and never have the chance to know for sure?" I thought to myself. "What if there is something there that you have prevented yourself from seeing? What if there is something you can do about it? You could go on forever wondering . . . but . . . but wouldn't it be better to finally know?"

I remorsefully went back to Craigslist and replied to some posts. I even met with a few guys, but I couldn't get myself to go much further than talk. The idea of being with another guy made me shake and breathe profusely, as if I was in cardiac arrest. I had never met guys in this context and I knew I was crossing a point of no return. I once even left a guy at the end of a hike we had gone on and ran the two miles back to Peeta, my Jeep, as if running away from demons. My legs just kept moving. I thought that maybe if I ran fast enough I'd leave these feelings behind.

But eventually I found myself reading posts again and I could no longer just keep wondering, "What if?"

Tired of going by others' expectations, I decided that it was time for me to post my own ad. "Nervous and New to This" was the title. I wrote that I wanted to meet a good guy who was also new to this to talk about what was going on inside us and possibly to explore together.

I left my computer and returned a couple of hours later to find dozens of messages waiting in my inbox. The majority of them had lines such as, "you can rip my ass in half" and "fuck my brains out." I was not expecting to have such direct, experienced, and explicit offers. I rubbed my face in disbelief. I knew then that I had made a mistake. I tried it, and it didn't work. I moved my mouse over to deactivate the post when a new message came in. "Also New and Nervous" was the title. "What the hell?" I thought. "Okay, I'll read this last one and then delete it."

And that's when I read Bobby's message.

It included a picture of a beautiful, white, blond, blue-eyed, tall guy with a fit body. I immediately thought it was fake. This was a full-body picture, and the large majority of messages I had received included pictures of genitals or a headless torso. Plus, the message was very kind. He said he had connected with my message. Though a Mormon himself, he was also new to Mormon Utah and was also very curious about his sexuality. I responded and told him about my doubts. He responded quickly with another full picture. I couldn't believe my thoughts, "He is beautiful."

Despite what I told him, I couldn't continue. It was too much for me right then, and I respectfully declined the offer to meet. I went back to bed and spent an hour tossing and turning. Thoughts would not let me close my eyes. I was uncomfortable and realized I would not be able to sleep. And I also realized what I had to do. Yeah, I was scared out of my mind, but if I didn't figure out who I was, I'd regret it for the rest of my life. I knew I wouldn't live in Mormon Utah for more than three years. Nobody knew me there. If I ever had an opportunity to experiment with something like this, it would be now.

I jumped out of bed and hoped he was still online. It was midnight, but he was working on his computer and replied a few seconds later. We agreed to meet that morning in Provo. It was Sunday and we both had the day off.

I picked him up with no idea about what would happen next. Damn he looked nice. Tall, fit, wearing pink shorts that showed off his nice, firm legs, covered in a soft, dirty-blond coat of hair. I'm a sucker for nice legs, and his were a fine example. We drove around town with no destination in mind, but my eyes kept veering down to those gorgeous extremities. I wondered how they looked under those shorts. And those eyes—so bright and clean. That smile. Those lips, pink and slightly chapped. It didn't take long to see that he was indeed a noble spirit, humble and kind. What was he doing on that site? But then again, what was I?

We decided to drive up the Provo canyon and find a place to park. We talked inside Peeta for a couple of hours. It turned out we had a lot in common. We both came from a heavily religious background. We both had wondered about possibilities and were scared to death of what our interests could mean. It felt like I was talking to an old friend and not to a random stranger.

Since we were there, we decided to go for a walk and check out the mountain forest. The hills were covered with trees showing off their autumn dresses in bright shades of green, red, and yellow. It was beautiful. Neither one of us had hiking shoes on, but we decided to explore the area nonetheless.

Once we got a little deeper into the woods, we decided to sit on a log to take a breather. He sat next to me, and I could smell his perspiration. I didn't want to accept it, but his scent made my heart beat faster. "Can I hold your hand?" he asked me. I agreed. Though I was still nervous, I didn't feel as though I was experiencing a heart attack. His calm nature had made me feel comfortable.

I am holding another man's hand. Why did it feel so natural? So right?

Part of me was caught off guard, but part of me felt at peace when he asked me the next question, "Would it be okay if I give you a kiss?" Before I answered, I thought about what it would be like. I thought it would feel wrong, unnatural, but maybe, just maybe, I could get past it. I might even tremble, but he might not care. I don't recall at what point in my thought process I consented. He got close, gazing at me with those gleaming bluish-gray eyes, both gentle and fiery. I felt his warm breath under my nose. He was a gorgeous man. I thought, if I ever make out with a guy, I would certainly want him to look like this—but he was still *a guy*. And then he pressed his lips against mine. I was innately very conscious of the experience: the fleshy feeling of his lips, the moisture of the saliva on his tongue, the roundness of his mouth, the warmth of his skin, and, before long, I was lost in him, not knowing where my face ended and his began.

The kiss was surprisingly no different than kissing a girl. There was no unnatural feel. Only a soft, tender, moist play of lips and tongues that enveloped us in a delirium of passion, yearning, and ardor as we sat embraced, in the middle of nature, in the arms of one another.

We felt innocent, as if discovering love for the first time—but we were no children. Our hands traveled and explored. I couldn't get enough of his legs. I followed the contour of his shoulders and was continuously amazed with how beautiful he was. The soft hair on his legs felt like a soft blanket I wanted to be wrapped in. His hands touched my chest. He followed the outline of my pecs, rubbed his thumbs on my nipples, and followed the inside of my abs down to my waist. I felt his fingers tremble at my belt buckle—jitter.

This was new to both of us. We both thought about it. But he was certainly braver.

"Is this okay?" he asked as he slightly inserted his index finger into my orange boxer briefs. I breathed out heavily, swallowed, and nodded. He easily found the head of my penis, now fully erect, and gently began to rub it. I sat there frozen, breathing deeply, with my eyes closed. I could see the fireworks blowing up inside of me. They glowed in bright, beautiful colors—like those of the trees around us. When I opened my eyes I found his again, a couple of inches from my face. And then he asked me if he could do more. Though it was his first time, he then gave me the best mind-blowing oral magic I had ever experienced. Twice.

This was real now. I like him. I like this. Oh my dear word, I think I'm gay!

We went back to my Jeep after that and talked for another couple of hours before I dropped him off at his place.

I drove home in a daze.

Though I resisted the idea, we met again a couple of weeks later and went back to the bright-colored canyon. This time we drove to a more secluded part of the forest. We lowered Peeta's back seat, set a blanket down, and lay next to each other. We talked about how nervous we both were, about how our lives were changing, and about the possible consequences of what we were doing if people found out. We were both smart adults who should have nothing to fear, except the vengeful scruples of a religious majority. But in spite of those fears, we found shelter in the privacy of the woods and now, with more confidence, embraced each other and put our lips together as our hands caressed the firmness of our bodies.

A bit later I sat up to look outside the window. The scenery was as bright, colorful, and broad as ever. I looked back at Bobby. He was just as vibrant, handsome, and hot as ever. He looked at me endearingly with those radiant eyes of his. "How could they be so beautiful and emanate so much light?" I thought. As I gazed at his breathtaking eyes, he stretched out his hand to me. His lips then parted to softly say the words that would forever change our lives, "I want you to go inside of me."

The woods were witness to our innocent and passionate defiance of religious confines. Outside of that Jeep, Religion cursed our love as "unnatural" and as an "abomination." Inside, Reason defined it as natural and beautiful. Every drop of sweat that left our bodies was another sparkle that cleansed our souls from a past of guilt and shame. Every moan, every kiss, every grasp, every nibble, and every thrust sharpened us into a better version of ourselves. We forgot the cultural expectations we grew up with and melted into a fiery passion that transformed us into gold, that burnt off the impurities of inhibitions and fears.

Bobby was glowing when I dropped him off. I had never seen a smile that wide. We found freedom in exploration and power in acceptance.

We are human. We are beautiful. And we are free.

I met other guys in the months to come; some just as sweet, some far more lustful. I learned about their process of acceptance, their struggles, their fears, their humiliation, and their discrimination. Many of them were among the most sensitive people I had ever met. Living under the microscope and the guillotine of public opinion, especially in ever-judging Mormon Utah, had pushed them to a state of extreme nobility and sensitivity. Yet others had become desensitized to human dignity. They pushed each other to ridicule, gossip, belittling—the distasteful horror of trashing the other's name for the sake of temporary supremacy and the immediate satisfaction of carnal needs.

Bobby moved out of Mormon Utah a few months later. We stayed in touch through email, text, and Skype for a while. Our feet may have taken us in different directions, but just like so many before us, we will never forget the trials we have endured, and the fears we have overcome, to escape the cultural and religious oppression that demanded submission of our feelings. There is no greater gift we could have given each other, than that of becoming purified.

17

SON OF PERDITION

"Nearly all men can stand adversity,
but if you want to test a man's character, give him power."
—Abraham Lincoln

Hell

It is hard to describe the deep feeling of loss, of regret, of treason I felt driving out of Price—like coming to the end of a very long nightmare.

I couldn't afford to pay for a U-Haul to move back home. I sold some things at a fraction of their value, but mostly gave away—or even threw away—the belongings I had accumulated, through hard work, my entire life.

I had moved to Price with a full Jeep and a large U-Haul packed with enough stuff to fill a three-bedroom apartment. But more than furniture, I had filled it with dreams. I now left pulling a small trailer behind my car carrying not much more than my clothes and books. I didn't need room for my dreams; they had already been crushed.

I cried in silence, looking at those desert hills and rocks covered by the sunset's dim shade. I remembered the hopes I had when driving in. I drove away now, cast away, with a scarlet letter on my forehead.

Things were going so good, I though. So, what happened?

Unpardonable

For the new school year we developed programs for the college that we could all be proud of, from academic initiatives such as a new leadership minor, to social events such as themed dances and festive activities. Collectively, these programs led to increased participation in sporting events and school spirit. Our determination bore fruitful results. Retention rates improved. Student participation tripled. People said we had created the most dynamic events they had ever seen. What once was a desolate campus destined for foreclosure began to show solid signs of growth and life.

Though most were excited about the growth we saw, many were troubled when they learned that before my time in Mormon Utah, I had been a "big-time religious leader" who was now comfortably living life with no need for God. They openly wondered whether I had experienced some big fallout or some great tragedy. To such questions, I would typically respond, "I reasoned my way out of religion." For those looking for a longer answer, I'd even share, with complete sincerity, my journey of introspection, my ever-growing doubts, and my surrender to the weight of reason, whereby I choose to base my life decisions on facts rather than on great, ancient stories.

They would often sit quietly, respectful, thinking of their own path. "I have never questioned my faith before," one of them told me. "I was born and raised in it. That's all I've ever known. I've never even been outside of Utah."

"Exactly," I calmly replied.

Inside I couldn't help but feel a sense of pity. Family units are mostly strong in Mormon Utah. Community is strong. Traditions are strong. But how could they know what they really believe if they've only been shown one option—and never tested it?

As the months passed, I could see more clearly why my leadership class was so controversial for some.

Students who worked with me usually enjoyed my company and ideas, kept knocking on my door for advice, and milked every eccentricity they could out of me. I was a novelty at school. But it was hard not to notice the ongoing campaign to bring me back to the herd. While they enjoyed the energy I brought, the innovative programming, and the growth in student participation, they also worried about my soul. Ongoing invitations to Mormon events, random conversations with believers, and other similar situations made it obvious I was on a prayer list.

Why?

A quick visit to the LDS.org website offers a detailed description of what they believed I had become: a blasphemer. According to LDS doctrine, I had left religion behind in what Mormons call "the unpardonable sin" (Matthew 12:31–32, Alma 39:5–6). I had *denied the Holy Spirit after having received it, and . . . denied the Only Begotten Son of the Father, having crucified him unto themselves and put him to an open shame* (D&C 76:35). Having denied the Holy Ghost, and having no desire to return to the cross, I would get "*no mercy*" (3 Ne. 29:7). I had joined Satan's army and belonged to the only group in humanity who would not see forgiveness and be named an *"enemy to God"* (Mosiah 16:5). I *"must remain filthy still"* (D&C 88:35). Seen as someone with no repentance, I would be put *"to an open shame"* (Hebrews 6:4–6). And my final doom would be a never-ending torment (Mosiah 2:36–39).

Before Mormon Utah, I had been successful because I swam against the current, dared to speak my mind, and blazed my own path. In Mormon Utah, I was forced to walk on eggshells, concerned I'd upset the giant. Even so, once they learned I no longer adhered to the Holy Ghost camp, I was considered to be *unpardonable*. Though most of them liked my personality, I had become that which their faith considered most iniquitous, a *"son of perdition"* (John 17:12).

It was almost impossible to avoid the topic of religion in conversations. I came looking for our executive assistant one day and found a student, Saul, sitting in for her. "What do you need?" he asked. "Well, I need some answers," I said. In a tongue-and-cheek tone, he replied, "Read the Book of Mormon." I smiled but remained quiet to avoid an uncomfortable conversation.

As director of student life, I had the opportunity to meet, teach, work, and speak with numerous students each and every day. Those who often engaged me in the topic of religion included John, Miriam, and Judas.

John was a liberal non-Mormon, charming enough to often get away with behaviors frowned upon by the majority. Miriam was an open-minded Mormon who substituted judgment with an overwhelming positive attitude. Judas was a conservative and traditional Mormon, older than the average student, but with maturity beyond his years. Conversations often got heated among the students, with me acting as a moderator.

"The same reasons I had for leaving Christianity, are the same reasons I have for not wanting to join the LDS Church," I told Judas. John echoed my thoughts. Miriam respected our feelings and decided not to pick a side.

In time, both John and Judas became very close to me. John saw me as somewhat of an older brother figure. We'd share a drink and talk about his challenges with education, love, and temptation. Judas, on the other hand, perhaps saw me more as a father figure. We enjoyed talking about our ideas and dreams, along with our views on politics, social issues, and current events.

Whenever I had to go out of town to pick up a purchase or check out a location, Judas would volunteer to join me. He took me out shooting and offered to take me fishing (if I got my license), and, when the snow came, he took me up the mountain to check out the wild, fresh, new powder. "Why did you ask me to come?" I asked him. "I just wanted to spend time with you,

Fernando," he said. But both John and I knew Judas felt that with proper attention and care I would open my heart to the teachings of Joseph Smith, as many before me had done with the same approach.

Damnation

As Judas' appreciation for me grew, he began to open up about more private matters, including his issues with depression and anxiety. He told me his doctor would be changing his medication. Since I had earlier shared my own experiences with that struggle, he thought I'd understand what he was going through. "You know how that medication works," he added. "It takes about four weeks, maybe more, for the new meds to kick in." He wanted to give me a heads up because he knew his emotional state would most probably deteriorate significantly before it got better. I told him I loved him as a student and as a friend and that I had his back.

When the time came to sign up for the coming year's student leadership positions, Judas threw his name in the hat for one of them. "I want you to know that I'm doing it because I would like to work closely with you," Judas told me. There were many others who toyed with the idea, but when Friday came, Judas was the only applicant for that role.

Miriam and I saw each other during an event that night. She brought up the issue of the lone candidate. She said she knew someone who had recently returned from mission, Andrew, and believed he would be a good candidate. She offered to talk to him at an event at the Mormon Institute later in the day. I said, "Sure. But he needs his paperwork in by Monday."

I also ran into John the following day, who brought up the same issue. He offered to talk to Paul, who had fulfilled his missionary duties, and had a solid reputation as a leader and a man of character. He'd be seeing Paul later in the day. I told John the same thing I told Miriam.

When Monday came, both Andrew and Paul came to my office to ask for an application. They both mentioned they had run into Judas on the way up and had asked him some questions about it. As I remember, a few minutes later Judas stormed into my office, slamming the door behind him. "Can I ask you something, Fernando?!" he shouted. "Do you not want me to be in student leadership?!"

"Why would you say that? Of course not," I replied, setting some papers down. He quickly responded, "Well, I just talked to Andrew and Paul, they wanted to talk to you, and wanted applications for the position!" Watching the fire of rage burning in his eyes, I decided to leave Miriam and John out of it. "Anybody can apply for the position, Judas," I tried to explain. "I know you had it sealed as of Friday, but you have to understand that it is healthier for a campus when you have more than one candidate for a position." He was having none of that. "Well, it seems to me like you don't like the cards you got dealt and you're trying to reshuffle the deck here!"

A couple of days later, Judas knocked on my door and asked to talk with me. He seemed far more calm. "I have decided not to apply," he said. "I have decided it would be better for me to dedicate more time to my family." I told him that it would be a loss for the school and that he already was a great leader. I also told him my door would always be open to him, that I had come to appreciate him not only as a coworker, but also as a friend. He thanked me, shook my hand, and walked out of my office.

The next day I was asked to meet with a campus administrator and a human resources coordinator from another campus. After Judas left my office in apparent peace, he had apparently walked into another administrative office and said that he didn't want to be around me any more. He claimed that about three months earlier, I had offered him some of my medication for depression. They made it very clear to me that this was a severe accusation that could have paramount consequences.

It felt as if the floor beneath me opened up, and I began to fall quickly into an abyss. My vision became blurry and I was distracted by a deafening sound in my ears. "Please sit down," the administrator said. "Wait. What?" I snapped back, asking for clarification.

After explaining that my job was hanging by a thread, the administrator asked me to type a memo with my account of the story. I sat at my desk and opened up Word, but I couldn't focus. My story was clear. I hadn't even had the kind of medication he said I gave him since the cruise. But right now I was not thinking about my job.

Hold on a second. Judas. My friend. He did this.

I was visited by a thick vision of *Dante's Inferno*. I saw Dante walk into the sulfur-infested fires of the underworld through the nine circles of hell: Limbo, Lust, Gluttony, Greed, Anger, Heresy, Violence, Fraud, and the last one, believed to be the very worst of all sins, Treachery.

I had sacrificed my desires, my prosperity, in order to serve in this rustic place. I had endured discrimination, isolation, economic uncertainty, so I could empower young leaders like him. I had served him not only as an adviser, but also as a friend. I opened the doors to my home. I cooked for him. I took him on rides in my Jeep so he could vent and tell me his troubles.

I hugged him and let him cry on my shoulder when the ghosts of his past came to haunt him. I understood anger. I understand depression. Okay, maybe he saw me as a father figure and felt I chose a different son when I let others apply for office when he thought he had the deal sealed? But to go for my jugular because he felt I didn't support him?

It didn't matter the reason. He was my friend. Friends just don't do that.

The charge ultimately resulted in an administrative letter that would go in my file that stated I was too close to students and that, in the future, I should be more cautious. I was asked whether I wanted to pursue any action against Judas. "He is very well known in the Mormon community, and you are an outsider," I was told. "If we pursue action against him it may cost the college dearly, and we are already struggling with enrollment. But if you want to do it, we can consider it."

I declined. "I won't be here for many years," I said. "It wouldn't be worth it. And I don't want to hurt the college." We agreed that I would just let it go, and that I would not try to contact Judas.

When I got home, I crash-landed on my carpet and felt a heart attack had finally come. My weeping was interrupted by intense gasps for air. My heart palpitated. I clenched what I could grab from the rug, drooling on it and looking up for help. There was no one to answer.

A panic attack like this kept coming every few hours. Even through the night—waking me up like a deadly nightmare.

First it was the zealot students in leadership class, now Judas' betrayal. Somehow it felt that even though I had made progress, it'd be only a matter of time before they'd try again, this time with a fatal blow.

Open Shame

Many of the friends I had made in Price had moved away after they grew weary of the stagnant culture. I feared my depression and anxiety might come back due to my excess work and lack of community.

I shut the door to my office on one Thursday afternoon, closed the blinds, and laid my head on the desk. I had an interview coming up for a similar position in Vegas. Even though I was already doing what I loved, I hoped my time in Price would end sooner rather than later. And with that attitude, I got my stuff together to run to leadership class. That day we'd be talking about liberal vs. conservative philosophies of leadership. When I stepped out of my office, I saw one of the school's top administrators talking to some of the students. "How is it going today?" he asked. "Oh, you know," I replied, "changing the world, one eagle at a time." He frowned, giving a look I had seen before. "We need to talk," he said. "Let's go into my office."

He took a seat and asked me to sit down as well, but I decided to remain standing. I could see in his eyes that he dreaded saying what he had to say, knowing very well the words would cause me tremendous pain. "I just got out of a meeting," he said. "Judas has gotten a group of other students together and said they are going to the local newspaper tomorrow to write an article about how you are dangerous for the school."

Mushroom cloud. Though he kept talking, everything sounded like a blur. I experienced something I had been trying to prevent at all cost.

It was as if my soul had detached from my body, leaving my muscles weak and tingling. It was as if I stood in a dream, not knowing what was real and what wasn't. My heart began to beat irregularly. I brought my right hand to it, and my left to my forehead. I felt like I had forgotten how to breathe by instinct. I began to wobble toward the window. The floor kept moving from side to side. I placed my hand forward in case I'd have to hold on to something. "I . . . a . . . I . . . " I couldn't speak.

A thick fog had entered his office. I lost track of where he was sitting and where the furniture was. I knew the window was on my left side. I stepped forward and reached for it. I wasn't sure if it was real. It looked real. But I didn't know for sure at that time.

"I . . . I don't understand. I . . . "

"They hate you, plain and simple," I recall him saying, "and they won't stop until they have you fired."

Filthy Still

Things didn't began to make sense until I left the area and received the final report from the school's investigation—and saw the other names and charges.

I wasn't surprised to see that Saul had made charges against me, though the nature of the charges did. According to the report, he said he felt uncomfortable with me painting his chest before a basketball game. He accused me of touching his behind at a basketball game. And he said he felt attacked when I told him that I didn't want to "compare dicks with him."

I'm thinking, "Say what?" I went deep into my mind trying to understand what the hell he was referring to.

REWIND.

No. No. No. Wait, I think this might be it.

STOP.

PLAY.

I walked upstairs in the gym to unlock the locker where the paint and the wigs were. They were down a guy and had urged me to join them in cheering on the basketball team. To demonstrate our school spirit, we would each have our upper bodies painted blue and have a golden letter drawn on our chests so that, standing together, we could spell out a word. As part of this plan, we helped one another with the painting. Saul had been part of this group.

FAST FORWARD.

Next game. I came back from halftime swinging a bandana in my hand. Saul was stretching against the wall next to the cheer team and I flicked its tip against his rear. He jumped back, laughing. When I said, "I'm sorry," he replied with a smile on his face, saying, "Don't worry about it, the cheerleader guys loved it!"—a couple of the male cheerleaders were rumored to be gay.

PAUSE.

FAST FORWARD.

PLAY.

I developed an involvement fair at the beginning of the school year where we'd showcase all the new ways to get involved at the school and provide opportunities to create new clubs. To set an example, I started a dance club where we'd teach people flashmobs.

The logistical responsibilities for the fair had been given to a particular student. This included the ordering of all tables and chairs. When the day of the event came, we realized the student had forgotten to make the order, and we thus submitted a rush request and received them at the last minute. Saul, who had been assigned to set up the tables and chairs, was upset that such pressure had been laid at his feet with practically no time to spare.

I walked upstairs to my office to pick something up before rushing back down to the fair and found the student sitting on the carpet putting some papers together. I told him we'd have to talk about his lack of responsibility once the event was over. As we were talking, Saul walked in to make his complaint. I apologized to Saul for the added pressure on him and told him we'd be making efforts to make sure such a situation didn't happen again. He had been cooking for a while and wasn't gonna let go that easily. He complained about the setup, brought up once again several past grievances, and listed a number of things he felt he could do better if he were in charge.

There are only so many things I can take at one time, especially when I'm under pressure. In the moment, trying to end the conversation and finish what I had to do, I put my hands up and said, "I don't want to have another dick measuring competition with you right now. Can we please talk about this later?" He clenched his fists and lips, gave me a stern look, and walked out of the room. The other student glanced over at me with a guilty and apologetic manner. I put my hands up and simply said, "Later," before heading out of the room.

I looked for Saul the next day during lunchtime to talk things through. I found him with a group of people in front of the cafeteria and he had to go to class right after, so I had to postpone our conversation.

STOP.

I was still thinking, "Why?" The answer came when I read the rest of his testimony. He said he felt uncomfortable because he "already gets negative homosexual comments" as it is.

I took a deep breath. Looking back at the report, I felt a ball drop down my throat and into my gut. The charges didn't end with Saul. Charges from another person in the report really surprised me and hurt even deeper. I thought we had a great relationship, but he complained that I had squeezed his nipple at some point and that I had "taken an interest in [his] life" and that it made him uncomfortable.

The heavy tear that slid down my eyes and rested at the end of my nose brought memories I believed to be pure and brotherly.

PLAY.

Esau had asked me, with tears in his eyes, to hear his pain, to support him, and to offer him counsel, which I sincerely did.

END OF TAPE.

I can't say for certain why he would elect to make such charges about me then, but I couldn't help put think that the spreading news not only about my blasphemy but also about my sexual identity had something to do with it.

Indeed, for those whose views are tainted by religious doctrine, gay male often equals child predator.

The words I heard from other staffers attested to this. I recall the yelling, the ignorance, the intimidation, and the humiliation. I was believed to be something disgusting. I was belittled, frightened, ridiculed, and tossed into a dark corner. While in that corner, my memories reached deep into the archive, and I realized I had been here before, felt like this before—when I had been beaten in that bathroom, powerless, by those military guards who asked, "Are you a fag or something?"

Still, I had never really understood the word *homophobia*, until now. It really comes down to this: in its most fundamental sense, homophobia is found whenever actions, words, or intentions are not perceived as unwanted, invalid, or harmful—up until the point they come from someone who is gay.

I recalled the warnings I had received when I first arrived in Mormon Utah. I was an outsider. I was Latino. I was a Humanist. I was now gay. It was only a matter of time before they used me as target practice.

I reached out to an administrator at another USU campus and asked if they could please help me make contact with whoever was responsible for helping staff defend against charges by students. I specifically said that I had been a victim of "bigotry and homophobia" and that I had lost everything because of it. But my call ended up on deaf ears.

With chills in my bones, I remembered something else I learned early on in my time in Mormon Utah—regardless of how wrong one of them might be, they will never take the side of a heathen outsider over one of their own.

Love Again

When I told my family I had resigned my position, they could hear my desperation. They responded by saying the words any caring person would say to a loved one who has been torn apart, "Please, come home."

It was not easy getting back to "normal." I was like a wounded soldier, waking up terrified in the middle of the night and walking with the familiar company of ghosts—remnants of losses on the red-soaked battleground. Depression and panic attacks returned. Friends and family tried to get me back into the swing of things, to distract me and help me laugh, but flashbacks and dark memories fought harder.

I had talked to Bobby about this, about the possibility, about the consequences. And it happened as feared. Without even publicly coming out, I had experienced gay bashing firsthand.

Losing everything was the *Price* I paid for discovering my identity in the epicenter of a powerful theocracy that doesn't understand homosexuality—that fears it—that demonizes it.

With so many dark memories I couldn't yet fully comprehend, it took over a year for my post-traumatic stress to subside and for honest smiles to come forward. I found strength in the knowledge that—regardless of how much stamina they or others might have to punch me and throw shit at me—I'd been in a ditch before. I'd licked my own wounds, learned lessons, and gotten back on my feet. And now that I have found myself, I move forward in the world of the living—and I know that, though it may hurt, if I get the chance, I will learn to love again.

18

REVELATIONS

*"The word 'God' is for me nothing more than the expression
and product of human weaknesses, and religious scripture
a collection of honorable, but still primitive legends which are
nevertheless pretty childish. No interpretation,
no matter how subtle, can (for me) change this."*

—Albert Einstein

Conditioned

In 1901, a Russian physiologist, Ivan Pavlov, made a breakthrough discovery
in the area of psychology, known as classical conditioning. He eventually
won a Nobel Prize for his paramount discovery of human behavior, which
is now taught in colleges around the world. Researching the salivation rates
of dogs when they were fed, Pavlov discovered that, in time, the dogs started
salivating when he entered the room, before being fed. The dogs seemed to
have identified his presence with the sweetness of food.

He decided to continue researching to better understand this behavior.
He started ringing a bell every time he fed the dogs. After doing this a few
times, he noticed the dogs began salivating at the sound of the bell, even
when there wasn't food around.

Pavlov called food an *unconditioned stimulus*. We do not have to be
taught to react to it. We do it naturally. He called salivating an *unconditioned
response*. No one has to teach us to salivate when there is food around. It is
a natural response. A lab assistant or a bell, on the other hand, represent a
neutral stimulus. They don't cause us to salivate on their own. But when a lab
assistant enters the room or a bell is continuously played when we are given
food, we then begin to identify one with the other.

They are *paired*.

The lab assistant and the bell sound thus become a *conditioned stimulus*, which create a *conditioned reaction*. The word *conditioned* refers to those reactions we would not naturally have unless it was paired, continuously, with a *natural (unconditioned) stimulus*.

If you lost a loved one during the holiday season, for example, regardless of how long it's been, you may continue to identify the season with sadness. If you have a car accident at the corner of Main and 5th, you may get anxious whenever approaching that intersection. If you are severely allergic to cats, you may develop an intense animosity toward felines. If you have a few drinks every time you go out with friends, you may get thirsty when you see them. If you grew up cheering at the sound of the snow cone truck, you may get a smile on your face every time you hear the sound at a distance. If you drive by a restaurant you like and smell the food in the air, you may get immediately hungry. These are all *conditioned* responses to *natural* stimuli.

When you get married, the pastor speaks of Jesus. A human being performs the ceremony, but since he speaks of Jesus, you now identify great joy with Jesus. When you attend a funeral, a priest gives you comfort, but since he speaks of Jesus, you now pair comfort with Jesus. When you attend summer camp, you have a lot of fun, meet new people, get a camp crush, compete, and learn, but since you also talked about and worshipped Jesus, you now identity sweet coming-of-age stories with Jesus. When you have Thanksgiving dinner, you share it with loved ones, but since you pray before the meal in the name of Jesus, you now identify family unity with Jesus. When you drive or fly with good friends, you bond with them over travel, but since you pray in the name of Jesus before or after the trip, you now identify trips and friendship with Jesus.

The list of possible associations goes on and on. Jesus has never been physically present. But since I, you, us, our family, our friends, and our leaders have all included Jesus in every event, ceremony, trip, and meal, we identify his name with each of those events—with nearly every aspect of our lives. Weddings, funerals, road trips, and times of hardship and joy are *unconditioned* stimuli, which create *unconditioned* reactions—we cry, we laugh, we learn in response naturally. But when Jesus, prayer, and worship are continuously paired with those same events, Jesus, prayer, and worship become *conditioned stimuli*, which create *conditioned responses*—we cry, we laugh, we learn in response to Jesus, prayer, and worship. It now feels natural.

For Pavlov's dogs, the sound of bells and the guy in the lab coat, made the presence of food feel real, even when it wasn't in the room. In the same way, the name Jesus, prayer, worship, and churches make the presence of God feel real, even when he is not in the room—even if he doesn't exist. Animals and humans are hardwired to work like that. And as long as we continuously pair our experiences with that *presence*, it will keep working like that.

Church trained us, and it trained us well, to fall in love with God—a character we cannot see, we cannot touch, we cannot hear, and we cannot locate, but who somehow is real just the same. Consider how Tom Hanks' character in the movie *Cast Away* fell in love with "Wilson," the volleyball—an inanimate object brought to life in the mind of a desperate, lonely individual who believed in goodness and was holding on to hope of a better life. He created a whole personality around Wilson that bounced off his experiences on the island. Wilson became real. Similarly, churches provide us a framework of God's personality that we fill in with our own personal experiences.

You have just read in this book how I filled it with mine.

For many years I kept brushing off my doubts about Christianity because I was so in love with Jesus that I kept believing till death do us part—no matter the evidence, or lack thereof.

There is one thing about God that both freethinkers and religious people agree on: God will only be as real as we want him to be.

Can It Make Sense Now?

As a child, we believed that Mickey Mouse was alive and well. He owned a silly dog named Pluto, was in love with his pretty girlfriend Minnie, and had a moody best friend called Donald Duck. And the stories about fire-breathing dragons, Caribbean pirates, princesses in despair, heroes on white horses with big swords, evil witches, flying elephants, teacup houses, flying carpets, a living wooden boy, a beast in love—they all existed. We heard those stories at nighttime. We saw their movies right in our living rooms. If we were good kids our parents would take us to "The Happiest Place on Earth" and everything would be all right—*if we believed.*

When we grew up, life began to beat us hard across the face. It made us doubt the fantasy of "The Happiest Place on Earth." But once a year, sometimes more often than that, we'd get to go back. And though we now knew there was someone inside that plastic mouse outfit, we played along and said hi, took a picture with him, and smiled widely. The story in here is so good, and the world out there is so bad, that we'd rather hold on to this hope as long as possible. It's better to live in a happy fantasy, however improbable, than in a crude reality.

We found a new way to keep dreams alive outside of that park in houses of faith. We only have to pay a tenth of our wages and we get all the good feelings we can handle for a week. And many times we can get away with paying less than that—they don't notice. We get to make a lot of friends that support us and think of us when they are home. And they have music, festivals, skits, retreats, and so much more stuff that provides us with a community.

They say it doesn't matter what we do, Jesus always loves us—even if we never see him. Even when people do something for us, they say it wasn't them, that it was Jesus. When we do something for other people, they say it wasn't us, that it was Jesus. And if we don't love Jesus, we will burn in a lake of fire for all eternity where there is weeping and gnashing of teeth.

As the market for these houses of faith grew, leaders began creating their own franchises, with their own special traditions and history. Some spoke in tongues, some formed strict methods of worship, some had extra books and new prophets, some practiced polygamy, some murdered the infidels. And they all claimed to be the real deal.

The community created rules. The rules created systems. And the systems pushed away those who wouldn't adhere to their beliefs.

We kept hearing the astonishing stories, over and over, accepting them because everyone else did. In the back of my mind, I always felt that these ancient legends, though honorable, sounded pretty childish.

The world created in six days. The first two humans, created from dust and a rib, in a garden, with a walking-talking snake that influences them to eat from a tree, hence sentencing every human who will ever live to hell, forcing us to adhere to a religious system or be thrown in a lake of fire. An ark that holds two of each land animal and bird through a worldwide, life-swiping flood. A group of people that kills another group of people because they say God told them that a specific area of land is now theirs. A sun (not the earth) that stands still for twenty-four hours because someone held his hands up. A burning bush that doesn't burn. A tower that every language in the world comes from. A little kid who defeats a giant with a slingshot and cures headaches with a harp. A woman who is turned into salt for looking back. A sea that parts in half and swallows an army. A guy who gets supernatural strength from his long hair. A chariot of fire with horses of fire that raise a man into heaven. A guy in a fiery furnace and a lion's den who doesn't burn or get eaten. A guy who is swallowed and chills in the belly of a large fish for three days and three nights, and lives. The son of God, from a virgin, who walks on water, turns water into wine, and is crucified and resurrected. The Second Coming. The four horsemen of the Apocalypse. The Antichrist.

We are drilled weekly with extreme metaphors that exemplify the values found in II Corinthians 5:7, *"For we live by faith, not by sight."* And in John 20:29, *"Then Jesus told him, 'Because you have seen me, you have believed; blessed are those who have not seen and yet have believed.'"* Church teaches us that we are somehow more virtuous if we believe in what doesn't make sense.

Once I "broke up with Jesus," all of the questions I had stored in the closet labeled "Do Not Open" began to have clear answers. Once I ended my unconditional love affair with Jesus, a fog was cleared.

The creation story, the Jesus narrative, the rise of Christianity, and the history of religion are all plagued with holes, soaked in blood, and filled with fantasy and horror we choose to leave aside to "focus on the good parts."

I am now able to separate my conditioned responses to faith for what they really are, *conditioned reactions.* I can no longer ignore facts, betray reason, and replace common sense with hopes of love and promises that "it will make sense one day."

My friends, why shouldn't it make sense now?

The One True Salad
During one of my most desperate times in my battles with doubt, I reached out to one of my former APU professors, Dr. Bruce Baloian, one of the most beloved and respected Bible professors on campus. I was considered by some as a teacher's pet when I was s student. He liked my story and appreciated my insight and thirst for biblical knowledge. I sent him an email, told him that I was thinking of leaving the faith, and asked him if he'd be willing to talk.

We met a few times, and each time he tried to emphasize what he called "the power of the narrative." The great story of Jesus, the son of God who came to earth, died for our sins, and gave us eternal salvation. "But Dr. Baloian," I interjected, "there is also power in the story of Harry Potter. There are real sites in those books, such as London, but that doesn't mean everything else is true. Harry Potter has a powerful following, people dress like him when they watch the movies, the books have sold millions, and there are groups who discuss the connection between the storylines in the books and the development of the characters."

He then talked about "the power of the personal experience." I reminded him that I had experienced the personal experience—that's how he met me.

I asked him, "Imagine there is a group of people here having this discussion with us. There you are making the case for Christianity and how good and real it is to you. But there is Kim over there," and I pointed to the seat to his left, "and she is a Buddhist. And she believes that her faith is good and real because she feels it. And here you have Muhammed," and I pointed to the seat to my right, "and he believes that Islam is the real religion of the world because it is good to him. He knows in his heart this is the one true faith." And then I pointed elsewhere, "And there is Carl over there. He is an atheist. He feels a peace in his heart and believes that science proves what is fact. He can see that 2 plus 2 equals 4 and believes it to be good to rely on what can be proven. He knows in his heart that that is real. And you have Vicente, a Catholic. And you have Joseph, a Mormon. And you have Daria, a Hindu. And everyone is saying that their religion is good and real because they can feel it in their hearts. At some point you have to stop and say, 'Okay, you all feel something,' but it doesn't make all of them the *one true religion* just because you feel it. At the end something has to prove all but one wrong."

Dr. Baloian usually was very efficient teaching through reason based on scripture, to validate scripture. This time he sat there, silent. And since he seemed lost in thought, I continued.

"Imagine you talk to an American and ask him what his favorite salad is, and he responds that Caesar salad is *the one true salad*. That all other salads are fake. That Caesar salad makes him feel good, and that it tastes so delicious in his mouth that it has to be *the one true salad*." Dr. Baloian leaned forward, not sure where I was headed with this. I continued, "But image you go to the Middle East, and this girl says, 'Oh no. Tabouli is *the one true salad*. And the way I know this is because ours is really healthy. You have fattening dressing on yours and bread chunks. We have fresh vegetables, and we even add olive oil to it. Since ours is truly healthy, that's how I know tabouli is *the one true salad*.' But then Vicente over here puts his hand up and says, 'Oh no. You guys hold on. Let me tell you que pasa. What we have over here is called salsa. It is so good that people add it to all kinds of meals. It has such powerful ingredients, like jalapeños, that it creates a sense of festivity and celebration. We have entire cultural traditions built around it. This is how we can see, without a shadow of a doubt, that salsa is *the one true salad*.'"

His eyes became a bit glossy, but he kept his attention on me.

I finished my statement, "You see, every religion in the world keeps assuring everyone else that their religion is *the one true religion* because it feels so good to them that there is no way that any other faith can feel just as good. We've all built so many traditions around our religion, that indeed it is very real to us. But does that make it *the one true religion*? Haven't we seen that we share the same values we all celebrate? Community, charity, leadership, meditation, service, accountability, mentorship, compassion, etc. All those values are in all of us simply because we are *human*, not because we are *religious*. The reason why all of those salads are good, is not because they are *the one true salad*, it's because they are all made of *vegetables*. Vegetables are the values that we ought to celebrate, not a particular recipe. Much less build a whole religion around it."

I escorted him back to his place. But before he entered his house, I said, "The Judeo-Christian story is a great narrative, and there is power in feeling we belong, but we can't go along and subscribe to a story just because it is a good story. And we cannot align every element in our lives—morality, ethics, mission—because an aspect of it makes us feel good. As rational beings we have to know what is true, regardless of how it makes us feel. Otherwise we'd be betraying that intellect you believe is a gift from God. Don't you think?"

I had never seen him speechless. He stood there, stepping back and forth, mumbling some words, "Ah, well, I think . . ." And then he did what I expected least. He turned around and rushed inside his house, leaving me standing on his sidewalk.

Having faith doesn't prove anything is real; it only proves we have faith. Loving Jesus makes us feel really good inside, but a good story is not reason enough to build a whole system around it. I decided that, though painful and torturous, I couldn't remain part of a belief system that was so against common sense.

I'm open to trying all kinds of vegetables in my diet, but I cannot dare call any special combination of them, *the one true salad*. I am open to applying all kinds of human values in my life, but I cannot dare call any special combination of them, *the one true religion*.

Soup
Human personality is like a recipe for soup. We may all start as water, but life will keep adding ingredients that, through fire, become the flavors that define who we are.

I was a little Mexican boy afraid of crossing the border and starting anew. The stars and stripes didn't understand the festive rituals of my Aztec tradition. Their rules seemed to have limits on the fullness of my freedom. I was uprooted and planted in a soil I didn't understand. I wept looking at pictures of life as I remembered it, as I had dreamt it. The United States was an idea too complex for me to understand, but I played along.

When I went to college, I defined my identity as "Mexican," but when I drove to Mexico and began partnering with the government and community, they saw me as part of the American team. "No," I explained. "I am still one of you. I dress differently, I live differently, but my heart is still here. I promise, one day I will return."

When I had the chance to become an American citizen, I initially resisted. Most people I knew who had taken the naturalization oath—to *"absolutely and entirely renounce and abjure all allegiance and fidelity to any foreign prince, potentate, state, or sovereignty, of whom or which I have heretofore been a subject or citizen"*—seemed to have crossed their fingers as they did. They took a new citizenship to have a better life up north, but their identity remined south of the border. "It's just something you have to say. Who cares?" I was told. But I couldn't. If I took that oath, I would not lie. I respected America too much.

When 2009 came, I knew the time had finally come. I loved America. My best friends were American. The standards I valued were American. The lifestyle I lived was American. The dreams I had were American. And I humbly asked her people to take me in as one of their own, because inside I already was. Providence could not have a better sense of humor because the day I was born again as a citizen of this great nation, was the day of my birth, May 28.

Today, some Mexicans accuse me of treason. They feel I should just take America's money, but never change my allegiance to the motherland. If I adhere to the excellence, standards, and values that have made America great, I am told, "It's because you don't like Mexicans now."

When I accepted my new citizenship, I could take a brand new name. What should it be? I thought about it for weeks. First, I got rid of my first name, Juan. It was given to me at birth—my father's name. I owed nothing to him and it had to go. Fernando became my first name. And as a new middle name, I took the name of one of my greatest heroes and role models. It would be a testament of my faith and to my irrevocable conviction to serve, transform, and inspire a new generation of believers. I even took it in its Hebrew form, Mosheh.

I was a good Catholic boy who had defended the traditions of my country and allegiance to her saints. Who became a Christian who spoke with the tongues of heaven and fought the devil with sword and shield. Who became a spiritual leader who led thousands in a movement to make more Christians. Who became a missionary who traveled the world championing the story of the god-man who would save us all.

I was also a nice straight boy who dreamt of meeting the girl of his dreams and raising a family that wouldn't experience the darkness he had known. A boy who grew up without a father—the man who might have preferred I was a stain on a blanket instead of a stain on his reputation. A boy who was accused of not being manly enough. A boy who was raised by women, with no masculine role models. A boy who had to come before a priest, on the day before his first Holy Communion, and reveal the most painful and shameful secrets of his life.

When I went on a night hike with my friend Jacob, we had an interesting conversation. We teased each other back and forth. "When are you gonna come out?" I asked him. "Well, when are you gonna come out?" He asked back. We both laughed. "Let me ask you a serious question," I said. "About that whole thing, what do you think it is, nature or nurture?" He quickly answered with a statement that caught me off guard and started a whole new internal dialogue in me between tradition and reason. He said, "Honestly man, who gives a fuck?"

In the political infighting between conservatives and liberals, between churches and Hollywood, between families and activists, the argument had been reduced to this: if you're born gay it's okay, but if you were made gay then it's not.

When I fell off the boulder and came back to campus, I was not the same. I was skin and bones. I limped, walked with crutches, and hadn't yet had reconstructive surgery to fix my face. During a Christmas party someone told one of my coworkers, "Fernando looks really weathered, dark. He looks nothing like the way he was." I gasped, but remained silent.

Fernando before the fall was loved by everyone, was positive about everything, and believed he could do anything. Fernando after the fall was a darker, weaker version of that, and people missed him. I tried for a long time to go back to the Fernando I used to be, because I loved that guy too. But when I made it back to the boulder, I realized that no matter what happened, that would never be. I had fallen, and that would never change. I had to live as the new Fernando, with all my roses, and all my skulls.

Was I born gay, or made gay? To quote Jacob, who gives a fuck? I didn't want to grow up fatherless, but I can't change that. I didn't want to be raised by only women, but I can't change that. I sure as hell didn't want to experience what no child ever should, but I can't change that either. Even if my sexuality is a combination of nature and nurture, it is my life.

When I have conversations with gay guys, many say they had a good childhood and a good relationship with their father and see no psychological reasons for their sexual identity. That is great! But at least half of them told me they had experienced sexual abuse. And we all have something in common: we all want politicians and religious people to please accept that we are what we are now. Let's all try to make the world a better place, where families are not falling apart, and where no child experiences the feeling of brutality.

I was a boy, I was a Mexican, I was a Christian, and I was straight.

Now I am a man, I am an American, I am a Humanist, and I am gay.

And all this time, then and now, I remained human just the same.

Your soup may taste different than mine. Some soups are sour, some are spicy, and some are on the mild side. But when it comes to my soup, I know this much, I am not fighting with my past. I love who I am. And I have no greater desire than for you to love your soup just as much as I love mine.

In my gospel, my story, you have read how my soup was made. You have read my recipe and seen what was the outcome. You have seen how religion influenced every decision in my life, even when reason challenged it. You have seen how even in the peak of my Christian ministry, I remained haunted by questions. Questions that I pushed back because I loved the Jesus story as I knew it. You have also seen how people have used religion to create a divide and bring pain to those of a different belief—because they can.

Religion and Reason have been demons and angels standing on each of my shoulders fighting for my identity. I have made my choice, which I based on all available evidence, as I care for my heart. It is now time for you to make yours.

I know your story will be great. A wonderful soup. Make it a good one. Fight for love. Fight for reason. Fight for yourself. And when they try to strip you of everything for being different, know they never can. Once they peel every creed and every theory off you, you are still the beautiful, smart, talented, wonderful human being you have always been.

The values we pour into our lives matter. Let's make some good soup.

Back

I came out of darkness and into the light. A light so blinding, it did, in fact, consume me. Leaving me with no sweeter desire than to escape its splendor. And I realize I have come back. Back to that spot. That time when I decided to take the wafer under the light shining through those stained-glass windows.

I have no idea how my life would have turned out had I not pursued after the holy. Had I not gone down that rabbit hole. Had I not seen what I have seen. Done what I have done. It feels like it was just yesterday I left Mexicali, hopped over a wall, shared bedtime stories with my sweet kindergartener, chased after "the Jews" in Charay, let Marcos copy my answers, knocked on the Guzmans' door, heard Don's last heartbeat, got beat up by the Mexican Army, walked around the block with Joel, spoke in tongues and cast out demons, led a camp with Dan and Fred, held a shooting star in my hand, lived off cookies at APU, prevented a massive deportation, painted schools with Team Stephen, played guitar for Watay, pulled friends out of a totaled van, got handcuffed to the back of a pickup truck, fell off a cliff and learned how to walk again, trained young Methodists, became an American citizen, met my father, checked myself in for a 5150, went on a cruise with Ricky and Danny, became purified with Bobby, was a son of perdition, and survived the judging flames of hell.

And now I'm back.

Mexicali. El Centro. They look so different, but also very similar to how I left them. Maybe it is not those places that have changed. Maybe it is me. I let my feet sweep me off to destinations only my untamed heart had dreamt of, prayed of. The heat there is just as unforgiving. But it doesn't feel as hot now that I've spent time baking in the oven of life. I set out on a journey to find meaning, to find truth, to find reason. I tried to find it in the Bible, but instead I found it in the world. I tried to find it in the heavens, but instead I found it here on earth. I tried to find it in God, but instead I found it in humanity.

And I'm back. A bit tired and a bit weary. It's been a long journey. I drop on the couch and see dust fall off my clothes, torn in places. I don't have much to unpack and not much to show for. But I lean back, close my eyes, and I listen to the radio, which is now playing my song—*"All this time I was finding myself, and I . . . didn't know I was lost"*—Avicii's "Wake Me Up."

And it's all there.

I play the movie in my head and see the choices I have made and those life has made for me. And there at the end of it I see that skinny, ungroomed child, his above-average height, his low weight, his lack of masculinity—the little boy with those golden-brown, gentle yet sad puppy eyes, and I tell him I love him.

I open my eyes and realize that kid is still here, plus or minus a few scars.

I look behind me at the journey I've traveled. Fateful it has been. And though I give time for my heart to mourn, my mind to grieve, and my body to heal, I see now it is a good thing I traveled light. I get up, dust off, and run my fingers through my hair. There's a lil' less of it than when I started.

I pick up my bag again and wonder what new treasures I can store in it. I might lose some. I might win some. And there in the bag's pocket, what is this? An old glow-in-the-dark star. It reminds me to be careful of what I ask for. But now that I know power has been in us all along, and not in an invisible man above the clouds, I start the greatest journey of them all. Still a quest for meaning, for truth, for reason—for a power locked up in humanity, to create and to unite.

My story is not done yet. It is actually just beginning. I still have an adventure or two to live, and a word or two to say. Pain and love have taken me on a passionate and treacherous journey where two things have been defined: I can't, not ever, refuse to think, or forget to love.

Now that I know it is *our* choice if we do or don't, I know we can truly save the world. And this, my friends, is some *good news*.

I have learned in my journey that fanfare and rattles get attention, that our past has consequences, and that love knows no bound when pressed to save the lost. I have seen and fought those who wear a mask of godliness but who, following the test of history, are revealed to be nothing more than a spectacle. But I also walked with those who gave love a face, regardless of creed and doctrine, and added value to my life. I choose now to hold on to the latter, as I heal from the past and learn to see through masks. I hope you'll also want to be one of them, the rescuers, the real ones, the believers, the people of love.

For all intents and purposes, I am what I am. A voyager traveling from poor Mexican dirt streets, to Catholic images of sainthood, to fervent Pentecostal tongues, to the Promised Land of Capitalism, to the pinnacle of Christian education, to the prominence of missionary work, to the arms of nondenominational servants, to the top floor of liberal Methodism, through the thick walls of Mormonism, to freedom from religious and sexual bounds—surviving tragedy, prejudice, and discovering the healing power of Reason.

I am a holy heathen with a sense of awe, lessons learned, and a desire to tell my own story, and in my own words, of this—my fateful journey to the cross and back.

I hold the star in my hand, bring it to my lips and smile, because this kid—yeah—this kid heads toward the door again and softly whispers those words, "I will be a shooting star."

EPILOGUE: WHAT REALLY MAKES SENSE

"Darkness cannot drive out darkness: only light can do that.
Hate cannot drive out hate: only love can do that."
—Martin Luther King Jr., *A Testament of Hope*

I have never been married, and hence I have never been divorced. But several of my friends have, and I have counseled many kids whose parents have been through that ordeal. I have been witness to the emotionally catastrophic process of dividing your life into different parts that will now go their separate ways. Who will keep the house and the car? Who will keep the kids? Who will keep which friends? Who will stay at this gym? The family, the community, the finances. It's like watching a beating heart ripped apart and seeing ventricles and arteries burst into a bloody spectacle, leaving two useless halves as a remnant.

Divorce is like that. And it works the same way when you leave a community.

Everything that I did was Christian. The church I went to was Christian. The school I went to was Christian. The job I had was Christian. The people I worked out with were Christian. The girls I dated were Christian. The people I played volleyball in the evenings with were Christian. The people I went out dancing with were Christian. Everything in my life was, in one way or another, related to Christianity. When I began to separate myself from the faith, I experienced the torturous process of ripping my heart in half—just like in a divorce.

The process was so hurtful and difficult that I considered staying in Christianity, if only to keep the community. Because who would I hang out with now? Who would listen to me?

I began reaching out to former pastors, mentors, professors, and friends, and came clean about my intentions to depart from Christianity. Most people understood, except some friends—understandably, some of them felt betrayed.

I went home and realized, this process is painful, but it has to be done.

When I left Catholicism, my friends were surprised. They talked about me behind my back and I lost contact with them.

When I became a Pentecostal Christian, church leaders had me break every CD I owned, asked me to stop dancing, and told me to stop going to the movies. For the sake of an imagined purity, I lost more than people; I lost myself when I lost the things I loved.

When I left Mexico, I left the only identity I knew. I was lost in a new land and wondered who would take me in now.

When I rose from the dead, I felt I had a fair reason to hate life, to hide myself in the shadows and plot against my own future.

When I left APU, I left the most solid history I'd yet had, and I had thought that I would always be a missionary.

When I joined the United Methodist Church, I was told right away that people would hate me because I was not one of them. And even though I'd helped lead the denomination to one of the greatest peaks they'd had in youth movement, they kicked me out. I had challenged them to accept something different.

When I became an American, I took in a new culture that I had come to love and become part of. But that came with accusations from Mexicans, many American citizens themselves, of betraying my roots, and of not loving my own people. They called me a "coconut"—brown on the outside and white on the inside.

When I left Christianity, old friends told me I was going to hell and that God told them they couldn't commune with me any longer. Few things could hurt more than that.

When I moved to Mormon Utah, the Mormons I served with my blood, sweat, and tears took me out to the woodshed when they felt threatened by something they didn't understand, something they were raised to fear.

When I accepted my sexual orientation, I was filled with anger toward the religious establishment. I had entrusted my mind and heart to it, and now, because of it, I might have ruined my chances of meeting the man of my dreams.

I have more than enough reasons to be bitter. I have more than enough reasons to feel vindictive. I have more than enough reasons to hide in my bedroom and plan revenge. But when I look at the story of my life, I also see I have more than enough reasons to love.

Throughout history, humans have used the God story to claim superiority over others. The innocent have fallen—been humiliated, tortured, and murdered. I see the timeline of humanity, and I don't have it in me to add more to the bloodshed.

I have chosen to follow a lifestyle that believes in what makes sense. And I continue to be a man of faith. An unchanging, stubborn, hopeful faith that humanity can overcome its darkness, be it in our hearts or our minds.

This book may not end up changing anybody's views about faith or reason, about immigrants, about mental illness, or about the LGBT community, but if you would give one element of these pages a chance to resonate after you put it down, please, please, please let it be this: being different from me does not make you my enemy.

We've bled enough, cried enough, killed enough—it is time to move on. Let us finally rise above our differences. We are religious and we are freethinkers. We are conservatives and we are liberals. We are Americans and we are immigrants. We are healthy and we are sick. We are straight and we are gay. But, my friends, we are all human just the same.

The true evidence of love is that, regardless of differences, we stop finding ways to divide ourselves and finally give tolerance and common sense a fair chance.

That is one gospel worth living for.

ACKNOWLEDGMENTS

To those whom I love. To those who have loved me. And to those who continue to open their arms to me. I am nothing without you. This is your story as much as it is mine.

To my rock and mother, Teresa Foucar, I cannot convey in words that I would not be where I am now without your sacrifice. Whatever good I ever accomplish, it is because you invested your life with unquestionable faith in my potential. I dream of flying high to make you proud, and yet I realize there's pride in your eyes simply because I exist. I love you.

To my siblings, Carolina, Ernest, and Sharon, I've enjoyed growing up with you, fighting with you, learning with you, and living with you. We will always be there for one another. To my nieces Joakima, Savannah, Marlena, and Noelia, you are a light in my eyes, and a joy in my dreams. Mi familia y amigos en Charay, Mexicali y Los Angeles, in the school of life and the playground of mischief, I couldn't have asked for better classmates and playmates.

To my family in Siete Olivos, the Foursquare church, Azusa Pacific University, Mexico Outreach, and the United Methodist Church, you saw me grow from a fearful kid unto a confident man who could stand on his own two feet. You believed in me, trusted me, and empowered me to fulfill my dreams and make a difference in the world. I hope I continue to make you proud.

To Chris Stedman at Yale Humanist Community and Dan Barker at the Freedom From Religion Foundation, thank you for your mentorship, guidance, and friendship. To Kurt Volkan at Pitchstone, I had heard horror stories about publishers, but I've had nothing but a positive, synergetic, and empowering experience with you. Thank you for making this dream a reality.

To those who have bullied me, bashed me, hurt me, and ridiculed me for being different, weaker, and lost, I thank you for the hard-earned lessons, the purifying tears, and the opportunities to rise even stronger from the ashes.

To the man of my dreams (wherever you are), I am sorry I showed up late to the game—I didn't know who I was. I haven't met you, and yet I already want to be a better man for you.

And finally, to you—my reader. Thank you for taking the time to journey with me as I search for answers. I hope in the process you find some of yours.

ABOUT THE AUTHOR

Fernando Alcántar was born and raised in Mexico and immigrated to the United States as a teenager. He has a bachelor's degree in psychology and a master's degree in organizational leadership from Azusa Pacific University, one of the top Christian universities in the United States. He is an author, activist, public speaker, and adventurer.

He worked at APU's Mexico Outreach for eight years as senior coordinator of North American partnerships. There, he oversaw hundreds of churches in Mexico and helped mobilize over 9,000 missionaries a year from all over the United States and Canada. He innovated dozens of new ministries and developed unprecedented partnerships with government officials, nonprofits, schools, businesses, and churches. He has spoken in front of thousands, sharing his faith and motivating people into Christian ministry, and traveled around the world serving marginalized communities.

He left APU to take the role of director of leadership development for young people for the California-Pacific Annual Conference of The United Methodist Church. "Cal-Pac" oversees almost 400 churches for about 83,000 members across Southern California, Hawaii, Guam, and Saipan. In this role, he oversaw youth and young adult ministries across the region, served as an ambassador to ethnic caucuses, and developed breakthrough leadership programs for its constituents. He was considered by many as the spokesperson for emerging United Methodism.

It was toward the end of his term with the UMC that Fernando reached the twilight of his theological process out of Christianity. He left the religious community and returned to higher education where he served at Utah State University Eastern as director of student life. Moving to the Mormon epicenter proved to be a challenging experience, but it was the place where he finally realized his full sexual identity. He eventually resigned his position

223

after experiencing homophobic attacks from members of the Mormon community.

Once a high-profile religious leader, Fernando wants to use this book to come out as both Humanist and gay—"gaytheist"—to help strengthen a national narrative of understanding, tolerance, and acceptance. He also wants to help give a voice to those hiding in the shadows, afraid to publicly question their religious and sexual identity for fear of isolation and retaliation.